Student Solutions Manual to Accompany

Starting Out with Java 5: Early Objects

By Tony Gaddis

Prepared by
Diane Christie,
University of Wisconsin-Stout

Scott/Jones, Inc.
P.O. Box 696
El Granada, CA 94018
Voice: 650-726-2436
Facsimile: 650-726-4693
E-mail: marketing@scottjonespub.com

ZYX 543
ISBN: 1-57676-167-3

Printed in USA.

Composition: Diane M. Christie
Book Manufacturing: EPac, San Leandro, CA.

Scott/Jones Publishing Company
Editorial Group: Richard Jones, Denise Simon, and Patricia Miyaki
Production Management: Mario M Rodriguez
Marketing and Sales: Richard Jones
Business Operations: Michelle Robelet, Cathy Glenn, and Morena Timm

Additional Titles by Tony Gaddis from Scott/Jones

Starting Out with Visual Basic. NET
Standard Version of Starting Out with C++, Fourth Edition
Brief Version of Starting Out with C++, Fourth Edition
(with Barret Krupow)
Starting Out with Java
Starting Out with Java, Alternate Edition
by Tony Gaddis
Starting Out with C++, Fourth Alternate Edition
by Tony Gaddis, Judy Walters, and Godfrey Muganda

Preface

This Solutions Manual is designed to supplement *Starting Out With Java 5 Early Objects* by Tony Gaddis. It contains detailed and annotated solutions to selected Programming Challenges, along with a description of how each solution was designed.

This Student Solutions Manual is a resource for instructor's management of their time. Experienced teachers understand that in many ways their most precious educational resource is classroom time. Yet when many professors walk into their lectures, the first question they often ask is: "any trouble with the homework assignment?" A few students inevitably raise their hands. Then the instructor starts de-construction the solution to the assignments they didn't "get". This can take time. The professor then has much less time remaining to (a) introduce (b) motivate and (c) illustrate the next concept. This Solutions Manual is designed to minimize the time spent solving last night's homework assignment, thus allowing the instructor more time maximizing the prep for tonight's assignment.

Each Programming Challenge solution contains the following:

- **Problem Statement** – Each solution starts out with a statement defining the problem.
- **Program Definition** – Next follows the definition of what the program should do, including a description of the purpose, the input needed, the process used, and the output required.
- **Class Documentation** – Each class needed to accomplish this purpose is defined by a listing of fields, constructors, and other methods along with a description of each.
- **UML Diagram** – A UML diagram is provided to describe each class as well. When GUIs need to be created, a sketch of what is desired is shown.
- **Pseudocode** – Pseudocode for each task is presented before any actual code is shown.
- **Code Solution** – The Java code for the solution is provided. All code is thoroughly commented.
- **Program Output** – All output is detailed at the end of each Programming Challenge.

The parts of the solutions are presented in this order so that the student can use it as a step-by-step guide to solving problems. The student can start by attempting each problem without the help of the Solutions Manual. When help is needed, the student should read only as far into the solution as is necessary to get headed in the correct direction. Once the student has determined what they feel is a good plan to proceed, it can then be checked against the solution.

The solutions can also be used as extra examples to supplement the problems already worked in the text. Students can see the logical progression used to solve the problems. The problems have been selected so that in each chapter a simple problem is solved first, then a moderately difficult problem. After that problems were selected to highlight any new concepts added in each chapter.

NOTES

CHAPTER 2

Java Fundamentals

Solutions

- Programming Challenge 2: Names and Initials
- Programming Challenge 8: Sales Tax
- Programming Challenge 12: String Manipulation

Programming Challenge 2: Names and Initials

Problem Statement:

Write a program that has the following **String** variables: **firstName**, **middleName**, and **lastName**. Initialize these with your first, middle, and last names. The program should also have the following char variables: **firstInitial**, **middleInitial**, and **lastInitial**. Store your first, middle, and last initials in these variables. The program should display the contents of these variables on the screen.

Solution:

Define What The Program Is To Do

Purpose	**Display Programmer's Name and Initials**
Input	**None**
Process	**Declare local String variables for programmer's first name, middle name, last name; first initial, middle initial; char variables for last initials. Initialize variables to their appropriate values**
Output	**Display:** **Programmer's first name** **Programmer's middle name** **Programmer's last name** **Programmer's first initial** **Programmer's middle initial** **Programmer's last initial**

High Level Pseudocode for Program

1) Create variables for first name, middle name, and last name.

2) Create variables for first initial, middle initial, and last initial.

3) Set the value of the first name variable to your first name. Perform the same operation for the middle name variable and the last name variable.

4) Set the value of the first initial variable to your first initial. Perform the same operation for the middle initial variable and last initial variable.

5) Display your first name, middle name, and last name.

6) Display your first initial, middle initial, and last initial.

Detailed Pseudocode for Program

1) Declare String variables **firstName, middleName,** and **lastName.** To declare a String variable in Java, write:

```
String firstName;
```

   a) By convention, variable names in Java begin with a lower case letter. To make the use of the variable clearer, multiple words are used to describe its purpose. These words are appended to form the variable name, where each word (except for the first) has its initial letter capitalized.

2) Declare **char** variables **firstInitial, middleInitial,** and **lastInitial.** To declare a char variable in Java, write:

```
char firstInitial;
```

3) Initialize variables **firstName, middleName,** and **lastName** with appropriate String values.

   a) **String** values are enclosed with double quote characters. For example, the first name of the programmer in the solution source code is "Joanna". The initialization of the variable **firstName** would be written in Java as:

```
firstName = "Joanna";
```

   b) **String** constants must be written on one line of source code.

   c) If a **String** variable is missing either a beginning or closing double quote, the Java compiler will reject the statement with that **String.** A missing double quote can also appear as an error in the preceding or the following statement.

4) Initialize variables: **firstInitial, middleInitial,** and **lastInitial.**

a) Values of type char are enclosed in single quote ' characters. For example, the first initial of the programmer in the solution source code is 'J'. The initialization of the variable firstInitial would be written in Java as:

```
firstInitial = 'J';
```

b) If single quotes do not enclose exactly one char value, the Java compiler will not accept the statement.

c) Also, note that String values can not be interchanged with char values. Java is a strongly typed language. The general rule is that data of one type can not be used in the place of another type. There are notable exceptions, such as implicit conversions (promotions) from a "smaller" to a "larger" numeric data types, e.g. an int can be converted to a float; a float to a double, etc.

5) Display variables **firstName, middleName,** and **LastName.**

a) Data is presented on the user's screen using the **System.out.println** method. The **println** method displays its parameters and then starts a new line.

b) To distinguish the different items that are displayed on the screen, prefix a **String** label to the data being displayed.

c) The display of the variable **firstName** is written in Java as:

```
System.out.println("First Name:   " + firstName);
```

d) To add a blank line to the display, the **println** method with no parameters is used, e.g.

```
System.out.println();
```

Notes

Always add indentation to the source code as it is being written. Indentation identifies blocks of code, making it easier to read and easier to identify syntax (structural) errors. There are many (free) editor programs, intended to be used by programmers that perform indentation automatically. Also, Integrated Development Environments for Java include source editors that indent code automatically. Check with your instructor for more information, or search the Internet for Java editors.

Always add comments to source code as it is being written, while the purpose of the program is still fresh in your mind. Comments should describe the *purpose* of the lines of program and not the literal operation of the Java code. Comments should be written so that the person who has to update this class, months or years later, can quickly understand how the program should operate. Assume that this person (perhaps it may even be you) will have a solid understanding of Java, and not need to have each line of the program explained as if she or he was a novice.

In the case of either indentation or comments, adding them as the code is being written is a habit to reinforce. To an experienced programmer, source that lacks indentation or comments looks sloppy and does not reflect well on its author.

Code Listing 2-1 (NameInitials.java)

```
//*****************************************************
//  Written by Joanna Catherine Robertson             *
//  Chapter 2                                         *
//  Programming Challenge 2: Name and Initials        *
//*****************************************************

//*****************************************************
//  2.  Name and Initials                             *
//      Write a program that has the following String *
//      variables: firstName, middleName, lastName.   *
//      Initialize these with your first, middle, and *
//      last names.  The program should also have the *
//      following char variables: firstInitial,       *
//      middleInitial, lastInitial.  Store your first, *
//      middle, and last initials in these variables. *
//      The program should display the contents of    *
//      these variables on the screen.                *
//*****************************************************

//*****************************************************
//      Note: The Problem Statement is included with  *
//      each solution so that it is unnecessary to    *
//      refer back to the textbook to see the         *
//      Programming Challenge's requirements.         *
//*****************************************************
```

```
//  define class that contains the program
public class NameInitials
{
//  the file containing this code needs to be named
//  NameInitials.java - matching the name of the class
//  (case sensitive) defined within it

    //  method main is the starting point for all Java
    //  programs
    public static void main(String[] args)
    {
        //  declare String variables to store programmer's
        //  first, middle, and last name
        String  firstName;       // Programmer's first name
        String  middleName;      // Programmer's middle name
        String  lastName;        //  Programmer's last name

        //  declare char variables to store programmer's
        //  initials
        char    firstInitial;    //  Programmer's first initial
        char    middleInitial;   //  Programmer's middle
                                 //  initial
        char    lastInitial;     //  Programmer's last initial

        //  initialize variables to hold programmer's name
        firstName    = "Joanna";
        middleName   = "Catherine";
        lastName     = "Robertson";
                       //  String literals are enclosed by
                       //  " " (double quote character)

        //  initialize variables to hold programmer's initials
        firstInitial    = 'J';
        middleInitial   = 'C';
        lastInitial     = 'R';
                        //  char literals are enclosed by
                        //  ' ' (single quote character)

                        //  NOTE:
                        //  'J' is not the same as "J"
                        //  'J' is a char; "J" is a String
                        //  Java does not permit you to
                        //  interchange
                        //  String and char variables at will.

        //  Display the programmer full name and initials
        System.out.println("First Name:      " + firstName);
        System.out.println("Middle Name:     " + middleName);
        System.out.println("Last Name:       " + lastName);

        //  put a blank line between name and initials
        System.out.println();

        System.out.println("First Initial:  " + firstInitial);
        System.out.println("Middle Initial: "
            + middleInitial);
        System.out.println("Last Initial:   " + lastInitial);
```

```
        //  Programming Style Note
        //
        //  Comments should explain the operations being
        //  performed and not describe the literal Java
        //  operations in English

        //  Meaningful Comment:

        //  Display the programmer's full name
        //  followed by a blank line.

        //  Too literal; not meaningful Comments:

        //  Display the String "First Name: " concatenated
        //  with the value of String firstName.
        //  Then display the String "Middle Name: "
        //  concatenated with the value of the String
        //  middleName.
        //  Display the String "Last Name: " concatenated
        //  with the value of the String lastName.
        //  Finally, display a blank line.
    }
}
```

Program Output

```
C:\Gaddis\Ch02>java NameInitials
First Name:      Joanna
Middle Name:     Catherine
Last Name:       Robertson

First Initial:   J
Middle Initial:  C
Last Initial:    R

C:\Gaddis\Ch02>
```

Programming Challenge 8: Sales Tax

Problem Statement:

Write a program that will ask the user to enter the amount of a purchase. The program should then compute the state and county sales tax. Assume the state sales tax is 4 percent and the county sales tax is 2 percent. The program should display the amount of the purchase, the state sales tax, the county sales tax, the total sales tax, and the total of the sale (which is the sum of the amount of purchase plus the total sales tax). Hint: Use the value 0.02 to represent 2 percent, and 0.04 to represent 4 percent.

Solution:

Define What The Program Is To Do

Purpose	**Perform sales tax calculations on a user's purchase**
Input	**Amount of the purchase**
Process	**Calculate:** **County sales tax on the purchase** **State sales tax on the purchase** **Total amount of the sale (purchase price + county sales tax + state sales tax)**
Output	**Display:** **County sales tax on the purchase** **State sales tax on the purchase** **Total amount of the sale**

High Level Pseudocode

1) Create variables for purchase amount, county sales tax, state sales tax and total amount of sale.

2) Prompt user to enter amount of purchase. Store this value into the variable for purchase amount.

3) The variable containing the purchase price entered by the user should not be modified during the remainder of the program.

4) Compute state sales tax by multiplying purchase price by 0.04. Store the result in the variable for state sales tax.

5) Compute county sales tax by multiplying purchase price by 0.02. Store the result in the variable for county sales tax.

6) Compute the total sales amount by adding the purchase price, the state sales tax and county sales tax. Store the result in the variable for total amount of sale.

7) Display the: purchase price, state sales tax, county sales tax, and total amount of sale.

Detailed Pseudocode for Program

1) Declare variables of type **double: purchase, countyTax, stateTax, totalSale.**

   a) The type **double** is the most useful numeric type for storing values with decimal values. Type **double** has 15 significant digits while type **float** only has 7 significant digits.

2) User the **Scanner** class to read from the keyboard.

   a) Create a **Scanner** object connected to System.in to read from the keyboard.

   ```
   Scanner keyboard = new Scanner(System.in);
   ```

   b) Any program using the Scanner class must have the following statement at the beginning of the file, before any class definition:

   ```
   import java.util.Scanner;
   ```

3) Display a prompt for the user to enter the amount of their purchase.

   a) The **Scanner** class provides easy to use methods for collecting data of all the basic Java types, from the user. In this example, the purchase price is set using the statement:

   ```
   purchase = keyboard.nextDouble();
   ```

4) Multiply the purchase price by **0.04,** giving 4% of the purchase price. Store that amount in the variable **stateTax.**

a) The value **0.04** represents the decimal value equivalent to 4%. In Java, 4% cannot be used in arithmetic calculations. Java requires that numbers be represented as sequences of decimal digits. The sequence of digits may be preceded by a plus (+) or minus (-) sign. A number may contain a decimal point, when a value is needed that is not a whole integer.

5) Multiply the purchase price by **0.02**, giving 2% of the purchase price. Store that amount in the variable **countyTax**.

6) Add the values: **purchase, stateTax, countyTax** and store the result in the variable **totalSale**.

7) Display the value of the variables: **purchase, stateTax, countyTax** and **totalSale**.

   a) To make the output easier to read, display a label before each value, indicating what the number represents, and display each label and value on a separate line.

Notes

Several of the source code lines in the following program will not fit on one line. When that occurs, find a place in the source line where no syntax errors will be introduced if the rest of the source is written on the next line. Usually, the space before an operator or any white space on the line will work. To continue a source line, indent it one level more than the beginning of the start of the line.

Do **not** split **String** constants over two lines. That is not permitted in Java. If a **String** constant contains more characters than will fit on a line, split the **String** into smaller **String** constants and use the concatenation operator (+) to create the value needed.

Before you run a program that performs arithmetic calculations, create several test cases and determine what the program's output should be. Perform the calculations by hand, using a calculator, or a spreadsheet program. Don't assume that because a value is output by the computer that it is correct!

Code Listing 2 - 2 (SalesTax.java)

```
//*********************************************************
//  Written by  John Jillson                              *
```

```
//  Chapter 2                                           *
//  Programming Challenge 8                             *
//******************************************************

//******************************************************
//  Chapter 2                                           *
//  Programming Challenge 8                             *
//                                                      *
//  Write a program that will ask the user              *
//  to enter the amount of a purchase. The              *
//  program should then compute the state               *
//  and county sales tax. Assume the state              *
//  sales tax is 4 percent and the county               *
//  sales tax is 2 percent. The program                 *
//  should display the amount of the                    *
//  purchase, the state sales tax, the county           *
//  sales tax, the total sales tax, and the             *
//  total of the sale (which is the sum of the          *
//  amount of purchase plus the total sales             *
//  tax). Hint: Use the value 0.02 to represent         *
//  2 percent, and 0.04 to represent 4 percent.         *
//******************************************************

//******************************************************
//  Purpose:                                            *
//      Perform sales tax calculations on a user's      *
//      purchase.                                       *
//  Input:                                              *
//      Amount of the purchase                          *
//  Process:                                            *
//      Calculate county sales tax on the purchase.     *
//      Calculate state sales tax on the purchase.      *
//      Calculate the total amount of the sale (purchase *
//      price + county sales tax + state sales tax).    *
//  Output:                                             *
//      Purchase Price                                  *
//      County Sales Tax                                *
//      State Sales Tax                                 *
//      Total Sale Amount                               *
//******************************************************

import java.util.Scanner; //to read keyboard input

public class SalesTax
{

    public static void main(String[] args)
    {
        //  declare variables for purchase price, taxes,
        //  and total amount of sale
        double  purchase;
        double  countyTax;
        double  stateTax;
        double  totalSale;

        // create a Scanner object to read from the keyboard
        Scanner keyboard = new Scanner(System.in);

        //  ask user to enter the amount of their purchase
```

```
            System.out.println(
                "Please enter the amount of your purchase");

                //  NOTE:  When lines of source become too long,
                //  break the line into smaller parts and
                //  indent them beneath the beginning of the
                //  source code.
                //  Always be sure to break the line at the
                //  start or end of a syntax unit so that the
                //  source code will compile correctly.
                //  Also, where possible, begin the indented
                //  continuation lines with an operator.

            // use the Scanner object to read from the keyboard
            purchase = keyboard.nextDouble();

            //  calculate sales taxes
            countyTax  =   purchase * 0.02;    // county tax is 2%
            stateTax   =   purchase * 0.04;    // state tax is 4%

            //  add everything together for total amount of sale
            totalSale  = purchase + countyTax + stateTax;

            //  display results of program's calculations
            System.out.println("purchase:    " + purchase);
            System.out.println("county tax:  " + countyTax);
            System.out.println("state tax:   " + stateTax);
            System.out.println("total sale:  " + totalSale);
        }
}
```

Program Output

```
C:\Gaddis\Ch02>java SalesTax
Please enter the amount of your purchase
100
purchase:    100.0
county tax: 2.0
state tax:   4.0
total sale: 106.0

C:\Gaddis\Ch02>java SalesTax
Please enter the amount of your purchase
1492
purchase:    1492.0
county tax: 29.84
state tax:   59.68
total sale: 1581.52

C:\Gaddis\Ch02>java SalesTax
Please enter the amount of your purchase
3.14159
purchase:    3.14159
county tax: 0.0628318
state tax:   0.1256636
total sale: 3.3300853999999998
```

Programming Challenge 12:String Manipulation

Problem Statement:

Write a program that asks the user to enter the name of his or her favorite city. Use a String variable to store the input. The program should display the following:

- The number of characters in the city name
- The name of the city in all uppercase characters
- The name of the city in all lowercase characters
- The first character in the name of the city.

Solution:

Define What The Program Is To Do

Purpose	**Use methods of the String class to manipulate data that is entered by the user.**
Input	**The user's favorite city.**
Process	**Declare variables for:** **the name of the favorite city,** **the number of characters in the city's name,** **the city's name in uppercase,** **the city's name in lowercase, and** **the first character in the city's name.** **Calculate:** **the number of characters in the city's name;** **the name of the city in uppercase characters;** **the name of the city in lowercase characters;** **the first character in the name of the city.**

Output	**Display:** **the name of the user's favorite city** **the number of characters in the city's name;** **the name of the city in uppercase characters;** **the name of the city in lowercase characters;** **the first character in the name of the city.**

High Level Pseudocode for Program

1) Create variables for: the user's favorite city, the number of characters in that name, the city's name in all uppercase characters, the city's name in all lowercase characters, and the first character in the name of the city.

2) Prompt the user to enter the name of their favorite city. Store the data entered in the variable for the user's favorite city.

   a) Insure that the variable containing the name of the user's favorite city is not changed by any subsequent operations.

3) Calculate the number of characters in the city's name. Store the result.

4) Convert the city's name into all uppercase characters. Store the result.

5) Convert the city's name into all lowercase characters. Store the result.

6) Determine the first character in the city's name. Store the result.

7) Display to the user: The name of their favorite city; The number of characters in the city's name; The city's name in all uppercase characters; The city's name in all lowercase characters; and The first character in the city's name.

Detailed Pseudocode for Program

1) Declare String variables **favoriteCity**, **favCityUpperCase**, **favCityLowerCase** in which to store the user's favorite

city, the city name in upper case, and the city's name in lower case respectively.

2) Declare **int** variable **favCityChars** to hold the number of characters in the name of the user's favorite city.

3) Declare **char** variable **favCityFirstChar** to hold the first character in the name of the user's favorite city.

4) User the **Scanner** class to read from the keyboard.

   a) Create a **Scanner** object connected to System.in to read from the keyboard.

      ```
      Scanner keyboard = new Scanner(System.in);
      ```

   b) Any program using the Scanner class must have the following statement at the beginning of the file, before any class definition:

      ```
      import java.util.Scanner;
      ```

5) Collect String containing user's favorite city.

   a) Display a String to prompt the user to enter the name of their favorite city. Collect city name using **nextLine** method of Scanner class. Store the result in variable **favoriteCity**.

      ```
      favoriteCity = keyboard.nextLine();
      ```

6) Use the length method of the **String** class to find the number of characters in **favoriteCity**. Store the number of characters in the int variable **favCityChars**.

   ```
   favCityChars = favoriteCity.length();
   ```

   a) A class method is applied to an object of the class by appending a dot '.' followed by the method's name and the methods parameters enclosed in parenthesis. An empty parameter list is represented by an open and close parenthesis that enclose nothing.

7) Use the **toUpperCase** method of the **String** class to create a **String** whose value is the same as **favoriteCity**, but all characters are in upper case. Store that value in **String favCityUpperCase**.

8) Use the **toLowerCase** method of the **String** class to create a **String** whose value is the same as **favoriteCity**, but

all characters are in lower case. Store that value in **String favCityLowerCase.**

9) Use the **charAt** method to access the first character in the **String favoriteCity.** Store that value in char variable **favCityFirstChar.**

   a) The characters in a **String** are numbered: 0, 1, … length - 1. The first character in a **String** is at index 0. The second character in a **String** is at index 1, etc. The final character in a **String** is at index (the length of the String minus 1).

10) Display the results of the **String** manipulations, with each value appropriately labeled, and displayed on a separate line.

   a) Display the value of **favoriteCity.**

   b) Display the value of **favCityChars.**

   c) Display the value of **favCityUpperCase**

   d) Display the value of **favCityLowerCase**

   e) Display the value of **favCityFirstChar.**

Code Listing 2 - 3 (CityString.Java)

```
//*****************************************************
//  Written by  Robert Johnson                        *
//  Chapter 2                                         *
//  Programming Challenge 12                          *
//*****************************************************

//*****************************************************
//   Chapter 2                                        *
//  Programming Challenge 12. String Manipulator      *
//                                                    *
//  Write a program that asks the user to enter       *
//  the name of his or her favorite city. Use a       *
//  String variable to store the input. The           *
//  program should display the following:             *
//                                                    *
//     -The number of characters in the city name     *
//     -The name of the city in all uppercase         *
//      characters                                    *
//     -The name of the city in all lowercase         *
//      characters                                    *
//     -The first character in the name of the city.  *
//                                                    *
//*****************************************************

//*****************************************************
```

```
//  Purpose:                                                *
//      Demonstrate operations on Strings in Java           *
//      using the name of the user's favorite city.         *
//                                                          *
//  Input:                                                  *
//      Name of user's favorite city.                       *
//                                                          *
//  Process:                                                *
//      -  Calculate number of characters in city's name.   *
//      -  Convert the city's name to upper case            *
//      characters and store it in a local variable.        *
//      -  Convert the city's name to lower case            *
//      characters and store it in a different local        *
//      variable.                                           *
//      -  Get the first character in the city's name       *
//      and store it in yet another local                   *
//      variable.                                           *
//                                                          *
//      NOTE: By using local variables for the results      *
//      of the String operations, the String that the       *
//      user entered is preserved.                          *
//                                                          *
//  Output:                                                 *
//      -   The name of the user's favorite city.           *
//      -   The city's name in upper case.                  *
//      -   The city's name in lower case.                  *
//      -   The first character in the city's name.         *
//***********************************************************

import java.util.Scanner;

public class CityString
{
    public static void main(String[] args)
    {
        //      declare String variables for favorite city
        //      and its upper case and lower case values
        String  favoriteCity,
                favCityUpperCase,
                favCityLowerCase;

        //      the number of characters in a String is an int
        int     favCityChars;

        //      the first character in favorite city is a char
        //      (not a String!)
        char    favCityFirstChar;

        // create a Scanner object to read from the keyboard
        Scanner keyboard = new Scanner(System.in);

        //      ask user to enter a String, store it,
        //      display a blank line to separate this from
        //      future output
        System.out.println(
            "Enter the name of your favorite city.");
        favoriteCity = keyboard.nextLine();
        System.out.println();
```

```
        //      perform operations on String and save results
        favCityChars        =   favoriteCity.length();
        favCityUpperCase    =   favoriteCity.toUpperCase();
        favCityLowerCase    =   favoriteCity.toLowerCase();
        favCityFirstChar    =   favoriteCity.charAt(0);

        //      display results of operations on String
        System.out.println(
            "Your favorite city is: "
            + favoriteCity);
        System.out.println(
            "The number of characters in your favorite"
            + " city's name are:  "
            + favCityChars);
        System.out.println(
            "Your favorite city's name in uppercase is: "
            + favCityUpperCase);
        System.out.println(
            "Your favorite city's name in lowercase is: "
            + favCityLowerCase);
        System.out.println(
            "The first character in your favorite"
            + " city's name is : "
            + favCityFirstChar);
    }
}
```

Program Output

```
C:\Gaddis\Ch02>java CityString
Enter the name of your favorite city.
Rio de Janeiro

Your favorite city is: Rio de Janeiro
The number of characters in your favorite city's name are:  14
Your favorite city's name in uppercase is: RIO DE JANEIRO
Your favorite city's name in lowercase is: rio de janeiro
The first character in your favorite city's name is : R

C:\Gaddis\Ch02>
```

CHAPTER 3

A First Look at Classes and Objects

Solutions

- ✦Programming Challenge 2: Car Class
- ✦Programming Challenge 2: Car Class with javadoc comments (Optional)
- ✦Programming Challenge 4: RetailItem Class
- ✦Programming Challenge 6: Widget Factory

Programming Challenge 2: Car Class

Problem Statement:

Write a class named **Car** that has the following fields:

- yearModel: The **yearModel** field is an **int** that holds the car's year model.
- make: The make field is a **String** object that holds the make of the car.
- speed: The speed field is an **int** that holds the car's current speed.

In addition, the class should have the following methods.

- Constructor: The constructor should accept the car's year model and make as arguments. These values should be assigned to the object's **yearModel** and **make** fields. The constructor should also assign 0 to the **speed** field.
- Appropriate accessor methods to get the values stored in an object's yearModel, **make**, and **speed** fields.
- **accelerate**: The accelerate method should add 5 to the **speed** field each time it is called.
- **brake**: The brake method should subtract 5 from the **speed** field each time it is called.

Demonstrate the class in a program that creates a **Car** object, and then calls the **accelerate** method 5 times. After each call to the **accelerate** method, get the current speed of the car and display it. Then, call the **brake** method 5 times. After each call to the **brake** method, get the current **speed** of the car and display it.

Solution: Car Class

Define What The Car Class Is To Do

Purpose	Model Properties And Behaviors Of A Simple Car	
Fields	yearModel	the car's model year
	make	the make of the car
	speed	the car's speed
Constructor		Set the values for **yearModel** and **make** according to the values provided by the input parameters. Initialize **speed** to zero.

Methods	getYearModel	Return the car's **yearModel**
	getMake	Return the car's **make**
	getSpeed	Return the car's **speed**
	accelerate	Increase the car's **speed** by 5
	brake	Decrease the car's **speed** by 5

High Level Pseudocode for Car Class

1) Define **Car** Class.
   a) Define fields for **yearModel, make,** and **speed.**
   b) Define the **Car** Class constructor.
      i) Initialize **yearModel field** and **make** field with values provided as constructor's parameters.
      ii) Initialize **speed** to zero.
2) Define Accessor methods.
   a) Define method **getYearModel**.
      i) Return value of field **yearModel**.
   b) Define method **getMake**.
      i) Return value of field **make**.
3) Define method **getSpeed**.
   a) Return value of the field **speed**.
4) Define **accelerate** method.
   a) Increase **Car** object's **speed** by 5.
5) Define **brake** method.
   a) Decrease **Car** object's **speed** by 5.

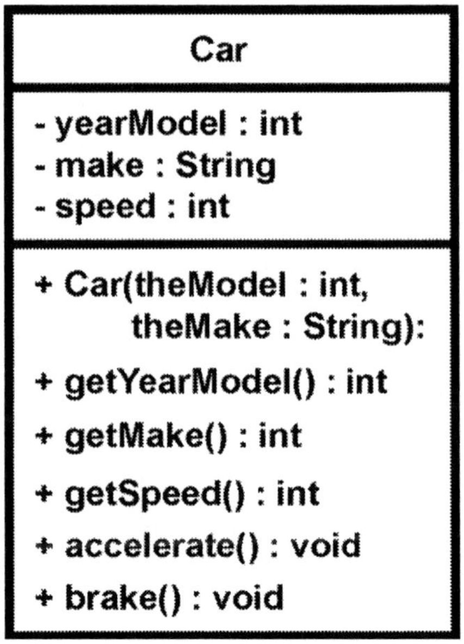

Figure 3 - 1 UML Diagram for Car Class

Detailed Pseudocode for Car Class

1) Define **Car** Class.

   a) The Java syntax to define a class is:

   ```
   public class Car
   {
           // define fields
                   // Java data definitions

           // define constructor(s)
                   // Java constructor definition

           // define methods
                   // Java method definitions
   }
   ```

   b) All class names begin with a capital letter.

   c) The name of the Java file that defines a class **must** be the name of the **public** class defined in the file, followed by ".java". The Java file that defines the **public** class **Car**, must be named "Car.java".

   d) Only one public class can be defined in any one file.

   e) All the fields and methods of a class must be included in the one file that defines the class.

2) Define fields for **yearModel**, **make**, and **speed**.

   a) Each field of an object is defined using Java data declarations. The definition of the **yearModel** field for the **Car** class is:

   ```
   private int yearModel;  // The car's model year
   ```

b) The keyword **private** is an access specifier. It indicates that the **yearModel** field can only be accessed by methods of the **Car** object. This protects the **Car** object's fields and insures that they can not be modified except through the methods of the **Car** class. Data Encapsulation is provided by the appropriate use of access specifiers on class' fields.

c) Fields of a class always have **private** access.

3) Define the **Car** Class constructor.

a) A class constructor is a method that is automatically called when an instance of a class is created using the **new** operator. The constructor method for the **Car** class has the name **Car**. The constructor method can not have a return type (not even void) and can not have a return value. The constructor for the **Car** class is defined in Java as:

```
public Car(int theModel, String theMake)
{
    yearModel    =    theModel;
    make         =    theMake;
    speed        =    0;
}
```

b) A constructor can have zero or more parameters, indicated by the name of a data type and a name for the parameter. The values of the parameters can be used when a new object is being initialized.

i) In the sample code above, the parameter **theModel's** value is being used to set the value of the **Car** object's **yearModel** field.

ii) The **speed** field of the **Car** object is set to zero using an assignment statement.

4) Define Accessor methods. Accessor methods are those that return the value of a field within an object.

a) Define the **getYearModel** Accessor method.

i) The header for the **getYearModel** accessor method is:

```
public int getYearModel()
```

ii) The keyword **public** is an access specifier indicating that this method may be used by any statement outside the **Car** class. Accessor methods always have **public** access. The purpose of accessor methods is to make the value of an object's field available to other programs.

iii) The keyword **int** designates the data type of the **yearModel** field, whose value is returned by this method. By their nature, accessor methods always return a value. The return data type is always the same as that of the field for which the method is the accessor.

iv) The name **getYearModel** is the name of the method. By convention, accessor methods are named **"get"** followed by the name of the field being accessed.

v) The open and close parenthesis "( )" indicate there are no parameters to this method. Accessor methods do not normally have parameters.

vi) The body of the **getYearModel** accessor method looks like:

```
{
    return yearModel;
}
```

vii) The method only has one statement, which provides the value of the field **yearModel** to the calling program. Most accessor methods have this pattern.

b) Define **getMake** accessor method.

i) The **getMake** accessor method returns the value of the **make** field. It is built in the same way as was the **getYearModel** method. In Java it looks like:

```
public String getMake()
{
    return  make;
}
```

5) Define **accelerate** method.

a) The **accelerate** method increases the **speed** of the **Car** object by 5. This method is a mutator method because it changes the value of a field.

b) In the body of the **accelerate** method, the value of the **speed** field is increased using Java arithmetic statements.

```
public void accelerate()
{
    //  regular addition expression
    speed   =   speed + 5;
}
```

6) Define **brake** method.

a) The **brake** method decreases the **speed** of the **Car** object by 5.

b) The **brake** method is written in the same way as the **accelerate** method, except the arithmetic statement is written so that the **speed** field is decreased by 5.

Code Listing 3 - 1 (Car.java)

```
//*****************************************************
//  Written by Jorge Menandoz                          *
//  Chapter 3, Programming Challenge 2, Car Class      *
//*****************************************************

//*****************************************************
//  2.  Car Class                                      *
//                                                     *
//  Write a class named Car that has the following     *
//  fields:                                            *
//                                                     *
```

```
//  •   yearModel                                       *
//      The yearModel field is an int that holds the    *
//      car's year model.                               *
//                                                      *
//  •   make                                            *
//      The make field is a String object that holds    *
//      the make of the car.                            *
//                                                      *
//  •   speed                                           *
//      The speed field is an int that holds the car's  *
//       current speed.                                 *
//                                                      *
//  In addition, the class should have the following    *
//  methods.                                            *
//                                                      *
//  •   Constructor                                     *
//      The constructor should accept the car's year    *
//      model and make as arguments. These values       *
//      should be assigned to the object's yearModel    *
//      and make fields. The constructor should also    *
//      assign 0 to the speed field.                    *
//                                                      *
//  •   Appropriate accessor methods to get the values  *
//      stored in an object's yearModel, make, and      *
//      speed fields.                                   *
//                                                      *
//  •   accelerate                                      *
//      The accelerate method should add 5 to the       *
//      speed field each time it is called.             *
//                                                      *
//  •   brake                                           *
//      The brake method should subtract 5 from the     *
//      speed field each time it is called.             *
//                                                      *
//*******************************************************

public class Car
{
    private int yearModel;  //  the car's model year
    private String make;    //  the car's make
    private int speed;      //  the car's speed

    //*****************************************************
    //  The Car class constructor creates a new object   *
    //  of type Car, initializing the yearModel field to *
    //  the value of parameter theModel, the make field  *
    //  to the value of the parameter theMake, and       *
    //  setting the speed field to the int value zero.   *
    //*****************************************************

    public Car(int theModel, String theMake)
    {
        yearModel   =   theModel;
        make        =   theMake;
        speed       =   0;
    }
```

```
    //***********************************************
    //  Accessor methods                            *
    //***********************************************

    //***********************************************
    //  The getYearModel method returns the int value    *
    //  of the Car object's field yearModel.        *
    //***********************************************

    public int getYearModel()
    {
        return  yearModel;
    }

    //***********************************************
    //  The getMake method returns the String value of   *
    //  the Car object's make field.                *
    //***********************************************

    public String getMake()
    {
        return  make;
    }

    //***********************************************
    //  The getSpeed method returns the int value of     *
    //  the Car object's speed field.               *
    //***********************************************

    public int getSpeed()
    {
        return  speed;
    }

    //***********************************************
    //  Mutator methods                             *
    //***********************************************

    //***********************************************
    //  The accelerate method increases the value of     *
    //  the speed field by five.                    *
    //***********************************************

    public void accelerate()
    {
        //  regular addition expression
        speed   =   speed + 5;
    }

    //***********************************************
    //  The brake method decreases the value of the      *
    //  speed  field by five.                       *
    //***********************************************

    public void brake()
    {
        //  for variety, use the auto-subtract operator
        speed   -=  5;
    }
}
```

Solution: CarDemo Class

Define What The Class Is To Do

Purpose	Demonstrate capabilities of **Car** class
Input	None
Process	Create an object of type **Car**. Use the **accelerate** method 5 times. Use the **brake** method 5 times
Output	Display: ✦ After each use of the **accelerate** method, display the Car object's speed. ✦ After each use of the **brake** method, display the Car object's speed.

High Level Pseudocode for CarDemo Class

1) Create a sample object of type **Car**.
2) Display the **Car** object and the value of its fields.
3) Repeat the following activities five times:
   a) Use the **accelerate** method to increase the Car object's speed.
   b) Display the Car object's current **speed**.
4) Repeat the following activities five times:
   a) Use the **brake** method to decrease the Car object's **speed**.
   b) Display the Car object's current **speed**.

Note:

A UML diagram is not provided for the CarDemo class; it has no fields and only one method, **main**.

Detailed Pseudocode for CarDemo Class

1) Create a sample object of type **Car**.
   a) A variable, **demoCar**, of type **Car** must be declared.
      i) This variable could be named with any legal Java identifier. It is common for objects in Java to have names that include their type, e.g. **myCar**, **anOtherCar**, **redCar**, etc.
   b) A new object of type **Car** must be created. This requires the use of the **Car** class constructor.
      i) The **Car** class constructor has two parameters: an **int** specifying **demoCar's** model year, and a **String** specifying **demoCar's** make. Values for these parameters must be provided (they can not be omitted).

```
Car demoCar = new Car( 2006, "DemoCar Rx");
```

2) Display the value of **demoCar's** fields.

   a) Use the **Car** class' accessor methods to retrieve the value of **demoCar's** fields.

      i) To apply a method to an object, write the object's name, a dot '.', and the name of the method including open and close parenthesis and any necessary parameters.

      ```
      demoCar.getYearModel();
      demoCar.getMake();
      demoCar.getSpeed();
      ```

      ii) No parameters are required (and are not allowed) on the accessor methods of the Car class. Nevertheless, the open and close parenthesis "( )" are required following the method's name.

      iii) The value returned by an accessor method can be used in any way that its type can be used in a Java statement. To display the make of object **demoCar**, write

      ```
      System.out.println("  Make    :" + demoCar.getMake());
      ```

3) Repeat the following activities five times. (In this program, repetition of action is accomplished by repeating the same Java statements five times in a row.)

   a) Use the **accelerate** method to increase the **demoCar's** speed. This is written:

      ```
      demoCar.accelerate();
      ```

   b) Display the **demoCar's** current speed. This is written:

      ```
      System.out.println("demoCar's speed:
             + demoCar.getSpeed());
      ```

4) Repeat the following activities five times. As before, the statements to accomplish this are written five times in a row.

   a) Use the **brake** method to decrease the **demoCar's** speed This is written:

      ```
      demoCar.brake();
      ```

   b) Display the **demoCar's** current speed. This is written in the same way it was in the previous step when the **demoCar** was accelerating.

Code Listing 3-2 (CarDemo.java)

```
//*****************************************************
//  Written by Jorge Menandoz                         *
//  Chapter 3, Programming Challenge 2, Car Class     *
//*****************************************************
```

```
//*****************************************************
//  Demonstrate the Car class in a program that creates *
//  a Car object, and then calls the accelerate         *
//  method 5 times. After each call to the accelerate   *
//  method, get the current speed of the car and        *
//  display it. Then, call the brake method 5 times.    *
//  After each call to the brake method, get the        *
//  current speed of the car and display it.            *
//*****************************************************

public class CarDemo
{
    //*************************************************
    //  create car object, show its properties,       *
    //  make it speed up and slow down                *
    //*************************************************
    public static void main(String[] args)
    {
        Car demoCar = new Car( 2006, "ExpressoMobile Rx");

        System.out.println("Demonstration of Car Class");
        System.out.println("");

        System.out.println("demoCar");
        System.out.println("  Model Year: "
            + demoCar.getYearModel());
        System.out.println("  Make      : "
            + demoCar.getMake());
        System.out.println("  Speed     : "
            + demoCar.getSpeed());
        System.out.println();

        //  make demoCar go faster - accelerate 5 times
        System.out.println("Speed Up!");
        demoCar.accelerate();
        System.out.println("demoCar's speed: "
            + demoCar.getSpeed());

        demoCar.accelerate();
        System.out.println("demoCar's speed: "
            + demoCar.getSpeed());

        demoCar.accelerate();
        System.out.println("demoCar's speed: "
            + demoCar.getSpeed());

        demoCar.accelerate();
        System.out.println("demoCar's speed: "
            + demoCar.getSpeed());
        demoCar.accelerate();
        System.out.println("demoCar's speed: "
            + demoCar.getSpeed());
        System.out.println();

        //  let's slow down again - brake 5 times
        System.out.println("Slow Down!");
        demoCar.brake();
        System.out.println("demoCar's speed: "
            + demoCar.getSpeed());

        demoCar.brake();
```

```
        System.out.println("demoCar's speed: "
            + demoCar.getSpeed());

        demoCar.brake();
        System.out.println("demoCar's speed: "
            + demoCar.getSpeed());

        demoCar.brake();
        System.out.println("demoCar's speed: "
            + demoCar.getSpeed());

        demoCar.brake();
        System.out.println("demoCar's speed: "
            + demoCar.getSpeed());
        System.out.println();

        System.out.println(
            "End of the Road for Car Class Demonstration");
    }
}
```

Program Output

```
Demonstration of Car Class

demoCar
  Model Year: 2006
  Make      : ExpressoMobile Rx
  Speed     : 0

Speed Up!
demoCar's speed: 5
demoCar's speed: 10
demoCar's speed: 15
demoCar's speed: 20
demoCar's speed: 25

Slow Down!
demoCar's speed: 20
demoCar's speed: 15
demoCar's speed: 10
demoCar's speed: 5
demoCar's speed: 0

End of the Road for Car Class Demonstration
```

(Optional) Car and CarDemo Classes with Javadoc

Introduction

Section 2.11 of the textbook describes the use of comments in Java. This Solutions Manual will follow the same comment style as is used in the textbook. This makes the two books consistent and permits easier comparison of programs from one to the other.

Block style comments are used to describe each class and each method. A block style comment has leading "//" characters on each line, and a box of asterisk '*' characters on the top, right side, and bottom of the comment. An example of a block style comment taken from the source code of the **Car** class is:

```
//*****************************************************
//  The Car class constructor creates a new object    *
//  of type Car, initializing the yearModel field to *
//  the value of parameter theModel, the make field  *
//  to the value of the parameter theMake, and       *
//  setting the speed field to the int value zero.   *
//*****************************************************
```

This section describes the use of another popular comment style, **javadoc**, which is unique to the Java language.

Javadoc comments are structured so that they can be processed by a separate program (named **javadoc**) that creates a set of pages written in Hyper Text Markup Language (**HTML**.) Each **HTML** page documents a class, describing its overall use, its fields, constructors, and methods. Using a World Wide Web Browser, **javadoc** documentation is easy to read and convenient to use for reference. Because the reference documentation for the class is included as comments in the same file as that of the source code that defines the class, it is likely to be an accurate description of the class' operation. If the class documentation were maintained in a separate file, using a process other than routine program development steps, it might not be kept complete and up to date.

An additional reason to learn about **javadoc** comments is that are used to describe the Java 2 Platform Standard Edition 5.0 Application Programming Interface (API) Specification. Please see: http://java.sun.com/j2se/1.5.0/docs/api/. The Java 2 API documentation is large and complex, but contains the definitive description of the Java class library. Additionally, it contains a wealth of information on the use of these classes (although it is not a tutorial). With some practice and patience, many programmers quickly find that the API **javadoc** is the first place to look when they have questions regarding the use of the Java Platform.

Here is the **javadoc** comment for the **Car** class constructor that was presented in block comment style at the beginning of this section:

```
/**
 *  Create a new object of type Car.
 *  Initialize the yearModel field to the value
 *  provided in the theModel parameter.
 *  Initialize the make field to the value provided
 *  in the theMake parameter.
 *  Initialize the speed field to zero.
 *
 *  @param      theModel    model year of Car object
 *  @param      theMake     make of the Car object
 */
```

The following figure shows this documentation after it has been formatted by the javadoc program.

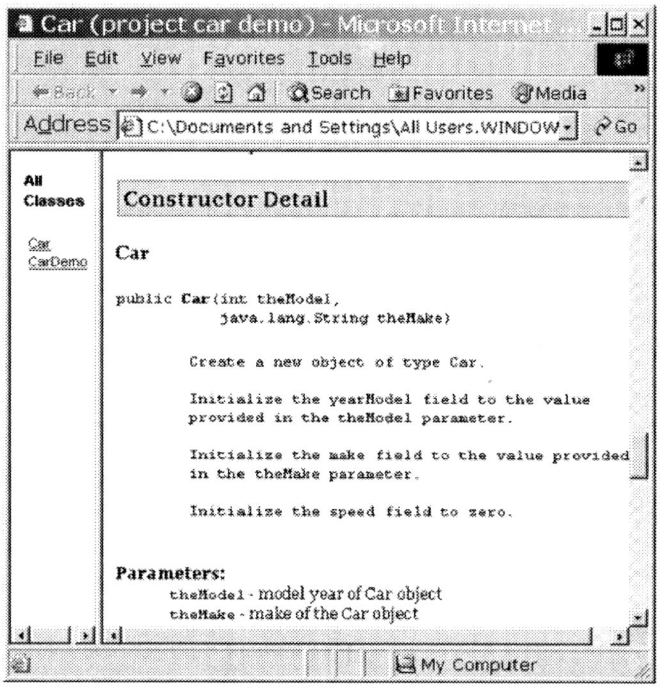

Figure 3 - 2 Javadoc Documentation for Car Class

Javadoc comments are built using a simple variation on Java's multi-line comment syntax (which Java adopted from the C Programming Language.)

Multi-line comments:

- begin with the character sequence "/*"
- end with the character sequence "*/"
- by convention:
    - are indented to the same level as the source code statements they describe,
    - are placed immediately before the section of source code to which they belong,

- o have the opening "/*" and the closing "*/" written on separate lines,
- o have intermediate lines that begin with a '*' character aligned with the first '*' in the opening "/**" and the last '*' in the closing "*/",
- o (These conventions need not be followed in order to use javadoc.)

Javadoc comments begin with the character sequence "/**" (that's one extra '*') but otherwise are the same as multi-line comments. Within the **javadoc** comment, keywords (tags) are used to identify specific pieces of information. In the previous example, the **@param** tag indicates that the first parameter to the **Car** class constructor holds the value to be used for the new **Car** object's model year attribute. For programmers beginning to learn **javadoc**, there are only a handful of tags that need to be used: **@author**, **@param**, and **@return**.

It is the software tools that are part of the Java Software Development Kit (SDK) that make the difference between **javadoc** comments and routine multi-line comments or block comments. In particular, the program **"javadoc"** parses Java program source files. Using the definitions of the class, fields, constructors and methods (determined from the source code) and the notations provided in the **javadoc** comments, the **javadoc** program produces an **HTML** page for each source file. The collection of all **HTML** pages for the necessary and relevant classes is a hypertext-indexed reference document for a project.

The **javadoc** tools expect **javadoc** comments to contain **HTML** format tags. Where a program's comments have already been formatted with spacing, alignment and line breaks, the **<PRE>** and **</PRE>** HTML tags should be used. Javadoc are treated as **HTML**, where any sequence of blank, tab, or newline characters are converted to one blank ' ' character. The use of the **<PRE>** **</PRE>** tag pair is shown in the following excerpt from the **Car** class **javadoc** comments.

```
/**
 *  <PRE>
 *  The Car Class
 *
 *  Write a class named Car that has the
 *  following fields:
 *
 *  •   yearModel
 *      The yearModel field is an int that holds the
 *      car's year model.
```

(lines omitted)

```
 *   •   brake
 *       The brake method should subtract 5 from the speed
 *       field each time it is called.
 *   </PRE>
 */
```

Creating Javadoc HTML Pages

1) These are a ***brief*** set of instructions for generating javadoc.
2) Use javadoc when classes have compiled successfully
3) Assume all the necessary Java source code files (*.java files) are in a folder named "project car demo".
4) Using Windows (or the similar Unix) commands:
   a) Change working directory to that in which the Java source files are stored

      ```
      C:> cd "project car demo"

      #use complete path name of the directory where
      #your *.java files reside
      ```

   b) Create a subdirectory (new folder) beneath the source file directory.

      ```
      C:> mkdir doc

      #creates a directory to place the javadoc output
      ```

   c) Use the javadoc program to create javadoc HTML pages.

      ```
      C:> javadoc -d doc -windowtitle "project car demo"
      -private -author *.java

      #Type this command continuously, even though it may take
      #several lines to type at the command prompt.
      ```

      i) Make sure the program javadoc is included in the PATH for your command line, or use its complete (fully qualified) file name. Normally, javadoc will be located in the same directory as the java and javac programs used to compile and execute Java programs.

      ii) The flag **-d doc** tells javadoc to place its results in the doc folder that was created in a previous step. Because javadoc creates many files, organization of them is simpler when they are kept separate from Java source files.

      iii) The flag **-windowtitle "project car demo"** gives javadoc a meaningful label for a WWW browser to display while the documentation pages are viewed.

      iv) The flag **-private** tells javadoc to create documentation for fields with either **public or private** access modifiers. **Javadoc's** default setting is to only create documentation for **public** fields. But, for student projects, documentation for **public** and **private** fields is sometimes desirable.

      v) The flag **-author** tells javadoc to process the **@author** tag so that the programmer's (student's) name can be included with the documentation. **Javadoc's** default setting is to ignore the **@author** tag.

vi) The string **"*.java"** in the command line tells **javadoc** to process every Java source file in the current directory. Alternatively, the names of each Java source file to be processed could be listed at the end of the command line.

vii) For more information on the javadoc tools in the Sun Java SDK, see **http://java.sun.com/j2se/1.5.0/docs/tooldocs/windows/javadoc.html**

Opinions Regarding The Use Of Javadoc

People can have strong opinions on **javadoc**, for and against. Many Java textbooks do not introduce **javadoc**. Some instructors never mention the topic. Other instructors, especially those who use it in their own work, require students to use **javadoc** in all their programming projects.

Javadoc comments have an appearance that is unusual in comparison to the block comments used in the text and this Solutions Manual. Most notably, blanks, tabs, or new line characters (white space) are used in **javadoc** to set apart sections of a program. Block comments, in comparison, use banners of characters to highlight sections of program. That **javadoc** comments use white space to draw attention to the definition of a class, its fields and its methods, may seem odd to a person who is accustomed to scan source program files for comment sections highlighted with repeated character strings. In practice, many programmers find it easy to switch from banner comment style to **javadoc** style (and vice versa).

Javadoc is widely used in academic, government, and commercial organizations. Many Java tools: source program editors, Integrated Development Environments (IDE), and Object Oriented Modeling systems; provide shorthand menus or forms to generate **javadoc** comments. Your instructor may already know of some of these programs. Or these programs can easily be found on the Internet as: "freeware", open source programs, or "academic" editions of a commercial software development tool.

Code Listing 3 - 3 (Car.java with javadoc comments)

```
/**
 *  Chapter 3, Programming Challenge 2, the Car class.
 *
 *  @author: Billy Jones
 */

/**
 *  <PRE>
 *      <!--
 *          The <PRE> ... </PRE> tags permit the
 *          insertion of preformatted text inside
 *          an HTML document so that the existing
 *          formats (spaces, tabs, columns, etc )
 *          are shown as they are written.
```

```
 *
 *          All javadoc comments are treated as HTML
 *          documents.
 *      -->
 *
 *  The Car Class
 *  (notated with javadoc comments)
 *
 *  Write a class named Car that has the
 *  following fields:
 *
 *  •    yearModel
 *       The yearModel field is an int that holds the
 *       car's year model.
 *
 *  •    make
 *       The make field is a String object that holds the
 *       make of the car.
 *
 *  •    speed
 *       The speed field is an int that holds the
 *       car's current speed.
 *
 *  In addition, the class should have the
 *  following methods.
 *
 *  •    Constructor
 *       The constructor should accept the car's year
 *       model and make as arguments. These values should
 *       be assigned to the object's yearModel and make
 *       fields. The constructor should also assign 0 to
 *       the speed field.
 *
 *  •    Appropriate accessor methods to
 *       get the values stored in an object's yearModel,
 *       make, and speed fields.
 *
 *  •    accelerate
 *
 *       The accelerate method should add 5 to the speed
 *       field each time it is called.
 *
 *  •    brake
 *       The brake method should subtract 5 from the speed
 *       field each time it is called.
 */

//  Javadoc comments for a class must appear immediately before
//  the class definition.

public class Car
{
    /** The car's model year */
    private int yearModel;

        //  in general only public fields and methods
        //  have javadoc comments, but private fields and
        //  methods can be included in the javadoc output

    /** The car's make */
    private String make;
```

```
/** The car's speed */
private int speed;

/**
 *  Create a new object of type Car.
 *  Initialize the yearModel field to the value
 *  provided in the theModel parameter.
 *  Initialize the make field to the value provided
 *  in the theMake parameter.
 *  Initialize the speed field to zero.
 *
 *  @param      theModel    model year of Car object
 *  @param      theMake     make of the Car object
 *
 */

//  Javadoc comments for a class constructor must be placed
//  immediately before the constructor definition.

public Car(int theModel, String theMake)
{
    yearModel    =   theModel;
    make         =   theMake;
    speed        =   0;
}

    //  Note: it is unnecessary to include data type
    //  documentation for fields, parameters, or
    //  return values.  The javadoc tools automatically
    //  detect type documentation from the syntax of
    //  the Java language.


/**
 *  Accessor method for private field yearModel
 *
 *  @return         the model year of the Car object
 */

//  Javadoc comments for a class method
//  must appear immediately before the method definition.

public int getYearModel()
{
    return  yearModel;
}

/**
 *  Accessor method for private field make
 *
 *  @return         the make of the Car object
 */
public String getMake()
{
    return  make;
}

/**
 *  Accessor method for private field speed
 *
 *  @return speed   current speed of the Car object
 */
```

```
    public int getSpeed()
    {
        return  speed;
    }

    /**
     *  Increase the Car object's speed by five
     */
    public void accelerate()
    {
        speed    =    speed + 5;
   }

    /**
     *  Decrease the Car object's speed by five
     */
    public void brake()
    {
        /*  use the auto-decrement operator */
        speed    -=   5;
    }
}
```

Code Listing 3 – 4 (CarDemo.java with javadoc comments)

```
/**
 *   Chapter 3, Programming Challenge 2
 *   The CarDemo Class
 *
 *   @author   Billy Jones
 *
 *   Demonstrate the Car class in a program that creates
 *   a Car object, and then calls the accelerate
 *   method 5 times. After each call to the
 *   accelerate method, get the current speed of the
 *   car and display it. Then, call the brake method
 *   5 times. After each call to the brake method,
 *   get the current speed of the car and display it.
 */

//   The Javadoc comments for a class immediately
//   precede the definition of the class.

public class CarDemo
{
   /**
    *   Create a demoCar object; Show its properties;
    *
    *   Five times in a row, use the accelerate method to
    *   increase demoCar's speed, displaying its speed
    *   after every acceleration.
    *
    *   Then, five times in a row, use the brake method to
    *   decrease demoCar's speed, displaying its speed
    *   after every deceleration.
    */

   //   The Javadoc comments for a method immediately
   //   precede the definition of the method.
```

```
    public static void main(String[] args)
    {
        Car demoCar = new Car( 2006, "ExpressoMobile Rx");

        System.out.println("Demonstration of Car Class");
        System.out.println("");

        System.out.println("demoCar");
        System.out.println("  Model Year: "
            + demoCar.getYearModel());
        System.out.println("  Make       : "
            + demoCar.getMake());
        System.out.println("  Speed      : "
            + demoCar.getSpeed());
        System.out.println("");

        //  make demoCar go faster - accelerate 5 times
        System.out.println("Speed Up!");
        demoCar.accelerate();
        System.out.println("demoCar's speed: "
            + demoCar.getSpeed());
        demoCar.accelerate();
        System.out.println("demoCar's speed: "
            + demoCar.getSpeed());
        demoCar.accelerate();
        System.out.println("demoCar's speed: "
            + demoCar.getSpeed());
        demoCar.accelerate();
        System.out.println("demoCar's speed: "
            + demoCar.getSpeed());
        demoCar.accelerate();
        System.out.println("demoCar's speed: "
            + demoCar.getSpeed());
        System.out.println("");

        //  let's slow down again - brake 5 times
        System.out.println("Slow Down!");
        demoCar.brake();
        System.out.println("demoCar's speed: "
            + demoCar.getSpeed());
        demoCar.brake();
        System.out.println("demoCar's speed: "
            + demoCar.getSpeed());
        demoCar.brake();
        System.out.println("demoCar's speed: "
            + demoCar.getSpeed());
        demoCar.brake();
        System.out.println("demoCar's speed: "
            + demoCar.getSpeed());
        demoCar.brake();
        System.out.println("demoCar's speed: "
            + demoCar.getSpeed());
        System.out.println("");

        System.out.println(
            "End of the Road for Car Class Demonstration");
    }
}
```

Programming Challenge 4: RetailItem Class

Problem Statement:

Write a class named **RetailItem** that holds data about an item in a retail store. The class should have the following fields:

- description
  The **description** field is a **String** object that holds a brief description of the item.
- unitsOnHand
  The **unitsOnHand** field is an **int** variable that holds the number of units currently in inventory.
- price
  The **price** field is a **double** that holds the item's retail price.

Write appropriate mutator methods that store values in these fields, and accessor methods that return the values in these fields. Once you have written the class, write a separate program that creates three **RetailItem** objects and stores the following data in them.

	Description	Units On Hand	Price
Item #1	Jacket	12	59.95
Item #2	Designer Jeans	40	34.95
Item #3	Shirt	20	24.95

Solution: RetailItem Class

Define What The Class Is To Do

Purpose	Model Properties And Behaviors Of An Article For Sale	
Fields	description	brief description of the item
	unitsOnHand	number of items in inventory
	price	retail price of the item
Constructor		Create an object of class RetailItem. Initialize all fields to zero or empty value.

	setDescription	set the value of the **description** field to the value of the method's parameter
	setUnitsOnHand	set the value of the **unitsOnHand** field to the value of the method's parameter
Methods	setPrice	set the value of the **price** field to the value of the method's parameter
	getDescription	return the value of the **description** field
	getUnitsOnHand	return the value of the **unitsOnHand** field
	getPrice	return the value of the **price** field

High Level Pseudocode for RetailItem Class

1) Define **RetailItem** Class
   a) Define fields for **description, unitsOnHand,** and **price.**
2) Define **RetailItem** Class constructor
   a) Initialize **description** field with empty **String.**
   b) Initialize **unitsOnHand** field to zero (0).
   c) Initialize **price** field to zero (0).
3) Define Mutator Methods
   a) Define method **setDescription**
      i) set **description** field to value of method's parameter
   b) Define method **setUnitsOnHand**
      i) set **unitsOnHand** field to value of method's parameter
   c) Define method **setPrice**
      i) set **price** field to value of method's parameter
4) Define Accessor Methods
   a) Define method **getDescription**
      i) return value of **description** field
   b) Define method **getUnitsOnHand**
      i) return value of **unitsOnHand** field
   c) Define method **getPrice**
      i) return value of **price** field

RetailItem
- description : String - unitsOnHand : int - price : double
+ RetailItem() : + getDescription() : String + getUnitsOnHand() : int + getPrice() : double + setDescription(aDescription : String) : void + setUnitsOnHand(units : int) : void + setPrice(aPrice : double) : void + toString() : String

Figure 3 - 3 UML for RetailItem Class

Detailed Pseudocode for RetailItem Class

1) Define **RetailItem** Class
   a) The **RetailItem** class is defined in the same manner as the **Car** Class in the previous solution.

```
public class RetailItem
{
        // define fields

        // define constructor

        // define mutator methods

        // define accessor methods

        // define miscellaneous methods
}
```

2) Define fields for **description**, **unitsOnHand**, and **price**.
   a) The Programming Challenge Problem Statement provides the Java data type for each of these fields.

```
private String description;

private int unitsOnHand;
```

```
private double price;
```

b) Remember that fields in a Class should have private access in order to insure data encapsulation.

3) Define **RetailItem** Class constructor

a) The **RetailItem** Class constructor has the same basic structure as that of the **Car** Class described in the previous solution.

i) The design of this solution for the **RetailItem** Class is to define the constructor to have no parameters. The value of fields for objects in this class would be set using the mutator methods.

ii) An alternative design for the **RetailItem** Class constructor would be for it to have parameters for the **description**, **unitsOnHand** and **price** fields.

(1) Except for the most simple programs and Classes, there are several designs that can satisfy the requirements of the Problem Statement.

iii) The constructor explicitly initializes each field of the object.

(1) Fields of type **String**, and other non-primitive Java data types need to be initialized. If not, errors would be likely when the object was used later in the program.

iv) The **RetailItem** object's fields are initialized as follows:

```
description = "";
unitsOnHand = 0;
price = 0.00;
```

4) Define Mutator Methods

a) Mutator methods change the value of an object's field to the value of the mutator method's parameter.

b) Mutator methods always have **public** access.

i) The purpose of a mutator method is to allow other programs to modify the value of a field in an object. In these solutions, the mutator changes one field only. In general, however, there are situations where a change to one field may necessitate changes to other fields in the object.

c) Mutator methods do not return values. They are defined as having type **void.**

d) The parameter(s) to a mutator method have the same data type(s) as that of the object's field(s) to be modified.

i) Because Java implicitly performs data type conversions, such as widening, (also known as promotion) it might seem that several data types can be used as parameters to a mutator method. For example, the **setPrice** method (described in the next section) can be used with a parameter value of type **int, long, float** or **double.** That is possible because Java automatically converts primitive data of a narrow type to a wider type when necessary. Consequently, data of type **int**, **long**, and **float** can be used with the mutator provided, even though that method is defined to take a parameter of type **double**.

ii) In later chapters, the textbook will describe how multiple mutator methods can be described for the same field. In these cases, the different mutator methods must have parameters of different data types.

e) The operation performed in a mutator method is usually an assignment statement where the object's field is set to the value of the mutator parameter.

f) Typically, parameters to the mutator are given names that include the name of the field that is being modified. For example, in the **setDescription** method that follows, the parameter with the new value for the description field is named **aDescription**.

5) Define method **setDescription**

a) Using the guidelines provided in the previous section, the mutator method **setDescription** is written:

```
public void setDescription(String aDescription)
{
    description =  aDescription;
}
```

6) Define method **setUnitsOnHand** - Define method **setPrice**

a) The methods **setUnitsOnHand** and **setPrice** are defined in a manner similar to that used in the **setDescription** mutator method

7) Define Accessor Methods

a) The accessor methods: **getDescription**, **getUnitsOnHand**, and **getPrice** are written in the same manner as the accessor methods for the Car Class in the previous solution.

8) **Optional** - Miscellaneous Methods

a) The Programming Challenge asks that the **RetailItem** Class be demonstrated using a specific set of objects. For convenience, a **toString** method has been added to the **RetailItem** Class.

b) A **toString** method is **optional.**

c) Many classes benefit from having a method name **toString** which is implicitly called under certain circumstances.

d) A **toString** method takes all the fields in an object and converts them into an easily readable text phrase of type **String.** This text phrase is the return value of the **toString** method.

e) Using a **toString** method, an object can easily be added to a **System.out.println statement.**

i) **Without** a **toString** method, to display the object **aRetailItem** of type **RetailItem** would require a Java statement such as:

```
System.out.println("RetailItem: [description: \""
      + aRetailItem.getDescription() + "\"; "
      + "unitsOnHand: "
```

```
+ aRetailItem.getUnitsOnHand() + "; "
+ "price $" + aRetailItem.getPrice() + "]" );
```

ii) **With** a **toString** method the previous statement could be written as:

```
System.out.println(aRetailItem);
```

f) The value returned by the **toString** method is:

```
"Retail Item: [description: \"" + description
    + "\"; unitsOnHand: " + unitsOnHand
    + "; price: $" + price + "] "
```

g) **String** constants (such as "[description:", "unitsOnHand:", etc.) label values that are being returned. The value returned by the **toString** method is meant to be read easily, and not require decoding by the user.

h) Notice the character sequence \" in the **String** returned by the **toString method.** This sequence inserts a " (double quote) in the return value. Without the preceding \ (backslash) character, Java would interpret the " as the end of the return **String,** with the result that the statement would have incorrect syntax. The quote characters are inserted in the return **String** to highlight the value of the description field of objects of the **RetailItem** Class.

Code Listing 3 – 5 (RetailItem.java)

```
//*******************************************************
//                                                      *
//  Written by Earl Scott Jr.                           *
//  Chapter 3 - Programming Challenge 4, RetailItem Class *
//                                                      *
//*******************************************************

//*******************************************************
//  RetailItem Class                                    *
//                                                      *
//  Write a class named RetailItem that holds data      *
//  about an item in a retail store.                    *
//                                                      *
//  The class should have the following fields:         *
//                                                      *
//      description                                     *
//                                                      *
//      The description field is a String object that  *
//      holds a brief description of the item.          *
//                                                      *
//      unitsOnHand                                     *
//                                                      *
//      The unitsOnHand field is an int variable that  *
//      holds the number of units currently in          *
//      inventory.                                      *
//                                                      *
//      price                                           *
//                                                      *
//      The price field is a double that holds the      *
//      item's retail price.                            *
//                                                      *
```

```
//  Write appropriate mutator methods that store          *
//  values in these fields, and accessor methods          *
//  that return the values in these fields.               *
//*********************************************************

public class RetailItem
{

    //  text description of item
    private String description;

    //  current stock of item
    private int unitsOnHand;

    //  current price of item
    private double price;

    //*****************************************************
    //  The RetailItem class constructor creates a new    *
    //  object  of type RetailItem.  The description      *
    //  field is set to an empty string, the units on     *
    //  hand field is set to zero and the price field is  *
    //  set to zero.                                      *
    //*****************************************************

    public RetailItem()
    {
        description =   "";
        unitsOnHand =   0;
        price       =   0.00;
    }

    //****************************************************
    //  Mutator methods                                  *
    //****************************************************

    //******************************************************
    //  The setDescription method sets the description     *
    //  field to the value of the method's parameter.      *
    //******************************************************

    public void setDescription(String aDescription)
    {
        description =   aDescription;
    }

    //******************************************************
    //  The setUnitsOnHand method sets the unitsOnHand     *
    //  field to the value of the method's parameter.      *
    //******************************************************

    public void setUnitsOnHand(int units)
    {
        unitsOnHand =   units;
    }
```

```
    //****************************************************
    //  The setPrice method sets the price field to the   *
    //  value of the method's parameter.                  *
    //****************************************************

    public void setPrice(double aPrice)
    {
        price   =   aPrice;
    }

    //**************************************************
    //  Accessor methods                               *
    //**************************************************

    //****************************************************
    //  The getDescription method returns the value of    *
    //  the description field.                            *
    //****************************************************

    public String getDescription()
    {
        return  description;
    }

    //****************************************************
    //  The getUnitsOnHand method returns the value of    *
    //  the unitsOnHand field.                            *
    //****************************************************

    public int getUnitsOnHand()
    {
        return  unitsOnHand;
    }

    //****************************************************
    //  The getPrice method returns the value of the      *
    //  price field.                                      *
    //****************************************************

    public double getPrice()
    {
        return  price;
    }

    //****************************************************
    //  The toString method returns a String that         *
    //  describes a RetailItem object.  This method is    *
    //  not required but is convenient to use for         *
    //  demonstration of the RetailItem class.            *
    //****************************************************

    public String toString()
    {
        return "Retail Item: [description: \"" + description
            + "\"; unitsOnHand: " + unitsOnHand
            + "; price: $" + price + "] ";
    }
}
```

Solution: RetailItemDemonstration Class

Define What The Class Is To Do

Purpose	Demonstrate the use of the **RetailItem** Class
Input	None
Processing	Create three **RetailItem** objects and store the following data in them Description / Units on Hand / Price Item 1 Jacket 12 59.95 Item 2 Designer Jeans 40 34.95 Item 3 Shirt 20 24.95
Output	Display the items that were created

High Level Pseudocode for RetailItemDemonstration Class

1) Create three **RetailItem** objects.
2) Display the objects.
3) Store data from the problem statement into each object using the **RetailItem** Class mutator methods.
4) Display the objects.

Detailed Pseudocode for RetailItemDemonstration Class

1) Declare three variables of type **RetailItem** named **ri01, ri02,** and **ri03.**
2) Initialize **ri01, ri02,** and **ri03** using the **new** operator and the **RetailItem** constructor.
3) Step 1 and 2 can be combined in one statement:

```
RetailItem ri01 = new RetailItem();
```

4) Display **ri01, ri02, ri03.**
   a) The display of objects of type **RetailItem** is simplified because a **toString** method has been provided in that class. The **System.out.println** method will automatically use the **toString** method to display a formatted text description of each object.
5) Store data from the problem statement into object **ri01** using the **RetailItem** Class mutator methods. This is written as:

```
ri01.setDescription("Jacket");
ri01.setUnitsOnHand(12);
ri01.setPrice(59.95);
```

6) Display object **ri01.**
   a) An object can be displayed by using its accessor methods to determine the value of its fields. This could be written as:

```
System.out.println(
    "Retail Item 1 is a/an \""
```

```
        + ri01.getDescription()
        + "\" priced at $" + ri01.getPrice()
        + " with " + ri01.getUnitsOnHand()
        + " units on hand.");
```

b) Notice the character sequence \" in the display **String**. This sequence inserts a " (double quote) in the output. Without the preceding \ (backslash) character, Java would interpret the " as the end of the **String** to be displayed. The quote characters are inserted in the display **String** to highlight the value of the description field. (This technique was also used in the **toString** method of the **RetailItem** Class.)

7) Store data from the problem statement into objects **ri02** and **ri03**, using similar steps to those described to store data into object **ri01**.

8) Display objects **ri02** and **ri03**.

a) Since a **toString** method has been provided for the **RetailItem** Class, the variables **ri02** and **ri03** can be written directly in the **String** to be displayed using the **System.out.println** method.

Code Listing 3 - 6 (RetailItemDemonstration.java)

```
//*********************************************************
//                                                        *
//  Written by Earl Scott Jr.                             *
//  Chapter 3 - Programming Challenge 4, RetailItem Class *
//                                                        *
//*********************************************************

//*********************************************************
//  4.  RetailItem Class                                  *
//                                                        *
//  Once you have written the [RetailItem] Class, write   *
//  a separate program that creates three RetailItem      *
//  objects and stores the following data in them         *
//                                                        *
//          Description      Units On Hand   Price        *
//Item #1   Jacket               12          59.95        *
//Item #2   Designer Jeans       40          34.95        *
//Item #3   Shirt                20          24.95        *
//                                                        *
//*********************************************************

public class RetailItemDemonstration
{
    //****************************************************
    //  Create the RetailItem objects specified in the   *
    //  Programming Challenge.  Demonstrate that the     *
    //  accessor and mutator methods perform as          *
    //  necessary                                        *
    //****************************************************

    public static void main(String[] args)
    {
```

```
//**********************************************
//  create three retail items, as requested in    *
//  the Programming Challenge                     *
//**********************************************

RetailItem  ri01    = new RetailItem();
RetailItem  ri02    = new RetailItem();
RetailItem  ri03    = new RetailItem();

//**********************************************
//  Display the objects ri01, ri02, ri03          *
//  Note: the RetailItem toString method is       *
//  automatically used to display the contents    *
//  in each RetailItem object                     *
//**********************************************

System.out.println("ri01  " + ri01);
System.out.println("ri02  " + ri02);
System.out.println("ri03  " + ri03);
System.out.println();

//**********************************************
//  Use the mutator methods to change the object's*
//  fields as requested in the programming        *
//  challenge.                                    *
//**********************************************

ri01.setDescription("Jacket");
ri01.setUnitsOnHand(12);
ri01.setPrice(59.95);

//**********************************************
//  Display object ri01.                          *
//**********************************************

System.out.println("ri01  " + ri01);
System.out.println();

//**********************************************
//  Display object ri01.                          *
//  Use accessor methods to retrieve object's     *
//  fields values.                                *
//**********************************************

System.out.println(
    "Retail Item 1 is a/an \"" + ri01.getDescription()
    + "\" priced at $" + ri01.getPrice()
    + " with " + ri01.getUnitsOnHand()
    + " units on hand.");
System.out.println();

//**********************************************
//  Use the mutator methods to change object      *
//  ri02's fields as requested in the programming *
//  challenge.                                    *
//**********************************************

ri02.setPrice(34.95);
ri02.setUnitsOnHand(40);
ri02.setDescription("Designer Jeans");
```

```
        //***********************************************
        //  display object ri02                         *
        //***********************************************

        System.out.println("ri02 " + ri02);

        //***********************************************
        //  Use the mutator methods to change object    *
        //  ri03's fields as requested in the programming *
        //  challenge.                                  *
        //***********************************************

        ri03.setUnitsOnHand(20);
        ri03.setPrice(24.95);
        ri03.setDescription("Shirt");

        //***********************************************
        //  display object ri03                         *
        //***********************************************

        System.out.println("ri03 " + ri03);
        System.out.println();
    }
}
```

Program Output

```
ri01 Retail Item: [description: ""; unitsOnHand: 0; price: $0.0]
ri02 Retail Item: [description: ""; unitsOnHand: 0; price: $0.0]
ri03 Retail Item: [description: ""; unitsOnHand: 0; price: $0.0]

ri01 Retail Item: [description: "Jacket"; unitsOnHand: 12; price:
$59.95]

Retail Item 1 is a/an "Jacket" priced at $59.95 with 12 units on hand.

ri02 Retail Item: [description: "Designer Jeans"; unitsOnHand: 40;
price: $34.95]
ri03 Retail Item: [description: "Shirt"; unitsOnHand: 20; price: $24.95]
```

Programming Challenge 6: Widget Factory

Problem Statement:

Design a class for a widget manufacturing plant. The class should have a method whose argument is the number of widgets that must be produced. The class should have another method that calculates how many days it will take to produce the number of widgets. (Assume that 10 widgets may be produced each hour. The plant operates two shifts of eight hours each per day.)

Demonstrate the class by writing a separate program that creates an instance of the class. The program should pass a number of widgets to the object, and call the object's method that displays the number of days it will take to produce that many widgets.

Solution: WidgetFactory Class

Define What The WidgetFactory Class Is To Do

Purpose	Model a Widget Manufacturing Plant	
Fields	widgetsToBuild	The number of widgets to be produced by the plant
Constructor		Create an object of type **WidgetFactory**. Initialize object's fields to zero or empty value.
Methods	setWidgetsToBuild	Set the **widgetsToBuild** field to the value of the method's parameter.
	getWidgetsToBuild	Return the value of the **widgetsToBuild** field.
	getDaysToBuild	Return the number of days it takes to build the number of widgets in the **widgetsToBuild** field.

High Level Pseudocode for WidgetFactory Class

1) Define **WidgetFactory** Class
2) Define **widgetsToBuild** field
3) Define Named Constants for **WidgetFactory** Class
4) Define **WidgetFactory** constructor
5) Define **setWidgetsToBuild** mutator method
6) Define **getWidgetsToBuild** accessor method

7) Define **getDaysToBuild** method

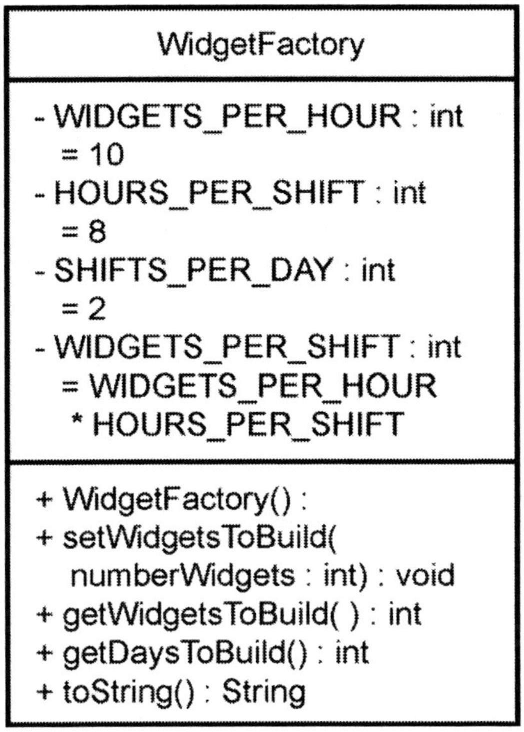

Figure 3 – 4 UML for WidgetFactory Class

Detailed Pseudocode for WidgetFactory Class

1) Define the **WidgetFactory** Class as in the previous Solutions, but with an additional section for the definition of Named Constants:

```
public class WidgetFactory
{
        // define fields

        // define Named Constants

        // define constructor

        // define mutator methods

        // define accessor methods

        // define miscellaneous methods
}
```

2) Define field for **widgetsToBuild.** The number of widgets is a whole number so a variable of type **int** is used.

```
private int widgetsToBuild;
```

3) Define Named Constants for **WidgetFactory** Class

   a) The problem statement for this Programming Challenge gives several values that define the characteristics of the factory's production capacity:

- 10 widgets may be produced each hour
- the plant has 2 shifts
- each shift has 8 hours

b) The Java statements in the **WidgetFactory** Class could use these values directly. However, if the problem statement were to change, it might be hard for a programmer to identify all the places in the source code where the values have been used.

c) Named Constants provide a mnemonic term for a particular value. (See Chapter 2, Section 2.7.) In Java, Named Constants have the syntax:

```
final double INTEREST_RATE = 0.069;
```

d) By convention, Named Constants in Java are given names using all capital letters. Where the most meaningful name for a constant uses two or more words, a '_' (underline) character is placed in the name to separate the words.

e) Named Constants defined in a Class often are given public access, so that they can be used by other programs. In Java, the value of **π** (the ratio of a circle's circumference to its diameter) is provided by the **Math** Class. It can be used in any program, for example:

```
double circumference;
double diameter = 10.00;

circumference = Math.PI * diameter;
```

f) Looking at the Java 2 API for the **Math** class (in package **java.lang**), it shows that the definition of **Math.PI** is:

```
public static final double PI = 3.141592653589793;
```

g) **Math.PI** is defined to be a **public static** value. Having public access, the constant is available to any Java statement. Being defined as a static value means that it exists independently of any object in class Math. That means the term **Math.PI** can be used in a program without first having to create an object in the **Math** Class.

h) Using these guidelines for the **WidgetFactory** solution, Named Constants can be defined for each of the numeric values given in the problem statement.

```
public static final int   WIDGETS_PER_HOUR = 10;
public static final int   HOURS_PER_SHIFT = 8;
public static final int   SHIFTS_PER_DAY = 2;
```

i) These constants can be used to define other values that can be used in the Class:

```
public static final int   WIDGETS_PER_SHIFT =
    WIDGETS_PER_HOUR * HOURS_PER_SHIFT;
public static final int   WIDGETS_PER_DAY =
    WIDGETS_PER_SHIFT * SHIFTS_PER_DAY;
```

4) Define **WidgetFactory** Class constructor

   a) The constructor for **WidgetFactory** is similar to the constructor for the **RetailItem** solution. The **WidgetFactory** constructor has no parameters. Its only function is to set all fields of the new object to a safe initial value.

5) Define **setWidgetsToBuild** mutator method

   a) The **setWidgetsToBuild** method is similar to the mutator methods described for the RetailItem Class in the previous solution.

6) Define **getWidgetsToBuild** accessor method

   a) The **getWidgetsToBuild** method is similar to the accessor methods described for the **Car** and **RetailItem** Classes in the previous solutions.

7) Define **getDaysToBuild** method

   a) The **getDaysToBuild** method returns an **int** value that is the number of days it takes to build the number of widgets in the **widgetsToBuild** field of the Class.

   b) The number of days it takes to build a certain number of widgets is the number of widgets needed divided by the widgets the factory can produce in a day. Perform this calculation so that a decimal value is returned.

   c) If the result of the calculation is a whole number, then that is the value to be returned by this method.

   d) However, if the calculation does not result in a whole number value, then the value returned by this method should be the next larger whole number than the value of the calculation.

      i) For example, it would take 24 factory hours to produce 240 widgets. That means it would take 3 shifts, over 2 days, to produce 240 widgets. In this case, the **getDaysToBuild** method would return the value 2.

   e) In order to perform this calculation, the **Math.ceil** (or ceiling) method is used. The **Math.ceil** method takes a **double** as its parameter and returns a **double** (that has a whole number value.) If the Math.ceil's parameter had a whole number value, then that is the value returned. But if the Math.ceil's parameter is not a whole number, then the value returned is the next higher whole number value.

   f) To calculate the decimal value of days it would take to build the number of widgets given in the field **widgetsToBuild,** the Java statement needed is:

```
// local variables used in the calculations

int daysToBuild;
double timeToBuild;

timeToBuild =
    ((double) widgetsToBuild) / WIDGETS_PER_DAY;
```

i) Note that to calculate a decimal value, at least one of the values in the division operation has to have a **float** or **double** data type. This is accomplished using a cast operation to widen the **int** value of **widgetsToBuild** to a **double** value.

g) Having computed a decimal value for the number of days needed by the factory, the **Math.ceil** method is used to convert that value to the next higher whole number value. Then, a narrowing cast operation is used to change the value returned by the **Math.ceil** method into an **int** value.

```
daysToBuild = (int) Math.ceil(timeToBuild);
```

h) The value of the variable **daysToBuild** is returned by the **getDaysToBuild** method.

8) Define **toString** method (**optional**)

a) As in the solution to the **RetailItem** Class Programming Challenge, a **toString** method is provided for convenience in a program that uses the **WidgetFactory** Class.

Code Listing 3 - 7 (WidgetFactory.java)

```
//*****************************************************
// Written by Lynda Bryant                            *
// Chapter 3                                          *
// Programming Challenge 6: Widget Factory            *
//*****************************************************

//*****************************************************
//  6.  Widget Factory                                *
//                                                    *
//  Design a class for a widget manufacturing         *
//  plant. The class should have a method whose       *
//  argument is the number of widgets that must       *
//  be produced. The class should have another        *
//  method that calculates how many days it will      *
//  take to produce the number of widgets.            *
//  (Assume that 10 widgets may be produced each      *
//  hour. The plant operates two shifts of eight      *
//  hours each per day.)                              *
//*****************************************************

public class WidgetFactory
{
    //*************************************************
    //  Define the factory's production capacity as   *
    //  given in the problem statement.               *
    //                                                *
    //  These constants have public access so that they *
    //  can be used by programs that use the          *
    //  WidgetFactory Class.  They are also defined as *
    //  static so that they can be used independently of *
    //  a WidgetFactory object.                       *
    //                                                *
    //  Use Named Constants so that the meaning of the *
    //  values is apparent to a programmer who may    *
    //  need to modify them should the problem statement *
    //  change.                                       *
    //                                                *
```

```
//  Where ever possible, Named Constants should be     *
//  used in programs instead of literal values.        *
//*****************************************************

public static final int   WIDGETS_PER_HOUR = 10;

public static final int   HOURS_PER_SHIFT = 8;

public static final int   SHIFTS_PER_DAY = 2;

public static final int   WIDGETS_PER_SHIFT =
    WIDGETS_PER_HOUR * HOURS_PER_SHIFT;

public static final int   WIDGETS_PER_DAY =
    WIDGETS_PER_SHIFT * SHIFTS_PER_DAY;

//  the number of items the factory should produce
private int widgetsToBuild;

//*****************************************************
//   The constructor for the WidgetFactory class      *
//   initializes the widgetsToBuild field to zero.    *
//*****************************************************

public WidgetFactory()
{
    widgetsToBuild  =   0;
}

//*****************************************************
//   The setWidgetsToBuild method sets the field      *
//   widgetsToBuild to the value given by the         *
//   parameter numberWidgets.                         *
//*****************************************************

public void setWidgetsToBuild(int numberWidgets)
{
    widgetsToBuild  =   numberWidgets;
}

//*****************************************************
//   The getWidgetsToBuild method returns the value   *
//   of the field widgetsToBuild.                     *
//*****************************************************

public int  getWidgetsToBuild()
{
    return  widgetsToBuild;
}

//*****************************************************
//   The getDaysToBuild method returns the number of  *
//   days it will take the factory to produce the     *
//   number of widgets specified in the widgetsToBuild*
//   field.                                           *
//*****************************************************

public int getDaysToBuild()
{
    //  local variables used inside the getDaysToBuild
    //  method
```

```
        int daysToBuild;
        double timeToBuild;

        //  The number of widgets that can be produced
        //  per day is determined by the factory's
        //  parameters that were given in the problem
        //  statement.
        timeToBuild =
            ((double) widgetsToBuild )/ WIDGETS_PER_DAY;

            //  Note: This calculation is a division of
            //  decimal values.  The result saved in
            //  daysToBuild may be a whole number value, but
            //  may be a value with digits to the right of
            //  the decimal point.

        //  Since the number of days needed by the factory
        //  has to be a whole number, the Math.ceil method
        //  is used.  Math.ceil returns the whole number
        //  value of its parameter, or if the value is
        //  not a whole number, the next larger whole
        //  number value.  The value returned by
        //  Math.ceil is a double.  In order to store
        //  that value in variable daysToBuild, an
        //  explicit cast (narrowing) from type double
        //  to type int is required.

        daysToBuild = (int) Math.ceil(timeToBuild);

        return  daysToBuild;
    }

    //*************************************************
    //  The (optional) toString method returns a readable *
    //  text value showing the contents of a WidgetFactory*
    //  object.                                           *
    //*************************************************

    public String toString()
    {
        return  "Widget Factory [widgets to build: "
            + widgetsToBuild + "];" ;
    }
}
```

Solution: WidgetFactoryDemo Class

Define What The WidgetFactoryDemo Class Is To Do

Purpose	Demonstrate the correct operation of the WidgetFactory Class
Input	None
Process	Create **WidgetFactory** objects Determine the number of days it takes to produce a sample of widget batches

Output	Display the number of days it takes to produce each sample of widgets.

High Level Pseudocode for WidgetFactoryDemo Class

1) Declare variables of type **WidgetFactory**
2) Construct **WidgetFactory** objects.
3) Create a sample of test cases that demonstrate that the **WidgetFactory** Class performs correctly.
   a) Test case creation is an important step in the software development process. It is the part of the process where the *author* finds and fixes the errors and mistakes in her or his software.
   b) After working hours or days on a program (or in a professional environment perhaps months or years) it is natural for a programmer to believe the software is correct as written. However, it is important to develop the skill to stand back and take an objective look at the program and test it thoroughly before handing it in to your instructor, or turning over to a customer.
      i) Finding your own mistakes in a program can bruise your ego, but having other people find these mistakes is always more costly and far more embarrassing.
   c) Test case data should exercise the normal operation of a program, but should also test boundary conditions to insure the program's logic handles these situations correctly.
   d) For the **WidgetFactory** Class, the test cases selected are to determine the number of days it takes to build these number of widgets: 1, 160 (the maximum the factory can build in a day), 161, and 0.
   e) For all but the simplest programs, there is no limit to the number of test cases that may be created. As a practical matter, only a small number of tests can be performed. Where possible, one test case should cover each possible path through the program, but even that is often too many. Choosing a representative sample of test data is an important skill for a programmer to develop.
4) For the case where 1 widget is to be produced, determine the number of days required and display the value. That value should be 1, i.e. it takes at least one day to produce any number of widgets.
5) For the case where the number of widgets to be produced is the one day capacity of the WidgetFactory, calculate the number of days required and the display the value. That value should be 1.
6) For the case where the number of widgets to be produced is one more than the one day capacity of the WidgetFactory, calculate the number of days required and the display the value. That value should be 2.
7) For the case where zero widgets are to be produced, calculate the number of days required and display the value. That value should be

zero, i.e. it takes no time for the factory to produce zero widgets. If you look around, you'll see that you already ***have*** zero widgets.

Detailed Pseudocode for WidgetFactoryDemo Class

1) Declare two objects of Class **WidgetFactory: wf01** and **wf02.**
2) Declare local variables used in the demonstration program.
3) Use the **WidgetFactory** constructor to create the objects for **wf01** and **wf02.**
4) Display the **WidgetFactory** objects, showing their initial state.
5) With object **wf01,** use the **setWidgetsToBuild** method to modify the object's **widgetsToBuild** field to one (1).
6) With object **wf02,** use the **setWidgetsToBuild** method to modify the object's **widgetsToBuild** field to the widget factory's maximum daily output, as defined in the Programming Challenge's problem statement.
   a) Use the Named Constant **WIDGETS_PER_DAY** from the **WidgetFactory** Class.
   b) From the problem statement, the factory produces 10 widgets per hour. The factory has two (2) shifts of eight (8) hours each. Under those circumstances, the factory produces 10 times 8 times 2, or 160 widgets in one day.
   c) To use the WIDGETS_PER_DAY, the name of the Class in which it is defined must be provided.

```
wf02.setWidgetsToBuild(
    WidgetFactory.WIDGETS_PER_DAY);
```

7) Apply the **getDaysToBuild** method to **WidgetFactory** objects **wf01** and **wf02.** Save the values returned in temporary variables.
8) For each **WidgetFactory** object, display the number of widgets to be built (using the **getWidgetsToBuild** accessor method) and the number of days the factory take to produce them.
9) Using object **wf01,** use the **setWidgetsToBuild** method to change the value of **wf01's** widgetsToBuild field to one greater than a factory can produce in one day.
10) Apply the **getDaysToBuild** method to **wf01** and save the return value in a temporary variable.
11) Display the number of widgets to be built and the number of days the factory takes to produce them.
12) Using steps similar to those described above, set the **widgetsToBuild** field of object **wf01** to zero. Determine the number of days it will take the factory to produce zero widgets. Display the number of widgets to be produced, and the number of days it takes the factory to make them.

Code Listing 3 - 8 (WidgetFactoryDemo.Java)

```
//***********************************************************
// Written by Lynda Bryant                                  *
// Chapter 3                                                *
// Programming Challenge 6: Widget Factory                  *
//***********************************************************

//***********************************************************
//  6.  Widget Factory                                      *
//                                                          *
//  Design a class for a widget manufacturing               *
//  plant. The class should have a method whose             *
//  argument is the number of widgets that must             *
//  be produced. The class should have another              *
//  method that calculates how many days it will            *
//  take to produce the number of widgets.                  *
//  (Assume that 10 widgets may be produced each            *
//  hour. The plant operates two shifts of eight            *
//  hours each per day.)                                    *
//                                                          *
//  Demonstrate the class by writing a separate             *
//  program that creates an instance of the                 *
//  class. The program should pass a number of              *
//  widgets to the object, and call the object's            *
//  method that displays the number of days it              *
//  will take to produce that many widgets.                 *
//***********************************************************

public class WidgetFactoryDemo
{

    //  Demonstrate the WidgetFactory class
    public static void main(String[] args)
    {
        //  declare WidgetFactory objects
        WidgetFactory   wf01;
        WidgetFactory   wf02;

        //  days to produce a number of Widgets
        int daysWF01;
        int daysWF02;

        //  construct Widget Factory objects
        wf01    =   new WidgetFactory();
        wf02    =   new WidgetFactory();

        //  display the objects
        System.out.println("wf01: " + wf01);
        System.out.println("wf02: " + wf02);
        System.out.println();

        //  set number of widgets to build
        wf01.setWidgetsToBuild(1);
        wf02.setWidgetsToBuild(
            WidgetFactory.WIDGETS_PER_DAY);

        //  display the objects again
        System.out.println("wf01: " + wf01);
        System.out.println("wf02: " + wf02);
        System.out.println();
```

```
        //  calculate the number of days to build
        //  the widgets requested
        daysWF01     =   wf01.getDaysToBuild();
        daysWF02     =   wf02.getDaysToBuild();

        //  show results of calculations
        System.out.println("wf01: Days to Build "
            + wf01.getWidgetsToBuild()
            + " Widgets is: " + daysWF01);

        System.out.println("wf02: Days to Build "
            + wf02.getWidgetsToBuild()
            + " Widgets is: " + daysWF02);
        System.out.println();

        //  Calculate days to build a one more
        //  widget than can be built in one day.
        wf01.setWidgetsToBuild(
            WidgetFactory.WIDGETS_PER_DAY + 1);
        daysWF01     =   wf01.getDaysToBuild();

        System.out.println("wf01: Days to Build "
            + wf01.getWidgetsToBuild()
            + " Widgets is: " + daysWF01);
        System.out.println();

        //  check that the factory is smart enough
        //  to know it takes zero days to make
        //  zero Widgets
        wf01.setWidgetsToBuild(0);
        daysWF01     =   wf01.getDaysToBuild();

        System.out.println("wf01: Days to Build "
            + wf01.getWidgetsToBuild()
            + " Widgets is: " + daysWF01);
    }
}
```

Program Output

```
wf01: Widget Factory [widgets to build: 0];
wf02: Widget Factory [widgets to build: 0];

wf01: Widget Factory [widgets to build: 1];
wf02: Widget Factory [widgets to build: 160];

wf01: Days to Build 1 Widgets is: 1
wf02: Days to Build 160 Widgets is: 1

wf01: Days to Build 161 Widgets is: 2

wf01: Days to Build 0 Widgets is: 0
```

CHAPTER 4

Decisions Structures

Solutions

- ✦ Programming Challenge 2: State Abbreviations
- ✦ Programming Challenge 6: ShippingCharges Class
- ✦ Programming Challenge 10: Freezing and Boiling Points

Programming Challenge 2:State Abbreviations

Problem Statement: State Abbreviations

Write a program that asks the user to enter one of the following state abbreviations: NC, SC, GA, FL, or AL. The program should then display the name of the state that corresponds with the abbreviation entered (North Carolina, South Carolina, Georgia, Florida, or Alabama.) The program should accept abbreviations in uppercase, lowercase, or a mixture of both upper- and lowercase. Display an error message if an abbreviation other than what is listed is entered.

Solution

Define What The Program is To Do

Purpose	State Abbreviations
Input	A String
Process	Determine the name of the state whose abbreviation is the same as the String entered by the user. The abbreviation entered by the user may be in uppercase, lowercase, or mixed case.
Output	The State Name for the State Abbreviation, or An error message if the user's input was not a State Abbreviation.

High Level Pseudocode for State Abbreviation Program

1) Prompt user to input a String that is a state abbreviation.
2) Compare the user's entry (ignoring its case) to:
   a) "AL" (Alabama)
   b) "FL" (Florida)
   c) "GA" (Georgia)
   d) "NC" (North Carolina)
   e) "SC" (South Carolina)
3) If the user's entry matched any of the abbreviations accepted by this program, display the state name.
4) If the user's entry did not match any of the abbreviations in the program, display an error message.

Detailed Pseudocode for State Abbreviation Program

1) Declare local variables

a) String userInput - Used to store the text entered by the user.

b) String theStateName - Used to store the name of the state that has the abbreviation matching the text entered by the user.

c) boolean stateNameFound - Used as a flag: is true if the user's entry matches the abbreviation of a state used in this program; is false otherwise.

d) In this solution, the local variables are not initialized in order to demonstrate a Java feature in a later step. Otherwise, they could be initialized in the same source line where they are declared.

2) Prompt the user to enter a State Abbreviation for one of the states in this program. Store the String entered by the user in the variable userInput.

3) Compare the value of userInput to the abbreviations for the states in this program.

a) To compare Strings, a method of the String class must be used. The equality operator "==" can only be used with primitive data types in Java.

i) See Section 4.7 of the Textbook for description of ways to compare String objects.

ii) Referring to the Java 2 API, the String class has an equals method with a boolean result. The method returns true if two String variables have the same value. The use of the equals method of the String class is demonstrated in the following example.

```
String a = "ABC";
String b = "ABC";
String c = "aBc";


if ( a.equals(b) )
   System.out.println(
      "Strings a and b have the same value");


if ( !a.equals(c) )
   System.out.println(
      "Strings a and c don't have the same value");
```

iii) The String class also has a boolean method equalsIgnoreCase. This method returns true if two String variables have the same value, without regard to whether some letters are uppercase or lowercase in either variable. The equalsIgnoreCase method would be used:

```
// Continuing with the same String variables
// used in the previous example …

if ( a.equals(c) )
   System.out.println(
      "Strings a and c have the same value "
      + "without respect to the case of "
      + "the letters within them.");
```

iv) The equalsIgnoreCase method performs the comparison needed for this problem.

b) The comparison of variable userInput to the state abbreviations in this program is performed using an if-else-if decision structure.

   i) See Section 4.4 in the textbook for description of the if-else-if decision statement.

c) When performing the if-else-if decision structure, the variable userInput and a literal value for a state abbreviation have the same value (ignoring case), the true branch is taken at that if decision. In the code block for the true branch:

   i) Set the variable theStateName to the String whose value is the one corresponding to the abbreviation entered by the user.

   ii) Set the flag variable stateNameFound to the value true, so that the variable theStateName is displayed following the completion of the if-else-if decision structure.

d) When the variable userInput and the literal value for a state abbreviation do not have the same value (ignoring case), the else (false) branch is taken for this decision. The variable userInput is then compared to the next literal value for a state abbreviation.

e) The previous two steps are written in Java as:

```
if( userInput.equalsIgnoreCase("AL")
{
   theStateName = "Alabama";
   stateNameFound = true;
}
else if (userInput.equalsIgnoreCase("FL")

//  Continue if-else-if to test userInput
//  with all the state abbreviations.
```

f) If the program reaches the last else branch for the if-else-if, then userInput has not had the same value (ignoring case) as any of the state abbreviations in this program.

i) Set the variable theStateName to "Unknown".

ii) Set the variable stateNameFound to false.

g) The last step is written in Java as:

```
// end of last true branch
else
{
   theStateName = "Unknown";
   stateNameFound = false;
}
```

4) Display the results of the program.

a) If the variable stateNameFound is true, then display the state's name and the variable userInput, the String entered by the user.

b) If the variable stateNameFound is false, then display an error message, including userInput, the String variable entered by the user.

Uninitialized Variable Error in Java

The Java compiler will not compile a class if there is a variable that *may* not have been initialized before it is used. This hasn't been a consideration in previous chapters because the path through each solution was one single sequence of steps. However, when a class uses a decision structure, the Java compiler can not know ahead of time which branches in that structure may be performed for all possible situations.

In the solution to the State Abbreviations problem, the path taken in the program depends on the input provided by the user, which by its nature, is unpredictable.

Consider a simplified problem where the variable userInput is compared only to the value "AL" for Alabama.

Code Listing 4 – 1 (UninitializedVariable.java)

```
//*****************************************************
//  Written by Don Bardero                            *
//  Chapter 4                                         *
//  Programming Challenge 2: State Abbreviations      *
//                                                    *
//  Demonstrate Java Uninitialized Variable Error     *
//  using a simplified version of the solution to     *
//  State Abbreviations Programming Challenge.        *
//*****************************************************

import java.util.Scanner;
```

```
public class UninitializedVariable
{
    public static void main(String[] args)
    {
        //  Create a Scanner object to use for reading from
        //  the keyboard.
        Scanner keyboard = new Scanner(System.in);


        //  The String userInput stores the text
        //  entered by the user.

        String  userInput;

        //  The String theStateName is used to store
        //  the name of the state that matches the
        //  text.  In order to demonstrate the
        //  unintialized variable error, do *not*
        //  give a value to theStateName here.

        String  theStateName;

        //  The flag stateNameFound is set true if
        //  the text entered by the user matches "AL".

        boolean stateNameFound;

        System.out.print("Enter the state abbreviation "
            + "AL for Alabama.");
        System.out.println();

        userInput = keyboard.nextLine();

        if ( userInput.equals("AL") )
        {
            theStateName = "Alabama";
            stateNameFound = true;
        }
        else
        {
//      To cause an uninitialized variable error,
//      comment out the following line of source code.
          //  theStateName = "Unknown";

            stateNameFound = false;
        }

        if ( stateNameFound )
        {
            //  An uninitialized variable error may
            //  occur in the following line if
           //  there is *any* possibility that
            //  theStateName has not been given a
            //  value.

            System.out.println(theStateName
                + "'s abbreviation is "
                + userInput + ".");
        }
        else
        {
```

```
            System.out.println("The text entered, "
                + userInput + ", \n"
                + "is not the abbreviation "
                + "for Alabama.");
        }
    }
}
```

Program Output (for correctly compiled program)

```
Enter the state abbreviation AL for Alabama.
AL
Alabama's abbreviation is AL.
```

```
Enter the state abbreviation AL for Alabama.
FL
The text entered, FL,
is not the abbreviation for Alabama.
```

Analyzing the logic in UninitializedVariable.java, when userInput is equal to "AL" [line 39.], variable stateName is given the value "Alabama" [line 41.] and variable stateNameFound is given the value true [line 42.]. If userInput is not equal to "AL", stateNameFound is given the value false [line 50.]. The next if statement [line 53.] tests the value of stateNameFound and displays the appropriate message: when the state name has been found [lines 61.-63.]; and when the state name has not been found [lines 67.-70.]. This logic appears to satisfy the requirements of the simplified problem.

However, the Java compiler will generate the following error message when the program is compiled.

```
UninitializedVariable.java [61:1] variable theStateName might not have
been initialized
        System.out.println(theStateName
                           ^
```

Why does the Java compiler decide that this program has an error when the variable theStateName isn't given a value in the else (false) branch of the if statement? When theStateName is given the value "Unknown" (or any String value) in the else branch, the program never displays the value "Unknown". The value of theStateName is only used when the flag stateNameFound is true; which is clearly not true when the else branch of the previous if statement has been taken. Is the Java compiler's error checking deficient? Of course not.

The Java compiler performs more thorough analysis of variable initialization than most other programming language compilers. Many compilers will not flag an error for programs written with the same decision structure and variable assignment statements as UninitializedVariable.java. This saves the programmer the effort to insure that variables are always initialized, but introduces the possibility that a program *may* use a variable whose value is indeterminant, consequently producing incorrect results.

The Java compiler's checking for uninitialized variables is simple, but effective. If a variable is used *after* a decision structure has been executed, then:

- The variable shall have had its value set *before* the decision structure is entered, or
- The variable shall have its value set for *every possible* path through the decision structure.

In exchange for Java's protection against using a variable that has not been initialized, the programmer must take extra care that variables always have a value, no matter which path a program may take.

(Optional) It might seem desirable for the Java compiler to analyze the UninitializedVariable.java program and determine it isn't necessary for the variable theStateName to have a value when stateNameFound is false. Unfortunately, analysis of a program's use of variables, for all possible cases of input and data values, becomes unmanageably complex with the addition of only a few decision structures and variables to a program. In general, complete analysis of an arbitrary program's use of variables is an "undecidable" problem. This means there is no algorithm that can complete the analysis in a limited (finite) number of steps. For more information on decidable and undecidable problems, look for books, magazine articles, or WWW pages that discuss the work of Alan Turing and "The Halting Problem." Turing (1912-1954) was a pioneer of Computer Science.

Returning to the solution for the State Abbreviations problem, there are at least two ways to satisfy the Java compiler's requirement that all variables be initialized before they are used. In the solution presented in StateAbbreviations.java, the variables theStateName and stateNameFound are given values in *every* path through the if-else-if decision statement. Another method to insure that theStateName and stateNameFound are always initialized would be to assign them values when they were declared.

Code Listing 4 - 2 (StateAbbreviations.java)

```
//*****************************************************
//  Written by Barbara Dondero                        *
//  Chapter 4                                         *
//  Programming Challenge 2: State Abbreviations      *
//                                                    *
//  Write a program that asks the user to enter       *
//  one of the following state abbreviations:         *
//  NC, SC, GA, FL, or AL. The program should         *
//  then display the name of the state that           *
//  corresponds with the abbreviation entered         *
//  (North Carolina, South Carolina, Georgia,         *
//  Florida, or Alabama.) The program should          *
//  accept abbreviations in uppercase,                *
//  lowercase, or a mixture of both upper- and        *
//  lowercase. Display an error message if an         *
//  abbreviation other than what is listed is         *
//  entered.                                          *
```

```
//*****************************************************

import java.util.Scanner;

public class StateAbbreviations
{

    public static void main(String[] args)
    {
        //  Create a Scanner object to use for reading from
        //  the keyboard.
        Scanner keyboard = new Scanner(System.in);

        //  The String userInput stores the text
        //  entered by the user when the program asks
        //  for a State Abbreviation.

        String  userInput;

        //  The String theStateName is used to store
        //  the name of the state that matches the
        //  text entered by the user (provided there
        //  is a match).

        String  theStateName;

        //  The flag stateNameFound is set true if
        //  the text entered by the user matches
        //  an abbreviation that is in the set of
        //  abbreviations that this program can test.

        boolean stateNameFound;

        //  Collect User Input

        System.out.print("Enter a State Abbreviation "
            + "from the set \n"
            + "{AL, FL, GA, NC, or SC}:  ");
        System.out.println();

        userInput = keyboard.nextLine();

        //  Compare the String entered by the user
        //  against the state abbreviations known
        //  in this program.

            //  To determine if two String Objects

            //  have the same value, the equals

            //  method (or in the case of this

            //  program, the equalsIgnoreCase

            //  method) must be used. The "=="

            //  operator can only be used on

            //  primitive Java data types.

        if ( userInput.equalsIgnoreCase("AL") )
        {
```

```
//  Whenever a match is found between the
//  user's input and a state abbreviation
//  in this program, the variable theStateName
//  is given the value of the full name of
//  the state.

    theStateName = "Alabama";

//  The flag variable stateNameFound is given
//  the value true, so that at the end of this
//  if-else-if chain, the program can test
//  whether a match was found between the user's
//  input and the abbreviations known to the
//  the program.

    stateNameFound = true;
}
else if (userInput.equalsIgnoreCase("FL") )
{
//  Every state in this program is handled the
//  same way as the case for "AL" Alabama.

    theStateName    = "Florida";
    stateNameFound = true;
}
else if (userInput.equalsIgnoreCase("GA") )
{
    theStateName    = "Georgia";
    stateNameFound = true;
}
else if (userInput.equalsIgnoreCase("NC") )
{
    theStateName    = "North Carolina";
    stateNameFound = true;
}
else if (userInput.equalsIgnoreCase("SC") )
{
    theStateName    =   "South Carolina";
    stateNameFound = true;
}
else
{
    theStateName = "Unknown";
    stateNameFound = false;
}

    //  Before the variables theStateName
    //  and stateNameFound are used in an
    //  expression, Java *requires* that
    //  they have been initialized.
    //
    //  In this program, these variables
    //  have been given values in *every*
    //  path through the if-else-if decision
    //  structure.
    //
    //  Another way to insure that
    //  theStateName and stateNameFound
    //  have been initialized would be to
    //  give them values when they were
```

```
            //  declared.

        //  The program's output depends on whether or
        //  not the user's input matched the
        //  abbreviation for a state name.

        if ( stateNameFound )
        {
        //  The user's input matched a state
        //  abbreviation.  Display the state name.

            System.out.println(theStateName
                + "'s abbreviation is "
                + userInput + ".");
        }
        else
        {
        //  The user's input String did not match
        //  any of the state abbreviations.  Display
        //  an error message.

            System.out.println(
                "The abbreviation \""
                + userInput
                + "\" is not recognized by this program.");
        }
    }
}
```

Programming Challenge 6: ShippingCharges Class

Problem Statement:

The Fast Freight Shipping Company charges the following rates:

Weight of Package (in kilograms)	Rate Per 500 Miles Shipped
2 Kg or less	$1.10
Over 2 Kg but not more than 6 Kg	$2.20
Over 6 Kg but not more than 10 Kg	$3.70
Over 10 Kg	$4.80

The shipping charges per 500 miles are not prorated. For example, if a 2 Kg. package is shipped 550 miles, the charges would be $2.20.

Design a class that stores the weight of a package and has a method that returns the shipping charges.

Solution: ShippingCharges Class

Define What The ShippingCharges Class Is To Do

Purpose	Compute Charges to Ship a Package with Fast Freight Shipping Company.	
Fields	weight	The weight (in kilograms) of the package to be shipped.
Constructor	ShippingCharges(double)	Create a ShippingCharges object, setting the weight field to the value of the constructor's parameter.
Methods	setWeight	Set the weight field to the value of the method's parameter.
	getWeight	Return the value of the weight field of the object.
	getShippingCharge	Return the cost to ship a package whose weight is stored in the weight field; the distance to ship is the parameter of the method.

High Level Pseudocode for ShippingCharges Class

1) Define the weight field.

   private double weight;

2) Define constructor.

   a) Signature:

      public ShippingCharges(double packageWeight)

   b) Set the weight field to the value of packageWeight.

3) Define mutator method setWeight.

   a) Signature:

      public void setWeight(double packageWeight)

   b) Set the weight field to the value of packageWeight.

4) Define accessor method getWeight.

   a) Signature:

      public double getWeight()

   b) Return the value of the weight field.

5) Define method getShippingCharge.

   a) Signature:

      public double getShippingCharge(double milesToShip)

   b) Based on milesToShip, determine the Distance Factor for the shipping charge.

      i) The Distance Factor is defined in 500 mile increments. However, the Distance Factor for 1 mile is the same as the Distance Factor for 500 miles; for 501 miles the same as 1000 miles, etc.

      ii) For distances less than or equal 0, the Distance Factor is 0 (the package isn't going anywhere).

      iii) For distances greater than 0 and less than or equal 500, the Distance Factor is 1.

      iv) For distances greater than 500 and less than 1000, the Distance Factor is 2.

Distance Factor vs. Mileage

Minimum (<) Distance (Miles)	Maximum (≤) Distance (Miles)	Distance Factor
N / A	0	0
0	500	1
500	1000	2

1000	1500	3
1500	2000	4
and so forth …		

v) Calculate Distance Factor

(1) Performing integer division of milesToShip by 500 gives the following results:

Distance (miles)	Integer Quotient when Divided by 500	Remainder when Divided by 500
0	0	0
1	0	1
2 - 499	0	2 - 499
500	1	0
501	1	1
502 - 999	1	2 - 499
1000	2	0
and so forth …		

(2) When the distance divided by 500 has a remainder of 0 (the distance can be divided exactly by 500), the Integer Quotient is the ***same*** as the Distance Factor.

(3) When the distance divided by 500 has a non zero remainder, the Distance Factor is one ***more*** than the Integer Quotient.

c) Determine the shipping rate based on the package's weight. The shipping rate is defined by the following table.

Minimum (<) Weight (Kg)	Maximum (≤) Weight (Kg)	Shipping Rate per Distance Factor
N / A	0	$0.00
0 <	2.00	$1.10
2.00 <	6.00	$2.20
6.00 <	10.00	$3.70
10.00	N / A	$4.80

d) Multiply the Shipping Rate by the Distance Factor resulting in the charge to ship the package.

e) Return the charge to ship the package.

ShippingCharges
- weight : double
+ ShippingCharges(packageWeight : double) : + setWeight(packageWeight : double) : void + getWeight( ) : double + getShippingCharge(milesToShip : double) : double

Figure 4 – 1 UML Diagram for ShippingCharges Class

Detailed Pseudocode for ShippingCharges Class

1) The class' field, constructor, mutator and accessor have been described in the previous section.

2) Define the getShippingCharge method.

   a) Signature:

   ```
   public double getShippingCharge(double milesToShip)
   ```

   b) Declare local variables:

      i) The double variable shippingCharge is used to store the result of this method.

      ii) The int variable distanceFactor is determined by the miles the package to be shipped.

      iii) The double variable shippingRate is determined by the weight of the package.

   c) Calculate Distance Factor.

      i) Using integer division, divide milesToShip by 500. Store the result in distanceFactor.

      ii) If the variable distanceFactor is a whole number value, that value is the Distance Factor.

      iii) Otherwise, the division in step i) leaves a remainder. According to its definition, add one to the quotient to result in the Distance Factor value. This is necessary since the package is being shipped into the next 500 mile segment.

   d) Calculate Shipping Rate

      i) If weight field is ≤ zero, the shipping rate is zero.

ii) Otherwise, if the weight field is ≤ 2, the shipping rate is 1.10.

iii) Otherwise, if the weight field is ≤ 6, the shipping rate is 2.20.

iv) Otherwise, if the weight field is ≤ 10, the shipping rate is 3.70.

v) Otherwise, the weight field is ≥ 10, the shipping rate is 4.80.

e) Calculate Shipping Charge

i) The value of shippingCharge is distanceFactor multiplied by shippingCharge.

f) Return the value of shippingCharge.

Code Listing 4 – 3 (ShippingCharges.java)

```
//*******************************************************
//  Written by Stella Kowalski                          *
//                                                      *
//  Chapter 4 - Programming Challenge 6                 *
//                                                      *
//  ShippingCharges Class                               *
//                                                      *
//  The Fast Freight Shipping Company charges           *
//  the following rates:                                *
//                                                      *
//      Weight of Package        Rate Per 500           *
//      (in kilograms)           Miles Shipped          *
//                                                      *
//      2 Kg or less             $1.10                  *
//                                                      *
//      Over 2 Kg but            $2.20                  *
//      not more than 6 Kg                              *
//                                                      *
//      Over 6 Kg but            $3.70                  *
//      not more than 10 Kg                             *
//                                                      *
//      Over 10 Kg               $4.80                  *
//                                                      *
//  The shipping charges per 500 miles are not          *
//  prorated. For example, if a 2 Kg. package is        *
//  shipped 550 miles, the charges would be             *
//  $2.20. Design a class that stores the weight        *
//  of a package and has a method that returns          *
//  the shipping charges.                               *
//*******************************************************

public class ShippingCharges
{
    //  The weight field contains the weight of the
    //  package to be shipped.

    private double  weight; // in kilograms

    //***************************************************
    //  Constructor for ShippingCharges Class.  The     *
```

```
//  weight field for the object is set to the          *
//  value passed to the constructor.                    *
//*****************************************************

public  ShippingCharges(double packageWeight)
{
    weight  =   packageWeight;
}

//*****************************************************
//  The setWeight mutator method changes the           *
//  weight field to the value passed as its            *
//  parameter.                                          *
//*****************************************************

public void setWeight(double packageWeight)
{
    weight  =   packageWeight;
}

//*****************************************************
//  The getWeight accessor method returns the          *
//  value of the object's weight field.                *
//*****************************************************

public  double  getWeight()
{
    return  weight;
}

//*****************************************************
//  The getShippingCharge method returns the           *
//  cost to send the package over the number of        *
//  miles given as its parameter.                       *
//*****************************************************

public double   getShippingCharge(double milesToShip)
{
    //  The total shipping charge is stored in local
    //  variable shippingCharge

    double      shippingCharge;

    //  The number of 500 mile segments in the
    //  distance the package is being shipped.

    int distanceFactor;

    //  The shipping rate for a package whose
    //  weight is given by the value of the
    //  weight field.

    double      shippingRate;

    //  Determine distance factor in the trip by
    //  dividing milesToShip by 500.

    //  Note that a whole number (int) value
    //  is needed to calculate distance factor.
    //  Cast milesToShip to an int and divide
    //  by the int value 500.
```

```
distanceFactor = (int) milesToShip / 500;

//  But if 500 does not divide evenly into
//  the number of miles to ship, increment
//  the distance factor.

//  Again, whole number (int) calculation
//  is required.

if ( (int) milesToShip % 500 != 0 )
{
    distanceFactor++;
}

//  Calculate the package's shipping rate
//  based on its weight.

if ( weight <= 0 )

    //  There's no charge to ship a package
    //  that weights nothing.

    shippingRate = 0.00;

else if ( weight <= 2.00 )

    //  The rate to ship packages that are no
    //  heavier than 2 Kg is $1.10.

    shippingRate = 1.10;

else if ( weight <= 6.00 )

    //  The rate to ship packages that are
    //  heavier than 2 Kg, but no heavier than
    //  6 Kg is $2.20.

    shippingRate = 2.20;

else if ( weight <= 10.00 )

    //  The rate to ship packages that are
    //  heavier than 6 Kg, but no heavier than
    //  10 Kg is $3.70.

    shippingRate = 3.70;

else

    //  The rate to ship packages that are
    //  heavier than 10 Kg is $4.80 per 500
    //  mile segment.

    shippingRate = 4.80;

//  The shipping charge is computed by
//  multiplying the shipping rate by
//  the distance factor.

shippingCharge = shippingRate * distanceFactor;

return  shippingCharge;
```

```
    }
}
```

Solution: Shipping Charges Main Program

Define What The Program is To Do

Purpose	Demonstrate the use of the ShippingCharges Class
Input	The weight of a package and the distance it is to be shipped.
Process	Create a ShippingCharges object having the weight specified by the user. Compute the shipping charge for the package using the getShippingCharge method with the distance specified by the user.
Output	Display the package weight, distance to be shipped, and the charge for that service.

High Level Pseudocode for Shipping Charges Main Program

1) Declare local variables:
    a) aPackage - an object of class ShippingCharges
    b) inputWeight - a double where the package's weight, specified by the user, is stored.
    c) theMiles - a double where the distance the package is to be shipped, specified by the user, is stored.
    d) charge - the cost to ship the package, calculated by this program using the getShippingCharge method of the object aPackage.
2) From the user, collect the weight of the package.
3) From the user, collect the distance the package is to be shipped.
4) Instantiate the object aPackage, using the weight value provided by the user.
5) Calculate the shipping charge by applying the getShippingCharge method to aPackage.
6) Display the package weight, distance to be shipped and the charge for that service.

Detailed Pseudocode for Shipping Charges Main Program

1) Declare local variables. This written in Java as:

```
ShippingCharges aPackage;
double inputWeight;
double theMiles;
double charge;
```

2) (Optional) Create DecimalFormat objects to use in the presentation of the program's output. Decimal values in doubles will be displayed to two decimal places, with ',' as the separator character. Currency values will be displayed with the local currency symbol prefixed.
3) Collect package weight from the user. Store value in variable inputWeight.
4) Collect distance to be shipped from the user. Store value in variable theMiles.
5) Instantiate aPackage using inputWeight for the value of the object's weight field.
6) Use aPackage's getShippingCharge method with theMiles parameter to determine package's shipping charge. Store result in variable charge.
7) Display inputWeight, theMiles, and charge.

Test Input for ShippingChargesMain Program

Test data for the program should demonstrate correct operation of the ShippingCharges class. In the case of this program, only a few tests are needed to exercise all paths through the methods of ShippingCharges.

Test Case	Weight	Distance	Shipping Charge	Notes
1	0	500	$0.00	Zero weight - no charge.
2	100	0	$0.00	Zero distance - no charge.
3	1	1	$1.10	Minimum weight, minimum distance.
4	2	500	$1.10	Lowest weight interval short distance.
5	2	501	$2.20	Lowest weight interval, charge for 2nd 500 mile distance.
6	2.01	500	$2.20	Second weight interval, minimum distance.
7	6	501	$4.40	Second weight interval, charge for

				2nd 500 mile distance.
8	6	1000	$4.40	Still 2nd weight interval, 2nd 500 mile distance.
9	6.01	1000	$7.40	Third weight interval, 2nd 500 mile distance.
10	10	1500	$11.10	Third weight interval, 3rd 500 mile distance.
11	10	1501	$14.80	Third weight interval, 4th 500 mile distance.
12	10.01	2000	$19.20	Maximum weight interval, 4th 500 mile distance.
13	1000	2001	$24.00	Maximum weight interval, 5th 500 mile distance.

Code Listing 4 – 4 (ShippingChargesMain.java)

```
import  java.text.DecimalFormat;
import  java.text.DecimalFormatSymbols;
import java.util.Scanner;

//*********************************************************
//  Written by Stella Kowalski                            *
//                                                        *
//  Chapter 4 - Programming Challenge 6                   *
//                                                        *
//  ShippingCharges Class                                 *
//                                                        *
//  Demonstrate the use of the ShippingCharges Class.     *
//                                                        *
//  * User enters the weight of the package and the       *
//  distance it needs to be shipped.                      *
//  * Using an object of type ShippingClass, this program *
//  determines how much it will cost to send the package. *
//  * The program displays the weight of the package, the *
//  distance it is to be shipped, and the cost to send    *
//  the package.                                          *
//                                                        *
//  By designing this program so that the package's       *
//  weight and distance to be shipped are entered by the  *
//  user, it is relatively easy to test variety of sample *
//  data to verify the ShippingCharges class works        *
//  according to the requirements given in the problem    *
//  statement.                                            *
//*********************************************************
```

```
public class ShippingChargesMain
{
    public static void main(String[] args)
    {
        //  Create a Scanner object to use for reading from
        //  the keyboard.
        Scanner keyboard = new Scanner(System.in);


        //  The ShippingCharges object aPackage
        //  describes the package the user wishes
        //  to ship.

        ShippingCharges aPackage;

        //  The weight of the package in
        //  Kilograms; entered by the user.

        double  inputWeight;

        //  The distance the package is to be
        //  shipped; value of theMiles is entered
        //  by the user.

        double  theMiles;

        //  Cost to ship aPackage, weighting
        //  inputWeight, over a distance of
        //  theMiles.

        double  charge;

        //  Optional: Define formats for the display of
        //  numeric data.  This produces a "cleaner" display
        //  of the program's results.

        //  DecimalFormat decimal2Format
        //  displays a numeric value with 2 decimal places;
        //  with ',' as the grouping separator.

        DecimalFormat   decimal2Format
            =   new DecimalFormat("#,##0.00");

        //  String currencySymbol is Java's
        //  default currency symbol for the
        //  program's location.  In the US, the
        //  currency symbol is '$' for the Dollar.
        //  In the UK, the currency symbol would
        //  be '£' for Pounds Sterling. In parts
        //  of Western Europe the currency is the
        //  Euro, whose symbol is '€'.  In Japan,
        //  the currency symbol would be '¥' for
        //  the Yen.  And so forth ...
```

```
        String currencySymbol
            = (new DecimalFormatSymbols()).getCurrencySymbol();

        //  DecimalFormat currencyFormat
        //  displays a numberic value with 2 decimal places;
        //  ',' separators at the thousands digit,
        //  all preceded by the local currency symbol.

        DecimalFormat currencyFormat
            = new DecimalFormat(currencySymbol + "#,##0.00");

        System.out.println(
            "Shipping Charges Program\n"
            + "===========================================");

        //  Collect user input.

        System.out.print("Please enter package weight (Kg): ");
        inputWeight = keyboard.nextDouble();

        System.out.print(
            "Please enter distance to be shipped (Miles): ");
        theMiles   =  keyboard.nextDouble();

        //  Instantiate a new ShippingCharges
        //  object specifying the weight of the
        //  package to be shipped.

        aPackage = new ShippingCharges(inputWeight);

        //  Use the getShippingCharge method to
        //  determine the cost to ship the package
        //  over the distance specified by the
        //  user.

        charge  =   aPackage.getShippingCharge(theMiles);

        //  Display the program's results
        //      The package's weight.
        //      The distance to be shipped.
        //      The shipping charge for that service.

        System.out.println("\n"
            + "Weight: "
            + decimal2Format.format(inputWeight) + " Kg"
            + "; Miles: "
            + decimal2Format.format(theMiles)
            + "; Shipping Charge:  "
            + currencyFormat.format(charge));

        System.out.println(
            "==========================================\n");
    }
}
```

Program Output

Case 1

```
Shipping Charges Program
==========================================
Please enter package weight (Kg): 0
Please enter distance to be shipped (Miles): 500

Weight: 0.00 Kg; Miles: 500; Shipping Charge:  $0.00
==========================================
```

Case 2

```
Shipping Charges Program
==========================================
Please enter package weight (Kg): 100
Please enter distance to be shipped (Miles): 0

Weight: 100.00 Kg; Miles: 0; Shipping Charge:  $0.00
==========================================
```

Case 3

```
Shipping Charges Program
==========================================
Please enter package weight (Kg): 1
Please enter distance to be shipped (Miles): 1

Weight: 1.00 Kg; Miles: 1; Shipping Charge:  $1.10
==========================================
```

Case 4

```
Shipping Charges Program
==========================================
Please enter package weight (Kg): 2
Please enter distance to be shipped (Miles): 500

Weight: 2.00 Kg; Miles: 500; Shipping Charge:  $1.10
==========================================
```

Case 5

```
Shipping Charges Program
==========================================
Please enter package weight (Kg): 2
Please enter distance to be shipped (Miles): 501

Weight: 2.00 Kg; Miles: 501; Shipping Charge:  $2.20
==========================================
```

Case 6

```
Shipping Charges Program
==========================================
Please enter package weight (Kg): 2.01
Please enter distance to be shipped (Miles): 500

Weight: 2.01 Kg; Miles: 500; Shipping Charge:  $2.20
==========================================
```

Case 7

```
Shipping Charges Program
==========================================
Please enter package weight (Kg): 6
Please enter distance to be shipped (Miles): 501

Weight: 6.00 Kg; Miles: 501; Shipping Charge:  $4.40
==========================================Case 8
```

Case 8

```
Shipping Charges Program
==========================================
Please enter package weight (Kg): 6
Please enter distance to be shipped (Miles): 1000

Weight: 6.00 Kg; Miles: 1,000; Shipping Charge:  $4.40
==========================================
```

Case 9

```
Shipping Charges Program
==========================================
Please enter package weight (Kg): 6.01
Please enter distance to be shipped (Miles): 1000

Weight: 6.01 Kg; Miles: 1,000; Shipping Charge:  $7.40
==========================================
```

Case 10

```
Shipping Charges Program
==========================================
Please enter package weight (Kg): 10
Please enter distance to be shipped (Miles): 1500

Weight: 10.01 Kg; Miles: 2,000; Shipping Charge:  $11.10
==========================================
```

Case 11

```
Shipping Charges Program
==========================================
Please enter package weight (Kg): 10
Please enter distance to be shipped (Miles): 1501

Weight: 10.00 Kg; Miles: 1,501; Shipping Charge:  $14.80
==========================================
```

Case 12

```
Shipping Charges Program
==========================================
Please enter package weight (Kg): 10.01
Please enter distance to be shipped (Miles): 2000

Weight: 10.01 Kg; Miles: 2,000; Shipping Charge:  $19.20
==========================================
```

Case 13

```
Shipping Charges Program
==========================================
Please enter package weight (Kg): 1000
Please enter distance to be shipped (Miles): 2001

Weight: 1,000.00 Kg; Miles: 2,001; Shipping Charge:  $24.00
==========================================
```

Programming Challenge 10: Freezing and Boiling Points

Problem Statement: Freezing and Boiling Points

The following table lists the freezing and boiling points[†] of several substances.

Substance	Freezing Point	Boiling Point
Ethyl Alcohol	-173	172
Oxygen	-362	-306
Water	32	212

[†] Temperatures are in degrees Fahrenheit at normal atmospheric pressure.

Design a class that stores a temperature in a temperature field, and has the appropriate accessor and mutator methods for the field. The class should also have the following methods:

- isEthylFreezing: This method should return the boolean value true if the temperature stored in the temperature field is at or below the freezing point of ethyl alcohol. Otherwise, the method should return false.
- isEthylBoiling: This method should return the boolean value true if the temperature stored in the temperature field is at or above the boiling point of ethyl alcohol. Otherwise, the method should return false.
- isOxygenFreezing: This method should return the boolean value true if the temperature stored in the temperature field is at or below the freezing point of oxygen. Otherwise, the method should return false.
- isOxygenBoiling: This method should return the boolean value true if the temperature stored in the temperature field is at or above the boiling point of oxygen. Otherwise, the method should return false.
- isWaterFreezing: This method should return the boolean value true if the temperature stored in the temperature field is at or below the freezing point of water. Otherwise, the method should return false.
- isWaterBoiling: This method should return the boolean value true if the temperature stored in the temperature field is at or above the boiling point of water. Otherwise, the method should return false.

Write a program that demonstrates the class. The program should ask the user to enter a temperature, and then display a list of the substances that will freeze at that temperature and those that will boil at that temperature. For example, if the temperature is -20 the class should report that water will freeze and oxygen will boil at that temperature.

Solution: FreezingBoiling Class

Define What The FreezingBoiling Class Is To Do

Purpose	Determine If A Substance Is Freezing Or Boiling At A Temperature	
Fields	temperature	The temperature to use to determine if a substance is freezing or boiling.
Constructors	FreezingBoiling(double)	Create a FreezingBoiling object with the temperature field set to the value of the constructor's argument.
Methods	setTemperature	Set the temperature field to the method's parameter.
	getTermperature	Return the value of the temperature field.
	isEthylFreezing	Return true if temperature field is ≤ -173° F.
	isEthylBoiling	Return true if temperature field ≥ 172° F.
	isOxygenFreezing	Return true if temperature field is ≤ -362° F.
	isOxygenBoiling	Return true if temperature field ≥ -306° F.
	isWaterFreezing	Return true if temperature field is ≤ 32° F.
	isWaterBoiling	Return true if temperature field ≥ 212° F.

Pseudocode for FreezingBoiling Class

1) Fields:

   private double temperature;

2) Constants:

   a) The values for the freezing and boiling temperatures for each of the substances are defined as public static final double values. Using constants for these values will simplify program maintenance if, for example, it were necessary to change this class to use the Celsius or Kelvin temperature scales.

   b) The names of the temperature constants have the pattern:

      <substance>_FREEZING

      <substance>_BOILING

where the meta-symbol <substance> is replaced by the terms: ETHYL, OXYGEN, and WATER, respectively.

For example, the temperature at which water freezes is given by the constant WATER_FREEZING. The temperature at which water boils is given by the constant WATER_BOILING.

A meta-symbol is a term that is used to describe other symbols.

3) Constructor:

   a) Signature:

   ```
   public FreezingBoiling(double)
   ```

   b) Set the temperature field to the value of the constructor's argument.

4) Methods:

   a) Mutator method setTemperature:

      i) Set the temperature field to the value of the method's parameter.

   b) Accessor method getTemperature:

      i) Return the value of the temperature field.

   c) Boolean methods: is<substance>Freezing.

      i) Return true if temperature is ≤ the freezing point of <substance>, given by the constant <substance>_FREEZING. Otherwise, return false.

      ii) The return value of the method is equivalent to the value of the boolean expression: temperature ≤ <substance>_FREEZING. For example,

   ```
   return temperature <= ETHYL_FREEZING;
   ```

   d) Boolean methods: is<substance>Boiling.

      i) Return true if temperature is ≥ the boiling point of <substance>, given by the constant <substance>_BOILING. Otherwise return false.

      ii) The return value of the method is equivalent to the value of the boolean expression: <substance>_BOILING ≤ temperature. For example,

   ```
   return ETHYL_BOILING <= temperature ;
   ```

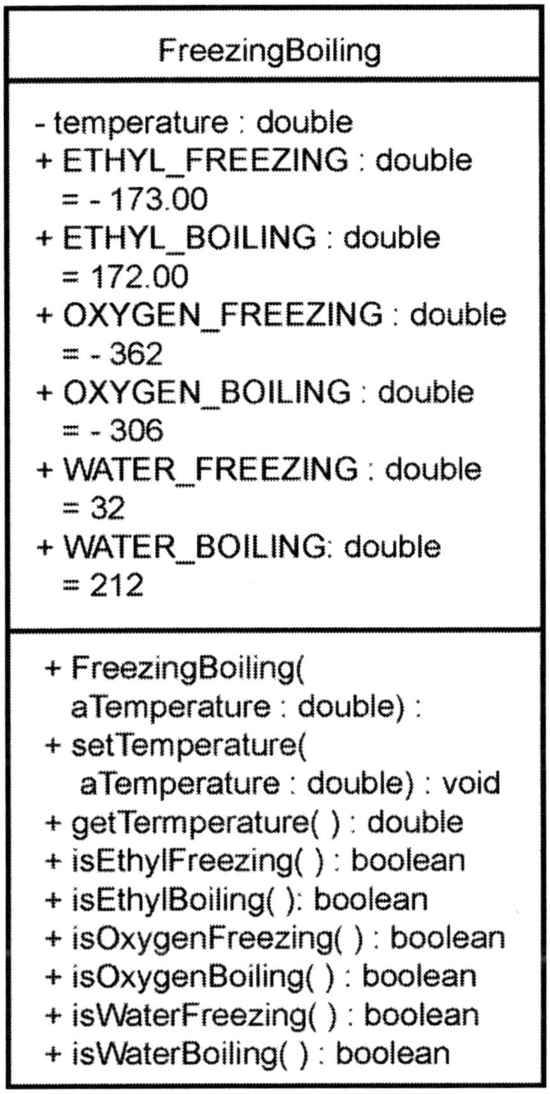

Figure 4 - 2 UML Diagram for FreezingBoiling Class

Code Listing 4 - 5 (FreezingBoiling Class.java)

```
//*****************************************************
//                                                    *
//  Written by Aditya Jabbour                         *
//  Chapter 4 - Programming Challenge 10              *
//                                                    *
//  Freezing and Boiling Points                       *
//                                                    *
//  The following table lists the freezing and        *
//  boiling points of several substances              *
//  [in degrees Fahrenheit, at normal atmospheric     *
//   pressure].                                       *
//                                                    *
//      Substance      Freezing   Boiling             *
//                      Point      Point              *
//      Ethyl Alcohol   -173       172                *
```

```
//      Oxygen          -362      -306                 *
//      Water             32       212                 *
//                                                     *
//  Design a class that stores a temperature in        *
//  a temperature field, and has the appropriate       *
//  accessor and mutator methods for the field.        *
//  The class should also have the following           *
//  methods:                                           *
//                                                     *
//  • isEthylFreezing: This method should              *
//    return the boolean value true if the             *
//    temperature stored in the temperature field      *
//    is at or below the freezing point of ethyl       *
//    alcohol. Otherwise, the method should return     *
//    false.                                           *
//                                                     *
//  • isEthylBoiling: This method should               *
//    return the boolean value true if the             *
//    temperature stored in the temperature field      *
//    is at or above the boiling point of ethyl        *
//    alcohol. Otherwise, the method should return     *
//    false.                                           *
//                                                     *
//  • isOxygenFreezing: This method should             *
//    return the boolean value true if the             *
//    temperature stored in the temperature field      *
//    is at or below the freezing point of oxygen.     *
//    Otherwise, the method should return false.       *
//                                                     *
//  • isOxygenBoiling: This method should              *
//    return the boolean value true if the             *
//    temperature stored in the temperature field      *
//    is at or above the boiling point of oxygen.      *
//    Otherwise, the method should return false.       *
//                                                     *
//  • isWaterFreezing: This method should              *
//    return the boolean value true if the             *
//    temperature stored in the temperature field      *
//    is at or below the freezing point of water.      *
//    Otherwise, the method should return false.       *
//                                                     *
//  • isWaterBoiling: This method should               *
//    return the boolean value true if the             *
//    temperature stored in the temperature field      *
//    is at or above the boiling point of water.       *
//    Otherwise, the method should return false.       *
//                                                     *
//*****************************************************


public class FreezingBoiling
{
    //*************************************************
    //  Field temperature contains the value that is  *
    //  used by the is<substance>Freezing and         *
    //  is<substance>Boiling boolean methods.         *
    //*************************************************
```

```
private double temperature;

//***************************************************
//  Define constants for the freezing and           *
//  boiling points of substances that are           *
//  given in the problem statement.                 *
//                                                  *
//  The use of constants will simplify              *
//  maintenance of this class should it be          *
//  decided that the Celsius or Kelvin              *
//  scales be used instead of the                   *
//  Fahrenheit scale.                               *
//                                                  *
//  Temperatures are given in degrees Fahrenheit at *
//  normal atmospheric pressure.                    *
//***************************************************

public static final double ETHYL_FREEZING  = -173.00;
public static final double ETHYL_BOILING   =  172.00;
public static final double OXYGEN_FREEZING = -362.00;
public static final double OXYGEN_BOILING  = -306.00;
public static final double WATER_FREEZING  =   32.00;
public static final double WATER_BOILING   =  212.00;

//***************************************************
//  Constructor for class FreezingBoiling.  Sets    *
//  the value of the temperature field to           *
//  aTemperature's value.                           *
//***************************************************

public FreezingBoiling(double aTemperature)
{
    temperature = aTemperature;
}

//***************************************************
//  The setTemperature mutator method is used to    *
//  change the value of the temperature field.      *
//***************************************************

public void setTemperature(double aTemperature)
{
    temperature = aTemperature;
}

//***************************************************
// The getTemperature access method is used to      *
// return the value of the temperature field.       *
//***************************************************

public double getTemperature()
{
    return temperature;
}

//***************************************************
```

```
//  A collection of boolean methods that return       *
//  either true or false, depending on the            *
//  comparison of the temperature field to one        *
//  of the constant values <substance>_FREEZING or    *
//  <substance>_BOILING.                              *
//                                                    *
//  All these methods have the same naming            *
//  pattern (i.e. is<substance>Freezing(),            *
//  is<substance>Boiling() ), and same                *
//  pattern for their decision structures.            *
//****************************************************

//****************************************************
//  Boolean method isEthylFreezing is true if         *
//  field temperature is less than or equal the       *
//  freezing temperature for Ethyl.                   *
//****************************************************

public boolean isEthylFreezing()
{
    return  temperature <= ETHYL_FREEZING;
}

//****************************************************
//  Boolean method isEthylBoiling is true if          *
//  boiling temperature for Ethyl is less than        *
//  or equal the temperature field.                   *
//****************************************************

public boolean isEthylBoiling()
{
    return  ETHYL_BOILING <= temperature;
}

//*****************************************************
//  Boolean method isOxygenFreezing is true if         *
//  field temperature is less than or equal the        *
//  freezing temperature for Ethyl.                    *
//*****************************************************

public boolean isOxygenFreezing()
{
    return  temperature <= OXYGEN_FREEZING;
}

//****************************************************
//  Boolean method isOxygenBoiling is true if         *
//  the boiling temperature for Oxygen is less        *
//  than or equal the temperature field.              *
//****************************************************

public boolean isOxygenBoiling()
{
    return  OXYGEN_BOILING <= temperature;
}

//*****************************************************
```

```
    // Boolean method isWaterFreezing is true if          *
    // field temperature is less than or equal the        *
    // freezing temperature for Water.                    *
    //*****************************************************

    public boolean isWaterFreezing()
    {
        return  temperature <= WATER_FREEZING;
    }

    //*****************************************************
    // Boolean method isWaterBoiling is true if the       *
    // boiling temperature for Water is less than         *
    // or equal the temperature field.                    *
    //*****************************************************

    public boolean isWaterBoiling()
    {
        return  WATER_BOILING <= temperature;
    }
}
```

Solution: FreezingBoiling Main Program

Define What The FreezingBoiling Main Program is To Do

Purpose	Demonstrate the operation of the FreezingBoiling class.
Input	A temperature in degrees Fahrenheit.
Process	Determine those substances that will freeze or will boil at the temperature entered.
Output	Display the substances that will freeze or will boil at the temperature entered.

Pseudocode for FreezingBoiling Main Program

1) Declare and initialize local variables.

   a) The double variable inputTemperature stores the temperature value entered by the user.

   b) The String outputString is used to accumulate information regarding which substances are found to be either freezing or boiling at the temperature given. The variable outputString is initialized to an empty String "".

   c) An object, aFreezingBoilingObject, of class FreezingBoiling is needed in order to determine the substances that are freezing or boiling at the temperature given.

2) Prompt the user to enter a temperature value. Store the result in variable inputTemperature.

3) Instantiate aFreezingBoilingObject using the constructor for the FreezingBoiling class with parameter inputTemperature.

4) For the three substances specified in this problem (Ethyl, Oxygen, and Water):

   a) Test if the substance is freezing at the temperature entered, using the is<substance>Freezing method of aFreezingBoilingObject.

      i) For example, the following boolean expression is true if the temperature entered by the user is less than or equal to -173° F, the freezing point of Ethyl.

      `aFreezingBoilingObject.isEthylFreezing()`

      ii) If the expression is true, (the substance is freezing) append the phrase "<substance> is freezing" to outputString.

   b) If the substance is not freezing at the temperature, test if it is boiling, using the is<substance>Boiling method of aFreezingBoilingObject.

      i) The following boolean expression is true if the temperature entered by the user is greater than or equal to 172° F, the boiling point of Ethyl.

      `aFreezingBoilingObject.isEthylBoiling()`

      ii) If the expression is true, (the substance is boiling) append the phrase "<substance> is boiling" to outputString.

   c) Nothing is added to the output string if the substance is neither freezing nor boiling at the temperature entered by the user.

5) If the variable outputString is empty (equal to ""), then no substance is freezing or boiling at the temperature entered. Display a message to the user indicating this situation.

6) Otherwise, the variable outputString contains a sequence of phrases showing which substances are freezing or boiling at the temperature given. Display that information to the user.

7) (Optional) Add punctuation between the phrases added to variable outputString.

   a) To improve readability, place a semicolon "; " between the phrases added to outputString.

   b) Use a boolean flag variable isFirst to indicate whether the phrase being added is the first one in outputString.

c) When isFirst is true, the output sequence is empty. Concatenate the phrase to outputString, and set isFirst to false.

d) If isFirst is false, the output sequence is not empty. Concatenate a "; " to outputString. This separates the prior contents of the output sequence from the new phrase being added to it.

e) When the output sequence is displayed to the user, put a period "." at its end.

Test Input for FreezingBoilingMain Program

To choose test data for the FreezingBoilingMain program, a number line is used to visualize the relationship of the freezing and boiling temperatures for the substances in the problem.

Substance	**Freezing Point**	**Boiling Point**
Ethyl Alcohol	-173	172
Oxygen	-362	-306
Water	32	212

Freezing and Boiling Points for Ethyl, Oxygen, and Water

```
-400      -300      -200      -100       0        100       200       300
 |         |         |         |         |         |         |         |
Oxygen
    F=====B
 |         |         |         |         |         |         |         |
Ethyl
                       F==================================B
 |         |         |         |         |         |         |         |
Water
                                           F=================B
 |         |         |         |         |         |         |         |
-400      -300      -200      -100       0        100       200       300
```

Temperature Scale (F°)

Test Cases:

1) Temperature less than -362:

   a) Oxygen is freezing; Ethyl is freezing; Water is freezing.

2) Temperature greater than or equal -362, but less than -306:

   a) Ethyl is freezing; Water is freezing.

3) Temperature greater than or equal -306, but less than -173.

   a) Oxygen is boiling; Ethyl is freezing; Water is freezing.

4) Temperature greater than or equal -173 but less than 32
   a) Oxygen is boiling; Water is freezing.
5) Temperature greater than or equal 32, but less than 172.
   a) Oxygen is boiling.
6) Temperature greater than or equal 172 but less than 212.
   a) Oxygen is boiling; Ethyl is boiling.
7) Temperature greater than or equal 212.
   a) Oxygen is boiling; Ethyl is boiling; Water is boiling.

Code Listing 4 - 6 (FreezingBoilingMain.java)

```
import java.util.Scanner;

//*******************************************************
//                                                      *
//  Written by Aditya Jabbour                           *
//  Chapter 4 - Programming Challenge 10                *
//                                                      *
//  Freezing and Boiling Points                         *
//                                                      *
//  Write a program that demonstrates the               *
//  [FreezingBoiling] class. The program should         *
//  ask the user to enter a temperature, and            *
//  then display a list of the substances that          *
//  will freeze [are a solid] at that                   *
//  temperature and those that will boil [are a         *
//  gas] at that temperature.                           *
//                                                      *
//  For example, if the user enters the                 *
//  temperature of -20 [F] the [FreezingBoiling]        *
//  class should report that water will freeze          *
//  and oxygen will boil.                               *
//                                                      *
//      [Ethyl is neither frozen or boiling at -20 F    *
//      (it's liquid) and will not be reported by the   *
//      program for this example.]                      *
//                                                      *
//*******************************************************

public class FreezingBoilingMain
{
    public static void main(String[] args)
    {
        //  Create a Scanner object to use for reading from
        //  the keyboard.
        Scanner keyboard = new Scanner(System.in);

        //  Temperature entered by user.  Program
        //  determines which substances are freezing or
        //  boiling at that temperature.

        double  inputTemperature;
```

```
//  String that will eventually contain the
//  list of substances that are either freezing
//  or boiling at the temperature entered.
//  Initialize it to an empty String

String outputString  =   new String("");

//  (Optional) Create a status variable to produce
//  output that has correct punctuation.  When
//  isFirst is true, the phrase added to
//  outputString is the first phrase to be
//  displayed.  When isFirst is false, the phrase
//  added to outputString follows another phrase. In
//  that case, ", " is added to outputString before
//  the next phrase that is to be displayed.

boolean isFirst  =   true;

//  Declare Object that will be instantiated to
//  determine the substances that are freezing,
//  neither freezing or boiling, or boiling, at
//  the temperature entered by the user.

FreezingBoiling aFreezingBoilingObject;

//  display program header

System.out.print(
    "=========================================\n"
    +
    "Freezing and Boiling Points of Substances\n"
    +
    "=========================================\n"
    );

//  Collect the temperature for which the substances
//  that are freezing, boiling (or neither) should
//  be determined.

System.out.print(
    "Please enter a temperature (Fahrenheit): ");
inputTemperature = keyboard.nextDouble();
System.out.println();

//  Instantiate FreezingBoiling object using the
//  temperature entered by the user.  Using this
//  object, the program can determine which
//  substances are freezing (solid), neither
//  freezing or boiling (liquid), or boiling
//  (gaseous).

aFreezingBoilingObject =
    new FreezingBoiling( inputTemperature );

//  The aFreezingBoilingObject is used to determine
//  whether, at the temperature entered by the user,
```

```
//  the substances: Ethyl, Oxygen, and Water are
//  freezing, boiling, or neither freezing or
//  boiling.

//  Compose String outputString to show which
//  substances are freezing of boiling. If a
//  substance is neither freezing or boiling at the
//  temperature field in aFreezingBoilingObject,
//  then nothing is added to outputString.

if ( aFreezingBoilingObject.isEthylFreezing())
{
    outputString += "Ethyl is Freezing";

    //  This phrase is the first one in
    //  outputString.  No punctuation
    //  is added before it.

    isFirst = false;
}
else if (aFreezingBoilingObject.isEthylBoiling())
{
    outputString += "Ethyl is Boiling";

    //  This phrase is the first one in
    //  outputString.  No punctuation
    //  is added before it.

    isFirst = false;

}

//  If a substance is neither freezing or boiling at
//  the temperature entered, then nothing is added
//  to the program's output.  If something should be
//  added to the program's output for the "neither
//  freezing nor boiling" condition, add an else
//  clause here and append that
//  information to outputString.

if ( aFreezingBoilingObject.isOxygenFreezing())
{

    if (!isFirst)

        //  This phrase is not the first one in
        //  outputString. Add punctuation "; " to
        //  outputString to separate this phrase
        //  from the previous one(s).

        outputString    += "; ";
    else

        //  This phrase is the first one in
        //  outputString.  No punctuation
        //  is added before it.
```

```
            isFirst = false;

        outputString += "Oxygen is Freezing";
    }
    else if (aFreezingBoilingObject.isOxygenBoiling())
    {
        //  Punctuation is added (or not) in
        //  the same way it was for the case
        //  where Oxygen is freezing.

        if (!isFirst)
            outputString    += "; ";
        else
            isFirst = false;

        outputString += "Oxygen is Boiling";
    }

    if ( aFreezingBoilingObject.isWaterFreezing())
    {
        //  Punctuation is added (or not) in
        //  the same way it was for the case
        //  where Oxygen is freezing.

        if (!isFirst)
            outputString    += "; ";
        else
            isFirst = false;

        outputString += "Water is Freezing";
    }
    else if (aFreezingBoilingObject.isWaterBoiling())
    {
        //  Punctuation is added (or not) in
        //  the same way it was for the case
        //  where Oxygen is freezing.

        if (!isFirst)
            outputString    += "; ";
        else
            isFirst = false;

        outputString += "Water is Boiling";
    }

    if (outputString.equals(""))

    //  If nothing has been added to outputString
    //  during the previous if-else-if decision
    //  statement, then no substance is freezing or
    //  boiling at the temperature entered by the
    //  user.  Display a message to show the user
    //  this situation.

    System.out.println("At temperature " + inputTemperature
        + ", no substance known by this program is "
        + " either freezing or boiling.");
```

```
        else
        {

        //  Display the substances that were determined
        //  to be either freezing or boiling at the
        //  temperature the user entered.  The String
        //  outputString contains the sentence fragment
        //  with that information.

            System.out.print("At temperature "
                + inputTemperature + ": ");

        //  Display the substances that are either
        //  freezing or boiling.  Add a "." to
        //  complete the sentence displayed.

            System.out.println(outputString + ".");
        }
    }
}
```

Program Output

Test Case 1

```
=========================================
Freezing and Boiling Points of Substances
=========================================
Please enter a temperature (Fahrenheit): -362

At temperature -362.0: Ethyl is Freezing; Oxygen is Freezing; Water is
Freezing.
```

Test Case 2

```
=========================================
Freezing and Boiling Points of Substances
=========================================
Please enter a temperature (Fahrenheit): -305

At temperature -305.0: Ethyl is Freezing; Oxygen is Boiling; Water is
Freezing.
```

Test Case 3

```
=========================================
Freezing and Boiling Points of Substances
=========================================
Please enter a temperature (Fahrenheit): -307

At temperature -307.0: Ethyl is Freezing; Water is Freezing.
```

Test Case 4

```
=========================================
Freezing and Boiling Points of Substances
=========================================
Please enter a temperature (Fahrenheit): -171

At temperature -171.0: Oxygen is Boiling; Water is Freezing.
```

Test Case 5

```
=========================================
Freezing and Boiling Points of Substances
```

```
==========================================
Please enter a temperature (Fahrenheit): 33

At temperature 33.0: Oxygen is Boiling.
```

Test Case 6

```
==========================================
Freezing and Boiling Points of Substances
==========================================
Please enter a temperature (Fahrenheit): 172

At temperature 172.0: Ethyl is Boiling; Oxygen is Boiling.
```

Test Case 7

```
==========================================
Freezing and Boiling Points of Substances
==========================================
Please enter a temperature (Fahrenheit): 212

At temperature 212.0: Ethyl is Boiling; Oxygen is Boiling; Water is
Boiling.
```

NOTES

CHAPTER 5

Loops and Files

Solutions

- Programming Challenge 2: Distance Traveled
- Programming Challenge 6: Population
- Programming Challenge 15: UpperCaseFile Class

Programming Challenge 2: Distance Traveled

Problem Statement:

The distance a vehicle travels can be calculated as follows:

Distance = Speed * Time

For example, if a train travels 40 miles-per-hour for 3 hours, the distance traveled is 120 miles.

Design a class that stores the speed of a vehicle (in miles-per-hour) and the number of hours it has traveled. It should have a method named getDistance that returns the distance, in miles, that the vehicle has traveled.

Demonstrate the class in a program that uses a loop to display the distance a vehicle has traveled for each hour of a time period specified by the user. For example, if a vehicle is traveling at 40 mph for a three hour time period, it should display a report similar to the one shown here.

Hour	Distance Traveled
1	40
2	80
3	120

Input Validation: Do not accept a negative number for speed and do not accept any value less than one for time traveled.

Solution

Define What The Vehicle Class is To Do

Purpose	Model the Behavior of a Vehicle in Motion	
Fields	speed	The Speed of the Vehicle in Miles Per Hour.
	time	The Number of Hours the Vehicle Travels.
Constructor	Vehicle( )	Create a Vehicle object, setting the field speed to zero, and the field time to zero.

Methods	setSpeed	Set the speed field to the value of the method's parameter.
	setTime	Set the time field to the value of the method's parameter.
	getSpeed	Return the value of the speed field of the object.
	getTime	Return the value of the time field of the object.
	getDistance	Return the distance the vehicle has traveled based on its speed and hours traveled.
	toString (optional)	Return a String that describes the Vehicle object.

Pseudocode for Vehicle Class

1) Fields

   Declare speed and time fields to be type int (whole number values).

   These fields could have been declared as type double. The decision to use type int was made from the example of the program's output that was shown in the problem statement. If type double were used for class Vehicle's fields, the double (instead of int) data type would be used in all the class' methods.

2) Constructor

   a) The Vehicle constructor is defined with no arguments.

   b) The speed and time fields are both initialized to 0.

3) Methods

   a) setSpeed

      Set the speed field to the value of the method's argument.

   b) setTime

      Set the time field to the value of the method's argument.

   c) getSpeed

      i) Return the value of the speed field.

   d) getTime

      i) Return the value of the time field.

   e) getDistance

i) Compute the distance the vehicle has traveled using the formula given in the problem statement:

distance = time * speed;

ii) Return the value of distance.

f) toString (optional)

i) Return a String value showing the Vehicle object's speed and time fields.

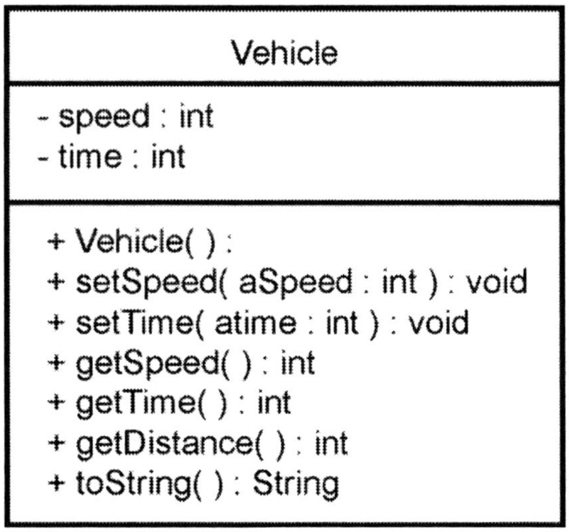

Figure 5 – 1 UML Diagram for Class Vehicle

Source Code Listing 5 – 1 Vehicle Class (Vehicle.java)

```
//*****************************************************
//  Written by:  Carl Holdsworth                      *
//  Chapter 5                                         *
//  Programming Challenge 2:  Distance Traveled       *
//                                                    *
//  The distance a vehicle travels can be             *
//  calculated as follows:                            *
//                                                    *
//      Distance = Speed * Time                       *
//                                                    *
//  For example, if a train travels 40                *
//  miles-per-hour for 3 hours, the distance          *
//  traveled is 120 miles.                            *
//                                                    *
//  Design a class that stores the speed of a         *
//  vehicle (in miles-per-hour) and the number        *
//  of hours it has traveled. It should have a        *
//  method named getDistance that returns the         *
//  distance, in miles, that the vehicle has          *
//  traveled.                                         *
//                                                    *
//  Demonstrate the class in a program that uses      *
//  a loop to display the distance a vehicle has      *
//  traveled for each hour of a time period           *
```

```
//  specified by the user. For example, if a              *
//  vehicle is traveling at 40 mph for a three            *
//  hour time period, it should display a report          *
//  similar to the one shown here.                        *
//                                                        *
//          Hour        Distance Traveled                 *
//          ----------------------------                  *
//          1            40                               *
//          2            80                               *
//          3           120                               *
//                                                        *
//  Input Validation: Do not accept a negative            *
//  number for speed and do not accept any value          *
//  less than one for time traveled.                      *
//*********************************************************

public class Vehicle
{
    //*****************************************************
    //  Field speed contains the current speed            *
    //  of the vehicle.                                   *
    //*****************************************************

    private int speed;

    //*****************************************************
    //  Field time contains the time the vehicle          *
    //  has been moving.                                  *
    //*****************************************************

    private int time;

    //*****************************************************
    //  Constructor for the Vehicle class.                *
    //  Initialize the speed and time fields to           *
    //  zero.                                             *
    //*****************************************************

    public Vehicle()
    {
        speed   = 0;
        time    = 0;
    }

    //*****************************************************
    //  Mutator method setSpeed changes the               *
    //  value of the speed field to that of the           *
    //  method's parameter.                               *
    //*****************************************************

    public void setSpeed(int aSpeed)
    {
        speed   =   aSpeed;
    }

    //*****************************************************
    //  Mutator method setTime changes the value          *
    //  of the time field to that of the                  *
    //  method's parameter.                               *
```

```
    //****************************************************

    public void setTime(int aTime)
    {
        time    =   aTime;
    }

    //****************************************************
    //  Accessor method getSpeed returns the              *
    //  value of the speed field.                         *
    //****************************************************

    public int getSpeed()
    {
        return speed;
    }

    //****************************************************
    //  Accessor method getTime returns the               *
    //  value of the time field.                          *
    //****************************************************

    public int getTime()
    {
        return time;
    }

    //****************************************************
    //  The getDistance method returns the                *
    //  distance the vehicle has traveled.                *
    //****************************************************

    public int getDistance()
    {
        return time * speed;
    }

    //****************************************************
    //  The optional method toString returns a            *
    //  String that describes the Vehicle                 *
    //  object.                                           *
    //****************************************************

    public String toString()
    {
        return "Vehicle[speed: " + speed + " mph; "
            + "time: " + time + " hours]";
    }
}
```

Solution: DistanceTraveled Program

Define What The Program is To Do

Purpose	Demonstrate the use of the Vehicle Class

Input	The speed of the vehicle. The time the vehicle is to travel.
Process	Collect and validate speed and time values from the user. Perform a loop, computing the distance traveled for each hour of the trip.
Output	Display a table showing, for each hour of the trip, the time and the total distance the vehicle has traveled.

High Level Pseudocode for DistanceTraveled Program

1) Create an object of class Vehicle.
2) Collect and validate speed and time values from the user.
    a) Prompt user to enter speed value.
    b) If the speed value entered is invalid (< 0), display an error message and ask the user to enter the speed data again.
    c) Once the user has entered valid data for speed, prompt the user to enter the number of hours to travel.
    d) If the time value entered is invalid (≤ 0), display an error message and ask the user to enter the time data again.
3) Set the speed value of the vehicle using the setSpeed method of the Vehicle class.
4) Display a table of the hours traveled and the total distance the vehicle has covered. Use a loop to execute once for each hour, up to the number of hours entered by the user. Use the int variable hr as the control variable in the loop.

    On each pass through the loop:

    - Set the time traveled by the vehicle object to the value of hr, using the setTime method.
    - Calculate the distance traveled using the getDistance method of the Vehicle class.
    - Display the value of hr and the distance traveled during that time.
    - Repeat the loop.

Detailed Pseudocode for DistanceTraveled Program

1) Declare local variables.

a) Variable theSpeed is the vehicle's speed (entered by the user.)

b) Variable theTime is the time the vehicle will travel (entered by the user.)

c) Variable v1 is an object of class Vehicle.

d) Variable speedOK is a status flag to indicate that the user has entered valid data for speed.

e) Variable timeOK is a status flag to indicate the user has entered valid data for time.

2) Collect speed value from the user. Validate that the value entered is ≥ 0. If data is invalid, display an error message and request speed value again.

a) Prompt the user to enter a value for speed. Save the value in variable theSpeed.

b) Enter a 'while' loop that will continue while theSpeed is invalid (< 0).

- ✦ Display an error message.
- ✦ Prompt the user to enter a value for speed.
- ✦ Save the value entered by the user in theSpeed.
- ✦ Perform next iteration of 'while' loop.

3) Collect time value from user. Validate that the value entered is ≥ 1. If data is invalid, display an error message and request time value again.

a) Use a 'do-while' loop that continue while theTime is invalid (< 0).

- ✦ Prompt the user to enter a value for time. Save the value in variable theTime.
- ✦ Determine whether the value of theTime is valid using a boolean expression. Save the result of the boolean expression in the status variable timeOK.

```
timeOK = theTime > 0;
```

- ✦ If timeOK is false, display an error message.
- ✦ If timeOK is false, perform another iteration of the 'do-while' loop.

4) Set the speed field of v1 to the value of theSpeed, using the setSpeed method.

5) Display a table of the hours traveled and the total distance the vehicle has covered.

a) Use a for loop, with index variable hr. The initial value of hr should be 1. The loop should continue while hr is <= theTime. At the end of each iteration of the loop, increment hr by one.

On each pass through the loop:

- Set the time field of v1 to the value of hr, using the setTime method.
- Use the getDistance method to determine the total distance traveled by v1 at time hr.
- Display the value of hr and the distance traveled during that time.
- Repeat the loop.

NOTE: Comparing the 'while' and 'do-while' Loops

In many programming situations, loops are constructed using a pretest loop, such as the 'while' loop or 'for' loop. Using a pretest loop, the loop's body is executed only if the loop's boolean expression is true. This boolean expression serves as a 'guard' so that the loop is performed only when that condition applies.

In contrast, the statements in a posttest loop, such as the 'do-while' loop, are always executed at least one time. This could be the source of unintended programming errors if the statements in the body of the 'do-while' loop expect the loop's boolean expression to be true.

However, a 'do-while' loop is an appropriate choice when:

- the boolean expression's value cannot be determined before a particular sequence of operations are performed, and
- that sequence of operations is repeated in the body of the loop.

This situation exists in the case where a user is prompted to enter data that must be validated. In the DistanceTraveled program, notice that, in the 'while' loop used to collect and validate the speed data, the operations before the loop begins are the same as those at the bottom of the loop's body. In comparison, the 'do-while' loop used to collect and validate the time data performs an equivalent function without duplication of statements. Where possible, duplication of statements should be avoided. Unintended programming errors are more likely to occur when one segment of the duplicated code is changed while the other is not.

Code Listing 5 - 2 (DistanceTraveled.java)

```
//*******************************************************
//  Written by:  Carl Holdsworth                        *
//  Chapter 5                                           *
//  Programming Challenge 2:  Distance Traveled         *
//                                                      *
//  Demonstrate the class in a program that uses        *
```

```
//  a loop to display the distance a vehicle has          *
//  traveled for each hour of a time period               *
//  specified by the user. For example, if a              *
//  vehicle is traveling at 40 mph for a three            *
//  hour time period, it should display a report          *
//  similar to the one shown here.                        *
//                                                        *
//          Hour        Distance Traveled                 *
//          ---------------------------                   *
//          1            40                               *
//          2            80                               *
//          3           120                               *
//                                                        *
//  Input Validation: Do not accept a negative            *
//  number for speed and do not accept any value          *
//  less than one for time traveled.                      *
//*********************************************************

import java.util.Scanner;

public class DistanceTraveled
{
    public static void main(String[] args)
    {
        //  Create a Scanner object to use for reading from
        //  the keyboard.
        Scanner keyboard = new Scanner(System.in);

        //  Variables used to determine a vehicle's
        //  motion over time.

        int theSpeed = 0;    //  speed of vehicle
                             //  entered by user

        int theTime = 0;     //  time of travel
                             //  entered by user

        //  Object v1 of type Vehicle.  The object's
        //  speed and time to travel are provided by
        //  user input.  The getDistance method is used
        //  to determine how far v1 has traveled over a
        //  specific time interval.

        Vehicle v1 = new Vehicle();

        //  Status variables are used to indicate
        //  validity of user input

        boolean speedOK = false;     //  true when speed
                                     //  input is valid

        boolean timeOK = false;      //  true when time
                                     //  input is valid

        //  All local variables have been initialized so
        //  they are assured to have values, no matter
        //  what path the program takes through the loop
        //  structures.

        //  Display program header.
        System.out.println(
            "-------------------------------\n"
```

```
    + "Distance Traveled Demonstration\n");

//  Collect vehicle speed value from user.

//  Demonstrate the use of a while loop
//  structure to perform this operation.

System.out.print("Enter vehicle speed (MPH): ");
theSpeed     =   keyboard.nextInt();

//  Insure that value entered for speed has
//  positive value.

while( theSpeed < 0 )
{
    System.out.println("Speed must be >= 0");

    System.out.print("Enter vehicle speed (MPH): ");
    theSpeed     =   keyboard.nextInt();
}

//  Since the previous loop has terminated, the
//  value of theSpeed must be equal to or
//  greater than zero.

//  Collect the value for the time to travel
//  from the user.
//
//  Demonstrate the use of a do-while loop
//  structure to perform the input-verify data
//  operation.

do
{
    System.out.print("Enter number of hours traveled: ");
    theTime      =   keyboard.nextInt();

    //  validity check

    timeOK = theTime >= 1;

    if (!timeOK)
        System.out.println("Time must be >= 1");
}
//  continue until time value is valid
while (!timeOK);

//  Since the previous loop has terminated, the
//  value of theTime must be equal to or greater
//  than 1.

//  Display the time and distance traveled table.

System.out.println(
    "\n"
    + "Hour          Distance Traveled\n"
    + "------------------------------");

//  Set the vehicle's speed.
```

```
        v1.setSpeed(theSpeed);

        //  Display the distance traveled for each hour of
        //  the trip.

        for (int hr = 1; hr <= theTime; hr++)
        {
            //  Set the vehicle's time of travel.
            v1.setTime(hr);

            //  Display the distance traveled line for
            //  this hour.

            System.out.println(
                hr
                + "                    "
                //Compute and display distance traveled.
                + v1.getDistance());
        }

        //  Distance traveled table display complete.
        System.out.println(
            "------------------------------");
    }
}
```

Program Output

```
------------------------------
Distance Traveled Demonstration

Enter vehicle speed (MPH): 1
Enter number of hours traveled: 10

Hour          Distance Traveled
------------------------------
1                   1
2                   2
3                   3
4                   4
5                   5
6                   6
7                   7
8                   8
9                   9
10                   10
------------------------------
------------------------------
Distance Traveled Demonstration

Enter vehicle speed (MPH): -10
Speed must be >= 0
Enter vehicle speed (MPH): 55
Enter number of hours traveled: 8

Hour          Distance Traveled
------------------------------
1                   55
2                   110
3                   165
4                   220
```

```
5                     275
6                     330
7                     385
8                     440
-------------------------------

-------------------------------
Distance Traveled Demonstration

Enter vehicle speed (MPH): 100
Enter number of hours traveled: 0
Time must be >= 1
Enter number of hours traveled: 4

Hour          Distance Traveled
-------------------------------
1                     100
2                     200
3                     300
4                     400
```

Programming Challenge 6: Population

Problem Statement:

Write a class that will predict the size of a population of organisms. The class should store the starting number of organisms, their average daily population increase (as a percentage), and the number of days they will multiply. The class should have a method that uses a loop to display the size of the population for each day. Test the class in a program that asks the user for the starting size of the population, their average daily increase, and the number of days they will multiply. The program should display the daily population.

Input Validation: Do not accept a number less than two for the starting size of the population. Do not accept a negative number for average daily population increase. Do not accept a number less than one for the number of days they will multiply.

Solution: Community Class

Define What The Community Class Is To Do

Purpose	Predict the Population of Organisms in a Community.	
Fields	population	The number of organisms in the community.
	growthRate	The (decimal) rate by which the population of the community grows per day.
Constructor	Community	Initialize the population field and the growthRate filed by the arguments provided.
Methods	getPopulation	Return the value of the population field.
	next	Advance the population field to its value for the next day.

High Level Pseudocode for Community Class

1) Fields:

   a) The population field contains a whole number value. An organism exists or it doesn't; fractional organisms are not realistic.

      Because the value of this field may be large, type long is used. For example, the world's population is greater than 6,000,000,000. This value will not fit in an int (largest value of an int is 2,147,483,647).

A double can represent very large numbers, but only to 15 digits of precision. Type long can hold values up to 92,233,720,368,547,758,071; large enough for practical purposes and having 20 digits of precision. Refer to Chapter 2 for explanations and comparisons of Java primitive data types.

b) The growthRate field contains the rate by which the population of the community grows each day. The growthRate value is a decimal, not a percentage.

2) Constructor:

The constructor for the Community class takes its arguments, starting population and rate of growth (decimal value - not a percentage) and initializes the population and growthRate fields.

3) Methods:

a) The getPopulation method returns the value of the population field.

b) The next method causes the population field to advance to the next day, increasing its value according to the growthRate field.

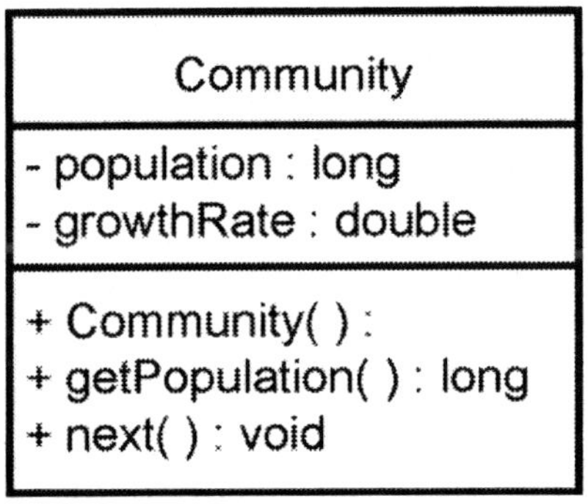

Figure 5 – 2 UML Diagram for Community Class

Detailed Pseudocode for Community Class

1) The population field is declared to be of type long. The growthRate field is declared to be of type double. Programs that use the Community class are expected to provide the object's growth rate in decimal, not percentage, terms.

2) The Community class constructor takes two arguments: the object's starting population (type long) and the object's population growth rate. The values of these parameters are stored in the population field and the growthRate field respectively.

3) The accessor method getPopulation method returns the value of the population field.

4) The next method is used to advance the Community object's population to the value it should have for the next day.

   The next day's population is calculated as the current population plus the current population times the object's growth rate. Conceptually this calculation is written:

   population = population + population * growthRate.

   This computation is simplified and rewritten:

   population = population * (1 + growthRate)

   Taking consideration of the data type conversions needed for this calculation, the calculation is written in Java as:

   ```
   population =
       (long) (population * (1.00 + growthRate));
   ```

Code Listing 5 – 3 (Community.java)

```
//*************************************************************
//  Written by: D. G. Samuel                                  *
//  Programming Challenge 6: Population                       *
//                                                            *
//  Write a class that will predict the size of a population  *
//  of organisms. The class should store the starting number  *
//  of organisms, their average daily population increase     *
//  (as a percentage), and the number of days they will       *
//  multiply. The class should have a method that uses a      *
//  loop to display the size of the population for each day.  *
//  Test the class in a program that asks the user for the    *
//  starting size of the population, their average daily      *
//  increase, and the number of days they will multiply. The  *
//  program should display the daily population.              *
//                                                            *
//  Input Validation: Do not accept a number less than two    *
//  for the starting size of the population. Do not accept a  *
//  negative number for average daily population increase.    *
//  Do not accept a number less than one for the number of    *
//  days they will multiply.                                  *
//*************************************************************

public class Community
{
    //*********************************************************
    //  Field population stores the current number of         *
    //  organisms in the community.  Type long is used so     *
    //  that large communities (for example the world         *
    //  population, currently over 6 Billion) can be          *
    //  modeled.  Initial value of population is provided by  *
    //  the class constructor.                                *
    //*********************************************************

    private long    population;

    //*********************************************************
    //  Field growthRate is the (decimal) rate by which the   *
```

```
    //  community grows per day.  The value of growth rate    *
    //  is provided by the class constructor.                 *
    //*********************************************************

    private double growthRate;

    //*********************************************************
    //  Community class constructor.  Take arguments          *
    //  provided and stores them in the object's fields.      *
    //*********************************************************

    public Community(
        long startingPopulation, double theGrowthRate)
    {
        population =   startingPopulation;
        growthRate  =   theGrowthRate;
    }

    //*********************************************************
    //  Accessor method getPopulation returns the value       *
    //  of the population field of the object.                *
    //*********************************************************

    public long getPopulation()
    {
        return  population;
    }

    //*********************************************************
    //  Method next advances the object to the next day.      *
    //  The population is increased by the growth rate.       *
    //*********************************************************

    public void next()
    {
        population  =
            (long) (population * (1.00 + growthRate));
    }
}
```

Solution: Population Program

Define What The Program is To Do

Purpose	Show the Population Growth of a Community, Day by Day
Input	The initial population of the community. The rate, in percent, by which the community's population grows on a daily basis.

Process	From the user, collect the value of the community's initial population. Validate the value entered to ensure that the initial population is ≥ 2. From the user, collect the value of the community's rate of population growth per day (as a percentage). Validate that the value for rate of growth is ≥ 0. Convert the value entered by the user from a percentage to a decimal value. From the user, collect the value of the number of days to calculate the community's population. Validate that the value for number of days is ≥ 1. Use a loop to calculate the community's population for each day until the number of days specified has been reached.
Output	For each day, display the number of the day and the community's population on that day.

Pseudocode for Population Program

1) Declare local variables:

   a) The variable startingNumber is used to store the initial population of the community. The community's population is represented by a whole number value; an organism exists or it does not. Because the initial population can be very large, type long is used.

   b) The variable percentGrowthRate is used to store the community's daily rate of growth, entered by the user, in terms of percentage.

   c) The variable populationGrowthRate is used to store the community's daily rate of growth, in terms of a decimal value.

   d) The variable numberDays is used to store the number of days that the user wants to have the community's population displayed.

2) The local variables listed in the previous step are initialized to 0. This prevents the program from using an uninitialized variable (and avoids a Java compiler error.)

3) (Optional) Create output format variables so that the program's display is easier to read.

   a) The format wholeCommaFormat is used to display values, using a comma ',' as the digit grouping symbol, and displays integer values (showing no decimal digits.)

   b) The format wholeDecimalFormat is used to display values, using a comma ',' as the digit grouping symbol, and displaying four (4) decimal digits.

4) From the user, collect the starting population. Validate the data entered for population is ≥ 2.

   a) Prompt the user to enter the starting population value. Store the data entered in the variable startingNumber.

   b) Determine whether the startingNumber is ≥ 2. Store the boolean result of that comparison in the status variable startPopOK.

   c) Begin a 'while' loop that will terminate when the value of startPopOK is true.

      ✦ The while loop's body is executed when startPopOK is false, meaning that the value of startingNumber is < 2.

      ✦ Display an error message to the user.

      ✦ Prompt the user to enter the value of the starting population again.

      ✦ Determine whether the startingNumber is ≥ 2. Store the boolean result of that comparison in the status variable startPopOK.

      ✦ Perform next iteration of the 'while' loop.

5) From the user, collect the value of the community's rate of population growth per day (as a percentage). Validate that the value of the rate of growth is ≥ 0.

   a) Prompt the user to enter the rate of growth. Store the data entered in the variable percentGrowthRate.

   b) Determine whether the percentGrowthRate is ≥ 0. Store the boolean result of that comparison in the status variable growthRateOK.

   c) Begin a 'while' loop that will terminate when the value of growthRateOK is true.

      ✦ The while loop's body is executed when growthRateOK is false, meaning that the value of percentGrowthRate is < 0.

      ✦ Display an error message to the user.

      ✦ Prompt the user to enter the value of the growth rate again.

      ✦ Determine whether the percentGrowthRate is ≥ 0. Store the boolean result of that comparison in the status variable growthRateOK.

      ✦ Perform the next iteration of the 'while' loop.

   d) Convert the growth rate entered from a percent value to a decimal value.

Divide percentGrowthRate by 100.00 and store the result in the variable populationGrowthRate.

6) From the user, collect the value of the number of days to calculate the community's population. Validate that the value of number of days is ≥ 1.

   a) Prompt the user to enter the number of days the program should display the population. Store the data entered in the variable numberDays.

   b) Determine whether the numberDays is ≥ 1. Store the boolean result of that comparison in the status variable nDaysOK.

   c) Begin a 'while' loop that will terminate when the value of nDaysOK is true.

      - The while loop is entered when nDaysOK is false, meaning that the value of numberDays is < 1.
      - Display an error message to the user.
      - Prompt the user to enter the value of number of days again. Store the data entered in the variable numberDays.
      - Determine whether numberDays is ≥ 1. Store the boolean result of that comparison in the status variable nDaysOK.
      - Perform the next iteration of the 'while' loop.

7) All the input has been entered and validated. Display the data entered to the user.

   (Optional) Use DecimalFormat objects to improve the appearance of the display.

   - Display startingNumber using wholeCommaFormat.
   - Display percentGrowthRate using decimalCommaFormat.
   - Display numberDays using wholeCommaFormat.

8) Declare and instantiate local variable aCommunity, an object of class Community, providing the class constructor with the startingNumber and populationGrowthRate; the community initial population and its daily growth rate respectively.

9) Display the community's population for each day, beginning at 1 and ending at the number of days entered by the user.

   A 'for' loop is a natural structure to control these repetitive steps.

   - The variable i is declared for use as the loop's control variable.

The scope of i is limited to this 'for' statement only. By declaring the control variable with this limited scope, it is easy for a programmer to see its intended use. This programming method also prevents the use of this variable in another part of the program where its value may not be what the programmer expects.

Initialization: The value of i is initialized to 1.

Test Expression: The test expression for the loop is:

i <= numberDays

Together with the initialization of i to 1, and the update expression i++, the loop will be performed numberDays times.

- Execute the Body of the 'for' statement (see next step).
- Update Expression: This 'for' loop has two (2) separate update expressions.

  Increment the value of i by 1.

  Use the next method of the Community class to increase the population to its value for the next day.
- In its completed form the 'for' statement to perform the loop is:

```
//  In the following example:
//      *   the declaration and initialization of
//          the control variable,
//      *   the test expression and
//      *   the update expressions (note plural)
//  are written on separate lines for emphasis.

for (int i = 1;
    i <= numberDays;
    i++, aCommunity.next())
{
    // body of loop (see below)
}
```

a) Body of 'for' loop:

- Determine the number of organisms in aCommunity using the getPopulation method of Community class. Note that in the solution provided, the value of the getPopulation method is used directly in an expression and not saved in a local variable.

- (Optional) Use the wholeCommaFormat to improve the readability of the display of the day's population.
- Display the day number (stored in index variable i) and the community's population for that day.
- Continue with the next iteration of the 'for' loop.

10) The Population program terminates when the display of the population data table is completes.

NOTE: Avoiding 'Off by One' Errors and Infinite Loops

It is easy to make an 'off by one' mistake when writing 'for' loops. The name 'off by one' refers to the situation where the loop is executed one less time, or one more time more than. Another mistake that is easy to make is writing an incorrect update expression. If the control variable is not updated correctly, an infinite loop (a loop that will not terminate) can occur. When this happens, the program can only be terminated by the user (for example, using a control-C in Windows, or a kill command in Unix / Linux.).

The following statements are incorrect, but, at quick glance, look deceptively similar to the correct solution.

```
// Sample mistake #1
// Incorrect initialization of control variable.
// Loop is performed one more time than it
// should.

for (int i = 0;    // Initial value should be 1.
    i <= numberDays;
    i++, aCommunity.next())

// Sample mistake #2
// Incorrect test expression. Loop is performed
// one less time that it should.
```

```
for (int i = 1;
    i < numberDays;       //  Boolean operator in test
                          //  should be <=.
                          //  Another common mistake
                          //  is to use negation of
                          //  the boolean expression
                          //  intended.
                          //  For example, writing >
                          //  when <= is intended.
    i++, aCommunity.next())

//  Not a mistake, just a different way to write
//  the loop so that it performs the correct
//  number of iterations.  There are many
//  situations in a program where the control
//  variable should start at 0, for example when
//  using Arrays(see Chapter 7).

for (int i = 0;
    i < numberDays;
    i++, aCommunity.next())

//  Sample mistake #3
//  Incorrect update expression for control
//  variable will cause the loop to never terminate.

for (int i = 0;
    i < numberDays;
    i + 1, aCommunity.next())  // Should be i++
```

Code Listing 5 – 4 (Population.java)

```
import java.text.DecimalFormat;
import java.util.Scanner;
//*****************************************************************
//  Written by: D. G. Samuel                                      *
//  Programming Challenge 6: Population                           *
//                                                                *
//  Write a class that will predict the size of a population      *
//  of organisms. The class should store the starting number      *
//  of organisms, their average daily population increase         *
```

```
//  (as a percentage), and the number of days they will       *
//  multiply. The class should have a method that uses a      *
//  loop to display the size of the population for each day.  *
//  Test the class in a program that asks the user for the    *
//  starting size of the population, their average daily      *
//  increase, and the number of days they will multiply. The  *
//  program should display the daily population.              *
//                                                            *
//  Input Validation: Do not accept a number less than two    *
//  for the starting size of the population. Do not accept a  *
//  negative number for average daily population increase.    *
//  Do not accept a number less than one for the number of    *
//  days they will multiply.                                  *
//*************************************************************

public class Population
{
    public static void main(String[] args)
    {
        //  Create a Scanner object to use for reading from
        //  the keyboard.
        Scanner keyboard = new Scanner(System.in);

        //  1) User enters starting number of organisms, their
        //  rate of population growth, and the number of days to
        //  display their population.
        //
        //  2) Validate data entered by user.
        //
        //  3) Create an object aCommunity of class Community
        //  using the starting number of organisms and the rate
        //  of their population growth.
        //
        //  4) For days 1, 2, ... number of days:
        //      a) display population on that day
        //      b) use Community method next to have
        //      aCommunity update population for next day.

        //  Starting number of organisms (whole number).
        //  Starting number must be >= 2;

        long    startingNumber;

        //  NOTE:  See Chapter 2 for definition of long data
        //  type. A long can store a value from:
        //
        //  -92,233,720,368,547,758,081 to
        //  92,233,720,368,547,758,071.
        //
        //  The int data type can store values from:
        //
        //  -2,147,483,648 to 2,147,483,647;
        //
        //  a range too small, for example, to store
        //  the world's current population (over 6
```

```
//  billion).
//
//  Type double is not used because the number of
//  organisms in a community must be a whole number. An
//  organism exists or it doesn't.  A fractional number
//  of organisms isn't realistic.  Additionally, type
//  long has greater precision so that it can accurately
//  represent larger populations than type double.


//  Rate (% per day) at which an organism produces a
//  new, independent organism.  Rate percentage is not
//  limited to whole number values only.  Rate must
//  be >= 0;

double  percentGrowthRate;

//  Rate (decimal value, per day) at which an organism
//  produces a new, independent organism.

double  populationGrowthRate;

//  Number of days the organisms will multiply.
//  Number of days must be >= 1;

int     numberDays;

//  The following variables need to be initialized so
//  that, no matter what path is taken in the program,
//  the compiler is certain each variable has been
//  explicitly given a value.  Otherwise a compiler
//  error will occur.

startingNumber = 0L;
percentGrowthRate = 0.00;
populationGrowthRate = 0.00;
numberDays  = 0;

//  status flags to control termination of input while
//  loops - flags set true when valid data is entered

boolean startPopOK = false;
boolean growthRateOK = false;
boolean nDaysOK = false;

//  Optional Output Formats
DecimalFormat wholeCommaFormat =
    new DecimalFormat("#,###");
DecimalFormat decimalCommaFormat =
    new DecimalFormat("#,###.####");

//  display header
```

```
System.out.println("Population Prediction");
System.out.println("---------------------------------");

//  Collect from the user the starting population of the
//  community.

System.out.print("Enter starting population: ");
startingNumber = keyboard.nextLong();
startPopOK = startingNumber >= 2;


//  Repeat request for input if starting
//  population is not >= 2.

while (!startPopOK)
{
    //  Display error message.
    System.out.println("Starting population must be >= 2");

    //  Request the user to enter starting population
    //  again.

    System.out.print("Enter starting population: ");
    startingNumber  = keyboard.nextLong();
    startPopOK  =   startingNumber >= 2;
}


//  Collect from the user the growth rate (%) for
//  the community.

System.out.print(
    "Enter daily population growth rate (%): ");
percentGrowthRate    = keyboard.nextDouble();
growthRateOK = percentGrowthRate >= 0;

//  Repeat request for input if growth rate is
//  not >= 0.

while (!growthRateOK)
{
    //  Display error message.
    System.out.println("Daily population growth rate "
        + "must be >= 0");

    //  Request the user to enter the growth rate again.

    System.out.print(
        "Enter daily population growth rate (%): ");
    percentGrowthRate    = keyboard.nextDouble();
    growthRateOK = percentGrowthRate >= 0;
}


//  Convert percentage to decimal.
```

```
populationGrowthRate = percentGrowthRate / 100.00;

//  Collect from the user the number of days to
//  display population growth.

System.out.print(
    "Enter number of days population will grow: ");

numberDays = keyboard.nextInt();
nDaysOK = numberDays >= 1;

//  Repeat request for input if number of days
//  not >= 1;

while (!nDaysOK)
{
    //  Display error message.
    System.out.println(
        "Number of days must be >= 1.");

    //  Request user to enter the number of
    //  days again.
    System.out.print(
        "Enter number of days population will grow: ");
    numberDays = keyboard.nextInt();
    nDaysOK =   numberDays >= 1;
}

//  Valid data has been entered by user

//  Display data entered by user

System.out.println(
    "Starting number of organisms: "
    + wholeCommaFormat.format(startingNumber));
System.out.println(
    "Population growth rate (%/day): "
    + decimalCommaFormat.format(percentGrowthRate));
System.out.println(
    "Number of days to display: "
    + wholeCommaFormat.format(numberDays));

//  Create community of organisms.

Community aCommunity = new Community(
    startingNumber, populationGrowthRate);

//  Display community's population for number of days
//  specified.

//  Display table header.
```

```
        System.out.println("");
        System.out.println(
            "Day                        Population");
        System.out.println(
            "---------------------------------");

        //  Start loop on day 1.  Continue loop until number
        //  of days requested have been displayed.  At the end
        //  each iteration, increment i and use the next method
        //  to have the Community object proceed to the
        //  next day.

        for (int i = 1;
            i <= numberDays;
            i++, aCommunity.next())
        //  ^^^  ^^^^^^^^^^^^^^^^^

        //  Note: Multiple operations are performed in the
        //  above for loop's update expression.

        {
            //  Display daily population data.
            System.out.println(
                i
                + "                          "
                + wholeCommaFormat.format(
                    //  gather community's population
                    //  and display it
                    aCommunity.getPopulation()) );
        }
        //  program complete
        System.out.println(
            "---------------------------------");
        System.out.println();
    }
}
```

Program Output

Test Case 1

```
C:\Gaddis\Ch05\Test>java Population
Population Prediction
---------------------------------
Enter starting population: 6000000001
Enter daily population growth rate (%): 1
Enter number of days population will grow: 10
Starting number of organisms: 6,000,000,001
Population growth rate (%/day): 1
Number of days to display: 10

Day                       Population
---------------------------------
1                            6,000,000,001
2                            6,060,000,001
3                            6,120,600,001
4                            6,181,806,001
5                            6,243,624,061
```

```
6                        6,306,060,301
7                        6,369,120,904
8                        6,432,812,113
9                        6,497,140,234
10                        6,562,111,636
---------------------------------
```

Test Case 2

```
C:\Gaddis\Ch05\Test>java Population
Population Prediction
---------------------------------
Enter starting population: 0
Starting population must be >= 2
Enter starting population: 2
Enter daily population growth rate (%): -1
Daily population growth rate must be >= 0
Enter daily population growth rate (%): 0
Enter number of days population will grow: 0
Number of days must be >= 1.
Enter number of days population will grow: 10
Starting number of organisms: 2
Population growth rate (%/day): 0
Number of days to display: 10

Day                    Population
---------------------------------
1                        2
2                        2
3                        2
4                        2
5                        2
6                        2
7                        2
8                        2
9                        2
10                        2
---------------------------------


C:\Gaddis\Ch05\Test>
```

Programming Challenge 15: UpperCaseFile Class

Write a class named UpperCaseFile. The class constructor should accept two file names as arguments. The first file should be opened for reading and the second file should be opened for writing. The class should read the contents of the first file, change all characters to uppercase, and store the results in the second file. The second file will be a copy of the first file, except all the characters will be uppercase. Use Notepad or another text editor to create a simple file that can be used to test the class.

Solution: UpperCaseFile Class

Define What UpperCaseFile Class Is To Do

Purpose	Copy a File Replacing All Characters With Changed to Uppercase.	
Fields	theInputFileName	The name of the file to be copied.
	theInputFileReader	FileReader object associated with the file to be copied.
	theInputFile	BufferedReader object from which lines of text are read.
	inputLine	A line of text from the input file.
	theOutputFileName	The name of the file to be created.
	theOutputFileWriter	FileWriter object associated with the file being created.
	theOutputFile	PrintWriter object to which lines of text from the input file are sent, after being converted to all upper case characters.
Constructors	UpperCaseFile	Create an UpperCaseFile object. Save the value of the first argument into field theInputFileName. Save the value of the second argument into field theOutputFileName.
Methods	start	Take lines of text from the input file, convert them to all upper case characters, and send them to the output file. Continue until all lines from the input file have been read.

Pseudocode for UpperCaseFile Class

1) Importing Class Libraries in Packages

   The fields and methods of the UpperCaseFile class make use of file input and output classes that are not included with the Java compiler for every program. To indicate that these additional classes are required, the UpperCaseFile.java source program file must 'import' the package that contains the additional classes. The file input and output classes needed by this program are contained in the package java.io. (See Java 2 Platform API Specification http://java.sun.com/reference/api/index.html). To indicate that the java.io package is required, the UpperCaseFile.java source program file begins with the statement:

   ```
   import java.io.*;
   ```

   If this import statement were not present, the Java compiler would produce an error message wherever a class from the Java IO library was used. When import statements are used in a Java source program file, they must appear as the first statements in the file.

2) Fields

   a) The field theInputFileName is a String whose value is the name of the input file, passed to the UpperCaseFile class constructor.

   b) The field theInputFileReader is a FileReader object created using the input file name given. An object of type fileReader is required to perform any input operations on a file. Methods of the FileReader class are used to perform low level file input operations.

   c) The field theInputFile is a BufferedReader object created using a FileReader object. A BufferedReader object permits reading lines of characters from an input file through the use of the readLine method.

   d) The field inputLine is a String that holds the line of characters that has been read from the input file, using the readLine method.

   e) The field theOutputFileName is a String whose value is the name of the output file passed to the UpperCaseFile class constructor.

   f) The field theOutputFileWriter is a FileWriter object created using the output file name given. An object of type FileWriter is required to perform any output operations on a file. Methods of the FileWriter class are used to perform low level file output operations.

   g) The field theOutputFile is a PrintWriter object created using a FileWriter object. A PrintWriter object has methods such as print and println that can be used to append the value of Strings to the output file.

3) The Constructor for the UpperCaseFile class has two arguments.

   a) The first argument is a String whose value is the name of the input file to be used by this object. The value of that string is saved in the field theInputFileName.

   b) The second argument is a String whose value is the name of the output file to be used by this object. The value of that string is saved in the field theOutputFileName.

4) The UpperCaseFile class has just one method, named start. This method has no parameters has no return value.

   a) Exception Handling

   Method start performs all the file operations and data manipulation in the class. The file input and output operations can cause exceptions to occur. These exceptions will propagate to the start method. In future chapters, processing of exceptions will be described in detail. For this solution, input and output exceptions will not be processed, but will instead be propagated (or 'thrown') the back to the start method's calling program. Java requires that the definition of a method indicate the exceptions it will throw. For the start method, this is indicated by writing

```
public void start() throws IOException
```

   b) Open input file and create the needed input objects so that the input file can be read a line at a time.

      i) In order to access data from an input file, an object of type FileReader must be created using the name of the input file passed to the UpperCaseFile constructor. This is written

```
FileReader theInputFileReader = new
    FileReader(theInputFileName);
```

      ii) If no file has the name theInputFileName, then the constructor for the FileReader class will throw an IOException. Given the design of the start method, its processing is terminated when a IOException occurs and the IOException is propagated to its calling program.

      iii) The object theInputFileReader can be used for low level input operations. In order to read characters from the file, one line at a time, a BufferedReader object is required. To create a BufferedReader object, the FileReader object is required. This is written

```
BufferedReader theInputFile = new
    BufferedReader(theInputFileReader);
```

   c) Create output file and the output file objects needed so that the output file can be written, one line at a time, using the print and println methods.

i) To write data to an output file, an object of type FileWriter must be created using the name of the output file passed to the UpperCaseFile constructor. This is written

```
FileWriter theOutputFileWriter = new
    FileWriter(theInputFileName);
```

ii) If there already exists a file with the name theOutputFileName, then the existing file will be deleted by this operation.

iii) The object theOutputFileWriter can be used for low level output operations. In order to write lines of characters using the print and println methods, an object of type PrintWriter is needed. This object is created using the OutputFileWriter,

```
PrintWriter theOutputFile =
    new PrintWriter(theOutputFileWriter)
```

d) Having created objects that can operate on the input and output files, the start method's primary processing loop can begin.

i) First a line of text is read from the input file using the BufferedReader method readLine. This is written

```
inputLine = theInputFile.readLine();
```

ii) A 'while' loop is entered to continue processing.

- ✦ The 'while' loop's body will be performed if there were characters read on the last input operation. If, however, the end of the input file has been reached, indicated by a null value in the String inputLine, the 'while' loop terminates and the start method's processing is complete (almost).

- ✦ The body of the 'while' loop takes the input line from the file and converts it to contain all uppercase characters using the String method, toUpperCase. The result of this conversion is saved in the String outputLine. The String outputLine is written to the output file using the PrintWriter method println. This is written

```
theOutputFile.println(outputLine);
```

- ✦ The next line of input is read using the readLine method and the while loop begins its next iteration.

- ✦ At the conclusion of the 'while' loop, both the input and output files are closed. The close operations are performed on FileReader and FileWriter objects. This is written

```
theInputFile.close();
theOutputFile.close();
```

```
UpperCaseFile
-------------------------------------------
- theInputFileName : String
- theInputFileReader : FileReader
- theInputFile : BufferedReader
- theOutputFileName : String
- theOutputFileWriter : FileWriter
- theOutputFile : PrintWriter
-------------------------------------------
+ UpperCaseFile(
    anInFileName : String,
    anOutFileName : String )
+ start( ) : void
```

Figure 5 – 3 UML Diagram for UpperCaseFile Class

Code Listing 5 – 5 (UpperCaseFile.java)

```
import java.io.*;

//*****************************************************
//  Written by W. I. Jessica                          *
//                                                    *
//  Chapter 5                                         *
//  Programming Challenge 15:  UpperCaseFile          *
//                                                    *
//  Write a class named UpperCaseFile.  The class;    *
//  constructor should accept two file names as       *
//  arguments.  The first file should be opened for   *
//  reading and the second file should be opened for  *
//  writing.  The class should read the contents of   *
//  the first file, change all characters to          *
//  uppercase, and store the results in the second    *
//  file.  The second file will be a copy of the      *
//  first file, except all the characters will be     *
//  uppercase.  Use Notepad or another text editor    *
//  to create a simple file that can be used to test  *
//  the class.                                        *
//*****************************************************

public class UpperCaseFile
{

    //  Field theInputFileName is the name of the input
    //  file, given in the class constructor.

    private String theInputFileName;

    //  Field theInputFileReader is a FileReader
    //  object that is associated with the input file.

    private FileReader theInputFileReader;

    //  Field theInputFile is a BufferedReader
    //  object associated with the input file.
```

```
private BufferedReader theInputFile;

//  Field inputLine is used to store a line of
//  text read from the input file.

private String inputLine;

//  Field theOutputFileName is the name of the
//  output file, given in the class constructor.

private String theOutputFileName;

//  Field theOutFileWriter is a FileWriter
//  object associated with the output file.

private FileWriter theOutFileWriter;

//  Field theOutputFile is a PrintWriter
//  object associated with the output file.

private PrintWriter theOutputFile;

//***************************************************
//  Constructor for class UpperCaseFile.  Store the   *
//  parameter values as the name of the input file and*
//  the output file, respectively.                    *
//***************************************************

public UpperCaseFile(String anInFileName, String anOutFileName)
{
    theInputFileName = anInFileName;
    theOutputFileName = anOutFileName;
}

//***************************************************
//  Method start reads a line from the input file     *
//  and stores that result in a local String          *
//  variable. The characters in the local String      *
//  variable are converted to all upper case and      *
//  written to the output file.  This process         *
//  continues until the input file is exhausted.      *
//  Because of the I/O methods used, the start        *
//  method may cause an IOException to be generated.  *
//  The exception is not processed by the start       *
//  method, but is instead propogated to the caller   *
//  of the method.                                    *
//***************************************************

public void start() throws IOException
{
    char    nextChar;
    char    nextCharAsString;
    String  outputLine;

    //  Create the file objects needed in this method.

    //  To read a file, one line at a time, a
    //  BufferedReader object is associated with the
    //  file.  In order to create a BufferedReader, a
    //  FileReader object must be created using the
    //  input file's name.

    FileReader theInputFileReader =
        new FileReader(theInputFileName);
```

```
        BufferedReader theInputFile =
            new BufferedReader(theInputFileReader);

        //  To write a file, one line at a time, a
        //  PrintWriter object is associated with the file.
        //  In order to create a PrintWriter, a FileWriter
        //  object must be created using the output file's
        //  name.

        FileWriter theOutFileWriter =
            new FileWriter(theOutputFileName);

        PrintWriter theOutputFile =
            new PrintWriter(theOutFileWriter);

        //  The start method's main processing loop. Read a
        //  line from the input file into String inputLine.
        //  If inputLine isn't null, convert all its
        //  characters to upper case storing the result into
        //  String outputLine.  Append outputLine to the
        //  output file using the println method. This loop
        //  terminates when the line read from the input
        //  file is null.

        //  read first line of input file
        inputLine = theInputFile.readLine();

        //  loop until nothing's left in input file
        while (inputLine != null)
        {
            //  convert output line to upper case
            outputLine = inputLine.toUpperCase();

            //  append output line to output file
            theOutputFile.println(outputLine);

            //  read next line of file
            inputLine = theInputFile.readLine();
        }

        //  The start method's processing is completed.  The
        //  input and output files used in the method are
        //  closed.

        theInputFile.close();
        theOutputFile.close();
    }
}
```

Solution: CreateUpperCaseFile

Define What The CreateUpperCaseFile Program is To Do

Purpose	From A Text File, Create Another File That Has All Characters In Upper Case.
Input	The name of the input file. The name of the output file.

Process	Perform the user interaction to obtain the name of the input file to be read, and the name of the new file to be created. Create an object of type UpperCaseFile using the input file and output file names. Invoke the appropriate method of UpperCaseFile to perform the creation of the output file.
Output	The output file contains the text from the input file with all characters converted to upper case.

Pseudocode for CreateUpperCaseFile Program

1) Importing an Exception defined in a Package.

   a) The CreateUpperCaseFile program uses the UpperCaseFile class, which has methods that may generate exceptions, namely IOException. The definition of this exception is contained in the package java.io. That definition must be 'imported' at the beginning of the CreateUpperCaseFile source file

   import java.io.IOException;

   b) Because the CreateUpperCaseFile program only needs the definition of this exception, the entire java.io package need not be imported.

   c) If this import statement were not present, the Java compiler would produce an error on the source line that uses IOException.

2) Excption Handling

   a) CreateUpperCaseFile calls the start method from class UpperCaseFile. The start method is defined showing that it may throw an IOException. For the purposes of this solution, the CreateUpperCaseFile program will not process this exception, but instead will throw it to the Java system. This is indicated by defining the main method

public static void main(String[] args) throws IOException

3) CreateUpperClassFile Program Steps

   a) The name of the input file to be process is collected from the user.

   b) The name of the output file that will be created (containing the text from the input file with all characters changed to upper case) is collected from the user.

   c) An object of type UpperCaseFile is created, giving the class' constructor the names of the input file and output file.

d) Invoke the UpperCaseFile object's start method.

i) If an exception occurs in the UpperCaseFile start method, it will be propagated to the main program. The main program is designed to propagate that exception to its calling program. When the main program throws an exception, the program is terminated and a set of error messages are displayed to the user.

ii) If the start method succeeds, the main program terminates.

4) To see the results of the CreateUpperCaseFile program, the user has to view the input file and the output file in a text editor.

a) Test Case 1

A text file, Moby01.txt is created with arbitrary text.

The program CreateUpperCaseFile is executed.

When the name of the input file is requested, Moby01.txt is entered.

When the name of the output file is requested, Moby01.out is entered.

The program continues and terminates normally.

The screen snapshots show the contents of Moby01.txt and Moby01.out after the program has been run.

b) Test Case 2

The program CreateUpperCaseFile is executed.

When the name of the input file is requested, the text "noFileHere.txt" is entered.

When the name of the output file is requested, the text "noFileHere.out" is entered.

The program terminates because of an exception in method main of class CreateUpperCaseFile. The error message shows that the system can not find the file "noFileHere.txt."

Code Listing 5 - 6 (CreateUpperCaseFile.java)

```
import java.io.IOException;
import java.util.Scanner;
//*******************************************************
//  Written by W. I. Jessica                            *
//                                                      *
//  Chapter 5                                           *
//  Programming Challenge 15:  UpperCaseFile            *
//                                                      *
//  Write a class named UpperCaseFile.  The class;      *
//  constructor should accept two file names as         *
//  arguments.  The first file should be opened for     *
//  reading and the second file should be opened for    *
//  writing.  The class should read the contents of     *
//  the first file, change all characters to            *
```

```
//  uppercase, and store the results in the second       *
//  file.  The second file will be a copy of the          *
//  first file, except all the characters will be        *
//  uppercase.  Use Notepad or another text editor       *
//  to create a simple file that can be used to test     *
//  the class.                                            *
//*******************************************************

public class CreateUpperCaseFile
{
    //  The main method uses the start method of
    //  class UpperCaseFile.  The start method may
    //  throw an IOException.  The main method does
    //  not process this exception, but instead
    //  propogates the exception to the program
    //  that called it.

    public static void main(String[] args) throws IOException
    {
        //  Create a Scanner object to use for reading from
        //  the keyboard.
        Scanner keyboard = new Scanner(System.in);

        String  inFileName;
        String  outFileName;

        //  Request input file name from user.

        System.out.print("Enter Input File Name: ");
        inFileName = keyboard.nextLine();

        //  Request output file name from user.

        System.out.print("Enter Output File Name: ");
        outFileName = keyboard.nextLine();

        //  Create UpperCaseFile object using the
        //  input and output file names entered by
        //  the user.

        UpperCaseFile anUpperCaseFile =
            new UpperCaseFile(inFileName, outFileName);

        //  Use the UpperCaseFile object's start
        //  method to create the output file whose
        //  contents is the same as the input file
        //  except that all characters are upper case.

        anUpperCaseFile.start();
    }
}
```

Program Output

Test Case 1

```
C:\Gaddis\Ch05\Test>dir

 Volume in drive C is ******
 Volume Serial Number is nnnnnnn

 Directory of C:\Gaddis\Ch05\Test

01/08/2004  04:56p      <DIR>          .
01/08/2004  04:56p      <DIR>          ..
```

```
01/08/2004  04:56p                 730 CreateUpperCaseFile.class
01/07/2004  11:14a               2,370 CreateUpperCaseFile.java
01/08/2004  04:56p               2,075 Keyboard.class
07/15/2003  07:40a               4,299 Keyboard.java
01/03/2004  01:10p               1,322 moby01.txt
01/08/2004  04:56p               1,166 UpperCaseFile.class
01/07/2004  04:41p               5,591 UpperCaseFile.java
               7 File(s)         17,553 bytes
               2 Dir(s)  38,986,490,368 bytes free

C:\Gaddis\Ch05\Test>java CreateUpperCaseFile
Enter Input File Name: moby01.txt
Enter Output File Name: moby01.out
C:\Gaddis\Ch05\Test>
```

Test Case Files

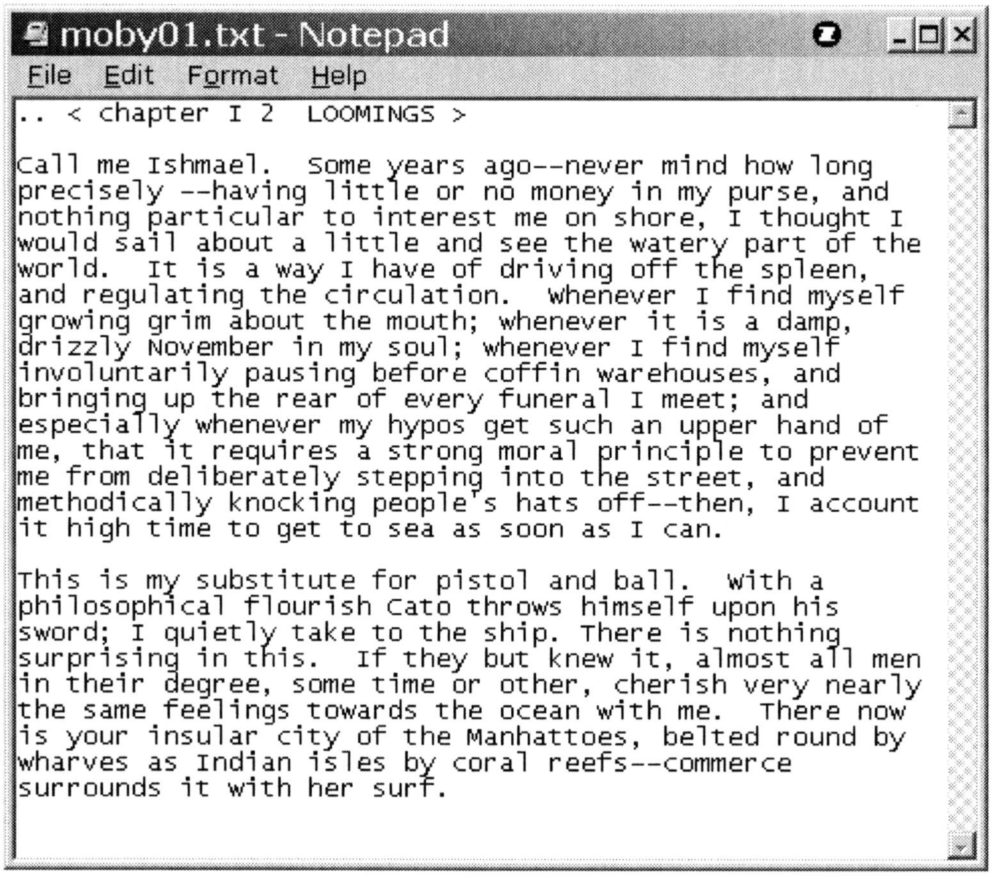


```
.. < chapter I 2  LOOMINGS >

Call me Ishmael.  Some years ago--never mind how long
precisely --having little or no money in my purse, and
nothing particular to interest me on shore, I thought I
would sail about a little and see the watery part of the
world.  It is a way I have of driving off the spleen,
and regulating the circulation.  Whenever I find myself
growing grim about the mouth; whenever it is a damp,
drizzly November in my soul; whenever I find myself
involuntarily pausing before coffin warehouses, and
bringing up the rear of every funeral I meet; and
especially whenever my hypos get such an upper hand of
me, that it requires a strong moral principle to prevent
me from deliberately stepping into the street, and
methodically knocking people's hats off--then, I account
it high time to get to sea as soon as I can.

This is my substitute for pistol and ball.  With a
philosophical flourish Cato throws himself upon his
sword; I quietly take to the ship. There is nothing
surprising in this.  If they but knew it, almost all men
in their degree, some time or other, cherish very nearly
the same feelings towards the ocean with me.  There now
is your insular city of the Manhattoes, belted round by
wharves as Indian isles by coral reefs--commerce
surrounds it with her surf.
```

Figure 5 – 4 Input File (moby01.txt)

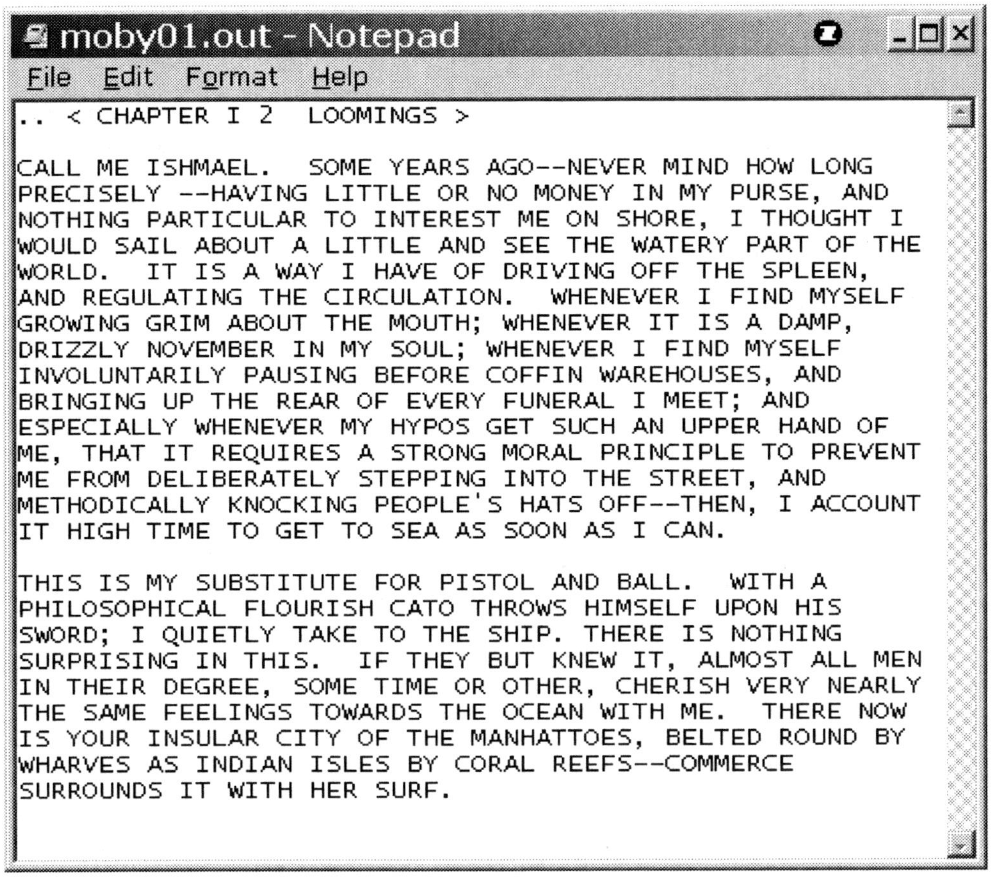

```
.. < CHAPTER I 2  LOOMINGS >

CALL ME ISHMAEL.  SOME YEARS AGO--NEVER MIND HOW LONG
PRECISELY --HAVING LITTLE OR NO MONEY IN MY PURSE, AND
NOTHING PARTICULAR TO INTEREST ME ON SHORE, I THOUGHT I
WOULD SAIL ABOUT A LITTLE AND SEE THE WATERY PART OF THE
WORLD.  IT IS A WAY I HAVE OF DRIVING OFF THE SPLEEN,
AND REGULATING THE CIRCULATION.  WHENEVER I FIND MYSELF
GROWING GRIM ABOUT THE MOUTH; WHENEVER IT IS A DAMP,
DRIZZLY NOVEMBER IN MY SOUL; WHENEVER I FIND MYSELF
INVOLUNTARILY PAUSING BEFORE COFFIN WAREHOUSES, AND
BRINGING UP THE REAR OF EVERY FUNERAL I MEET; AND
ESPECIALLY WHENEVER MY HYPOS GET SUCH AN UPPER HAND OF
ME, THAT IT REQUIRES A STRONG MORAL PRINCIPLE TO PREVENT
ME FROM DELIBERATELY STEPPING INTO THE STREET, AND
METHODICALLY KNOCKING PEOPLE'S HATS OFF--THEN, I ACCOUNT
IT HIGH TIME TO GET TO SEA AS SOON AS I CAN.

THIS IS MY SUBSTITUTE FOR PISTOL AND BALL.  WITH A
PHILOSOPHICAL FLOURISH CATO THROWS HIMSELF UPON HIS
SWORD; I QUIETLY TAKE TO THE SHIP. THERE IS NOTHING
SURPRISING IN THIS.  IF THEY BUT KNEW IT, ALMOST ALL MEN
IN THEIR DEGREE, SOME TIME OR OTHER, CHERISH VERY NEARLY
THE SAME FEELINGS TOWARDS THE OCEAN WITH ME.  THERE NOW
IS YOUR INSULAR CITY OF THE MANHATTOES, BELTED ROUND BY
WHARVES AS INDIAN ISLES BY CORAL REEFS--COMMERCE
SURROUNDS IT WITH HER SURF.
```

Figure 5 - 5 Output File (moby01.out)

Test Case 2

```
C:\Gaddis\Ch05\Test>dir

 Volume in drive C is **********
 Volume Serial Number is nnnnnnnnnn

 Directory of C:\Gaddis\Ch05\Test

01/08/2004  04:56p      <DIR>          .
01/08/2004  04:56p      <DIR>          ..
01/08/2004  04:56p                 730 CreateUpperCaseFile.class
01/07/2004  11:14a               2,370 CreateUpperCaseFile.java
01/08/2004  04:56p               2,075 Keyboard.class
07/15/2003  07:40a               4,299 Keyboard.java
01/08/2004  04:56p               1,322 moby01.out
01/03/2004  01:10p               1,322 moby01.txt
01/08/2004  04:56p               1,166 UpperCaseFile.class
01/07/2004  04:41p               5,591 UpperCaseFile.java
               8 File(s)         18,875 bytes
               2 Dir(s)  38,986,488,832 bytes free

C:\Gaddis\Ch05\Test>java CreateUpperCaseFile
Enter Input File Name: noFileHere.txt
Enter Output File Name: noFileHere.out
Exception in thread "main" java.io.FileNotFoundException: noFileHere.txt
(The system cannot find the file specified)
        at java.io.FileInputStream.open(Native Method)
        at java.io.FileInputStream.<init>(Unknown Source)
```

```
        at java.io.FileInputStream.<init>(Unknown Source)
        at java.io.FileReader.<init>(Unknown Source)
        at UpperCaseFile.start(UpperCaseFile.java:101)
        at CreateUpperCaseFile.main(CreateUpperCaseFile.java:60)

C:\Gaddis\Ch05\Test>
```

CHAPTER 6

A Second Look at Classes and Objects

Solutions

- Programming Challenge 3: Carpet Calculator
- Programming Challenge 5: Month Class
- Programming Challenge 7: Retail Item Class Modification

Programming Challenge 3: Carpet Calculator

Problem Statement:

The Westfield Carpet Company has asked you to write an application that calculates the price of carpeting for rectangular rooms. To calculate the price, you multiply the area of the floor (width times length) by the price per square foot of carpet. For example, the area of floor that is 12 feet long and 10 feet wide is 120 square feet. To cover that floor with carpet that costs $8 per square foot would cost $960. (12 x 10 x 8 = 960.)

First, you should create a class named RoomDimension that has two fields: one for the length of the room and one for the width. The RoomDimension class should have a method that returns the area of the room. (The area of the room is the room's length multiplied by the room's width.)

Next you should create a Room Carpet class that has a RoomDimension object as a field. It should also have a field for the cost of the carpet per square foot. The RoomCarpet class should have a method that returns the total cost of the carpet.

Figure 6-19 is a UML diagram showing possible class designs and depicting the relationships between the classes. Once you have written these classes, use them in an application that asks the user to enter the dimensions of a room and the price per square foot of the desired carpeting. The application should display the total cost of the carpet.

Solution: RoomDimension

Define What The Method is To Do

Purpose	Describe a room by its dimensions.	
Fields	length	The length of the room in feet.
	width	The width of the room in feet.
Constructors	RoomDimension(double,double)	Create a RoomDimension using the length and width.
Methods	getArea	return the area of the room

Pseudocode for the RoomDimension class

1) Define RoomDimension fields.

   a) The field length represents the length of the room in feet.

   b) The field width represents the width of the room in feet.

2) Define RoomDimension constructor.

   a) Create an object of the class RoomDimension by assigning the length and width passed in from the parameters to the instance fields.

3) Define the method for getArea.

a) Calculate and return the area using the formula A = lw.

4) Define the method for toString.

a) Return a string that contains a description of the room using the length and the width.

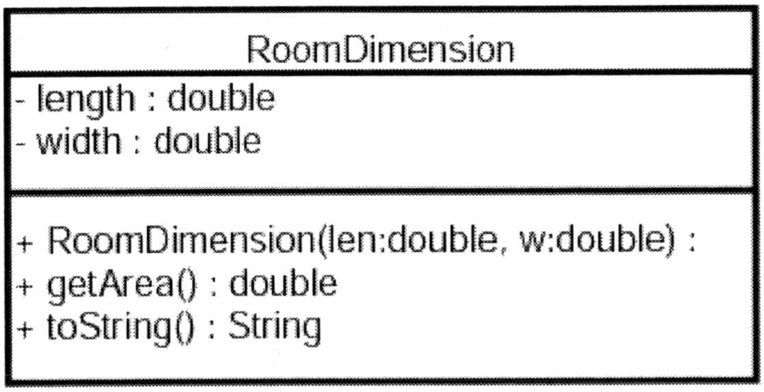

Figure 6 - 1 UML Drawing for RoomDimension Class

Code Listing 6 - 1 (RoomDimension.java)

```
//****************************************************
// Written by Diane Christie
// Chapter 6
// Programming Challenge 3:  RoomDimension Class
//****************************************************

//****************************************************
// The Westfield Carpet Company has asked you to write
// an application that calculates the price of carpeting
// for rectangular rooms.  To calculate the price, you
// multiply the area of the floor (width times length)
// by the price per square foot of carpet.  For example,
// the area of floor that is 12 feet long and 10 feet
// wide is 120 square feet.  To cover that floor with
// carpet that costs $8 per square foot would cost $960.
// (12 x 10 x 8 = 960.)
//
// First, you should create a class named RoomDimension
// that has two fields: one for the length of the room
// and one for the width.  The RoomDimension class should
// have a method that returns the area of the room.  (The
// area of the room is the room's length multiplied by
// the room's width.)
//
// Next you should create a Room Carpet class that has a
// RoomDimension object as a field.  It should also
// have a field for the cost of the carpet per square
// foot.  The RoomCarpet class should have a method that
// returns the total cost of the carpet.
//
// Figure 6-19 is a UML diagram showing possible class
// designs and depicting the relationships between the
// classes.  Once you have written these classes, use them
// in an application that asks the user to enter the
```

```
// dimensions of a room and the price per square foot of
// the desired carpeting.  The application should display
// the total cost of the carpet.
//****************************************************

public class RoomDimension
{
      private double length;  //The length in feet.
      private double width;   //The width in feet.

      //**************************************************
      //Constructor accepts a length and a width.
      //**************************************************
      public RoomDimension(double len, double w)
      {
            length = len;
            width = w;
      }

      //**************************************************
      //This method returns the product of the length and
      //and the width.
      //**************************************************
      public double getArea()
      {
            return length * width;
      }

      //**************************************************
      //This method returns a string indicating the room
      //dimensions.
      //**************************************************
      public String toString ()
      {
            return "The room is " + length + " feet long by "
                  + width + " feet wide.\n";
      }
}
```

Solution: RoomCarpet Class

Define What The Method is To Do

Purpose	Describe the cost of carpet for a room	
Fields	size	The RoomDimension object that contains the dimensions of the room to carpet.
	carpetCost	The price of the carpeting in $/square foot.
Constructors	RoomCarpet(RoomDimension ,double)	Create a RoomCarpet object using a RoomDimension object and the cost of the carpet.
Methods	getArea	return the area of the room

Pseudocode for the RoomCarpet class

1) Define RoomCarpet fields.
   a) The size represents the RoomDimension object containing the dimensions of the room to carpet.
   b) The carpetCost represents the price of the carpeting in $/square foot.
2) Define the constructor.
   a) The constructor creates a RoomCarpet object by taking in the cost of the carpet and the dimensions of the room in the form of a RoomDimension object and assigning them to the instance fields.
3) Define the method getTotalCost.
   a) The method calculates the total cost by multiplying the area of the room by the cost of the carpeting and returns the result.
4) Define the method toString.
   a) The method returns a string that describes the dimensions of the room and the cost of carpeting it.

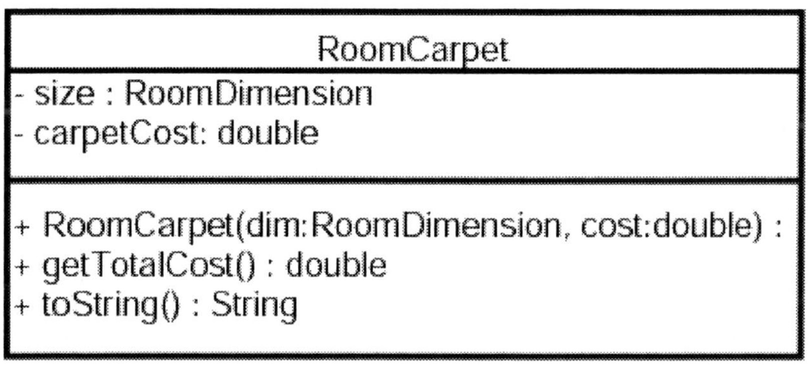

Figure 6 - 2 UML Drawing for RoomCarpet Class

Code Listing 6 - 2 (RoomCarpet.java)

```
//*****************************************************
// Written by Diane Christie
// Chapter 6
// Programming Challenge 3:  RoomCarpet Class
//*****************************************************

//*****************************************************
// The Westfield Carpet Company has asked you to write
// an application that calculates the price of carpeting
// for rectangular rooms.  To calculate the price, you
// multiply the area of the floor (width times length)
// by the price per square foot of carpet.  For example,
// the area of floor that is 12 feet long and 10 feet
```

```
// wide is 120 square feet.  To cover that floor with
// carpet that costs $8 per square foot would cost $960.
// (12 x 10 x 8 = 960.)
//
// First, you should create a class named RoomDimension
// that has two fields: one for the length of the room
// and one for the width.  The RoomDimension class should
// have a method that returns the area of the room.  (The
// area of the room is the room's length multiplied by
// the room's width.)
//
// Next you should create a Room Carpet class that has a
// RoomDimension object as a field.  It should also
// have a field for the cost of the carpet per square
// foot.  The RoomCarpet class should have a method that
// returns the total cost of the carpet.
//
// Figure 6-19 is a UML diagram showing possible class
// designs and depicting the relationships between the
// classes.  Once you have written these classes, use them
// in an application that asks the user to enter the
// dimensions of a room and the price per square foot of
// the desired carpeting.  The application should display
// the total cost of the carpet.
//*****************************************************

import java.text.DecimalFormat;

public class RoomCarpet
{
      private RoomDimension size;
      private double carpetCost;

      public RoomCarpet(RoomDimension dim, double cost)
      {
            size = dim;
            carpetCost = cost;
      }

      public double getTotalCost()
      {
            return carpetCost * size.getArea();
      }

      public String toString()
      {
            DecimalFormat money = new DecimalFormat("0.00");
            return size.toString() + "The carpet cost at $"
                  + money.format(carpetCost) + " per yard "
                  + "totals $" + money.format(getTotalCost());
      }
}
```

Solution: RoomCarpet Class

Define What The Class Is To Do

Purpose	Demonstrate the RoomDimension and RoomCarpet classes

Input	The length and width of the room, and the cost of the carpeting.
Process	Ask the user for the dimensions of the room. Create a RoomDimension object. Ask the user for the cost of the carpeting. Create a RoomCarpet object.
Output	Display information about the cost of carpeting the room specified by the user.

Pseudocode for CarpetCalculator Class

1) Prompt the user and collect the length and width of the room.
2) Create a RoomDimension object with the user input.
3) Prompt the user and collect the cost per square foot of the carpet.
4) Create a RoomCarpet object with the Room Dimension object and the carpet cost.
5) Print out the information about the room and the cost to carpet it.

Code Listing 6 - 3 (CarpetCalculator.java)

```
//****************************************************
// Written by Diane Christie
// Chapter 6
// Programming Challenge 3:  Carpet Calculator
//****************************************************

//****************************************************
// The Westfield Carpet Company has asked you to write
// an application that calculates the price of carpeting
// for rectangular rooms.  To calculate the price, you
// multiply the area of the floor (width times length)
// by the price per square foot of carpet.  For example,
// the area of floor that is 12 feet long and 10 feet
// wide is 120 square feet.  To cover that floor with
// carpet that costs $8 per square foot would cost $960.
// (12 x 10 x 8 = 960.)
//
// First, you should create a class named RoomDimension
// that has two fields: one for the length of the room
// and one for the width.  The RoomDimension class should
// have a method that returns the area of the room.  (The
// area of the room is the room's length multiplied by
// the room's width.)
//
// Next you should create a Room Carpet class that has a
// RoomDimension object as a field.  It should also
// have a field for the cost of the carpet per square
// foot.  The RoomCarpet class should have a method that
// returns the total cost of the carpet.
//
// Figure 6-19 is a UML diagram showing possible class
// designs and depicting the relationships between the
// classes.  Once you have written these classes, use them
```

```
// in an application that asks the user to enter the
// dimensions of a room and the price per square foot of
// the desired carpeting.  The application should display
// the total cost of the carpet.
//*************************************************************

import java.util.Scanner;

public class CarpetCalculator
{
      public static void main (String [] args)
      {
            Scanner keyboard = new Scanner(System.in);
            RoomDimension roomSize;
            RoomCarpet rug;
            double length;
            double width;
            double price;

            System.out.print("Welcome to the Carpet Calculator \n"
                  + "Courtesy of the Westfield Carpet Company \n"
                  + "Please enter the length of the room in feet:  ");
            length = keyboard.nextDouble();

            System.out.print("Please enter the width of the room"
                  + " in feet:  ");
            width = keyboard.nextDouble();

            roomSize = new RoomDimension(length, width);

            System.out.print("Please enter the price of the "
                  + " carpet per foot:  $");
            price = keyboard.nextDouble();

            rug = new RoomCarpet(roomSize, price);

            System.out.println (rug.toString());
      }
}
```

Program Output

```
Welcome to the Carpet Calculator
Courtesy of the Westfield Carpet Company
Please enter the length of the room in feet:  12
Please enter the width of the room in feet:  10
Please enter the price of the  carpet per foot:  $8
The room is 12.0 feet long by 10.0 feet wide.
The carpet cost at $8.00 per yard totals $960.00
```

Programming Challenge 5: Month Class

Problem Statement:

Write a class named Month. The class should have an int field named **monthNumber** which will hold the number of the month. For example, January would be 1, February would be 2, etc. In addition, provide the following methods:

- A default constructor that sets the **monthNumber** field to 1.
- A constructor that accepts the number of the month as an argument. It should set the **monthNumber** field to the value passed as the argument. If a value less than 1 or greater than 12 is passed, the constructor should set **monthNumber** to 1.
- A constructor that accepts the name of the month, such as "January", "February", etc., as an argument. It should set the **monthNumber** field to the corresponding value for the month named.
- A **setMonthNumber** method that accepts an **int** argument, which is assigned to the **monthNumber** field. If a value less than 1 or greater than 12 is passed, the method should set **monthNumber** to 1.
- A **getMonthNumber** method that returns the value in the **monthNumber** field.
- A **getMonthName** method that returns the name of the month. For example, if the **monthNumber** field contains 1, then this method should return "January".
- A **toString** method that returns the same value as the **getMonthName** method.
- An **equals** method that accepts a **Month** object as an argument. If the argument object holds the same data as the calling object, this method should return **true**. Otherwise, it should return **false**.
- A **greaterThan** method that accepts a **Month** object as an argument. If the calling object's **monthNumber** field is greater than the argument's **monthNumber** field, this method should return **true**. Otherwise, it should return **false**.
- A **lessThan** method that accepts a Month object as an argument. If the calling object's **monthNumber** field is less than the argument's **monthNumber** field, this method should return **true**. Otherwise, it should return **false**.

Solution: Month Class

Define What The Month Class Is To Do

Purpose	Describe a month of the year.	
Fields	monthNumber	The month's order in the year. January has value 1, February has value 2, … December has value 12.
Constructors	Month()	Create a **Month** object for January.
	Month(int)	Create a **Month** object corresponding to the nth month of the year where $(1 \le n \le 12)$. If n is not in that range, create a **Month** object for January.
	Month(String)	Create a **Month** object corresponding to the month that has the name specified as the constructor's input parameter: e.g. **"January"**, **"February"**, … **"December"** (case sensitive). If the input parameter **String** is not the name of a month, create a **Month** object for January.

	getMonthNumber	return the object's **monthNumber** field
	setMonthNumber	Validate the parameter to the method. If its value is acceptable, set the **monthNumber** field to that value. If the parameter's value is not valid, set the **monthNumber** field to 1 (January).
	getMonthName	Return the name of the month corresponding to the value of the **monthNumber** field, e.g."January" if the value is 1, "February" if the value is 2, etc. If by chance the **monthNumber** field has an invalid value, set the field to 1 and return the value "January".
Methods	toString	Returns the same value as the **getMonthName** method.
	equals	Returns **true** if the **monthNumber** field of the object is equal to the **monthNumber** field of the method's parameter. Otherwise, returns **false.**
	greaterThan	Returns **true** if the **monthNumber** field of the object is greater than the **monthNumber** field of the method's parameter. Otherwise, returns **false.**
	lessThan	Returns **true** if the **monthNumber** field of the object is less than the **monthNumber** field of the method's parameter. Otherwise, returns **false.**

High Level Pseudocode for Month Class

1) Define **Month** class fields.

   a) The only field in the **Month** class is an **int, monthNumber,** that represents the sequence of the month in the year. For January, the **monthNumber** is 1, for February the **monthNumber** is 2, … for December the **monthNumber** is 12. Ony the values 1, 2, 3, … 12 are valid in this field.

2) Define **Month** class (overloaded) constructors.

   a) Default constructor (having no arguments).

      i) Create an object of class **Month** having a **monthNumber** field set to 1 (for January).

   b) Constructor with integer argument.

      i) Validate the argument to insure its value is in the range 1, 2, … 12. If the argument is valid, create an object of class **Month** having a **monthNumber** set to the value of the integer argument. If the argument is invalid, create an object of class **Month** having a **monthNumber** field set to 1 (January).

c) Constructor with **String** argument.

i) Compare the value of the **String** argument against the names of the 12 months (case sensitive). When a match is found, create an object of class **Month** having a **monthNumber** corresponding to the month whose name was the method's argument. If the value of the method's argument does not match any month name, then create an object of class **Month** having a **monthNumber** field set to 1 (January).

3) Define accessor method **getMonthNumber**.

a) Return the value of the **monthNumber** field.

4) Define mutator method **setMonthNumber**.

a) Validate the method's argument to insure its value is in the range 1, 2, … 12. If the argument is valid, change the value of the **monthNumber** field to the value of the argument. If the argument's value is invalid, change the value of the **monthNumber** field to 1 (for January).

5) Define method **getMonthName**.

a) Return a **String** whose value is the name of the month that corresponds to the value of the **monthNumber** field.

6) Define method **toString**.

a) According to the problem statement, the **toString** method returns the same value as the **getMonthName** method.

7) Define method **equals**.

a) Return **true** if the **Month** object's **monthNumber** field is the same as the parameter **Month** object's **monthNumber** field. Otherwise, return **false**.

8) Define method **greaterThan**.

a) Return **true** if the **Month** object's **monthNumber** field is greater than the value of the parameter **Month** object's **monthNumber** field. Otherwise, return **false**.

9) Define method **lessThan**.

a) Return **true** if the **Month** object's **monthNumber** field is less than the value of the parameter **Month** object's **monthNumber** field. Otherwise, return **false**.

Month
-monthNumber : int
+Month() : +Month(aMonthNumber : int) : +Month(aMonthName : String) : +setMonthNumber(aMonthNumber : int) : void +getMonthNumber() : int +getMonthName() : String +toString() : String +equals(aMonth : Month) : boolean +greaterThan(aMonth : Month) : boolean +lessThan(aMonth : Month) : boolean -validMonthNumber(aMonthNumber : int) : boolean

Figure 6 - 3 UML Drawing for Month Class

Low Level Pseudocode for Month Class

1) Overloaded Constructors

See textbook Section 6.3 and Code Listing 6-9.

a) Programmer Defined Default Constructor

For this constructor, set the **monthNumber** field to 1

b) **Month** Constructor with Integer Parameter

i) Validation of Argument **aMonthNumber** - insure that its value is:

$1 \leq$ aMonthNumber ≤ 12

ii) To express this condition in Java:

```
( 1 <= aMonthNumber && aMonthNumber <= 12 )
```

NOTE: The tests of **aMonthNumber's** value are written in this manner so that they look, as much as possible, similar to the mathematical expression of the condition.

ALSO NOTE: The parameter **aMonthNumber** is compared to 1 and 12, the limits of the **monthNumber** field, as given in the problem definition. Using these literal values makes the expression easier to understand than if values outside the field's limits were tested:

```
( 1 <= aMonthNumber  && aMonthNumber <= 12 )
//    first month number is 1
//    last month number is 12
```

```
( 0 < aMonthNumber  && aMonthNumber < 13 )

//    How are 0 and 13 related to the concept of
//    a month?
```

c) **Month** Constructor with **String** Parameter

i) Compare a **String** parameter against the names of the 12 months. Set **monthNumber** to the value that corresponds to the month's order in the year. If there is no match, set **monthNumber** to 1, representing January, the default value for a **Month** object.

ii) The comparison of the **String** against the names of the 12 months is performed using an **if-else-if** conditional statement.

2) The **setMonthNumber** method

a) The **monthNumber** field is set to the parameter's value, provided that the parameter is in the range:

$$1 \leq \text{aMonthNumber} \leq 12$$

b) Otherwise, the **monthNumber** field is set to 1, its default value.

c) The test to check whether an integer has a meaningful value for use as a month number is the same as was performed in the **Month** constructor with an integer parameter. For consistency and to reduce the possibility of programming errors, a private **boolean** method **validMonthNumber** is defined. This method is used in the **Month** constructor and in the **setMonthNumber** method.

3) The getMonthNumber method

a) The **getMonthNumber** method returns the value of the object's **monthNumber** field.

4) The **getMonthName** method

a) The **getMonthName** method performs the inverse operation that is performed in the **Month** constructor that takes a **String** as its parameter. In the constructor, a **String** value was compared against all the month names and the integer corresponding to the matching name was found. In the **getMonthName** method, the integer value of the **monthNumber** field is used to determine the month's name for the month in that order in the calendar.

b) To find a **String** based on the value of an integer, the **switch** statement is a natural candidate. The value that controls the **switch** is the **monthNumber** field. For each legitimate value of the **monthNumber** field, a **case** label is created and for that case, the appropriate month name is stored in a temporary **String** variable. This temporary value will be the return value of the method.

i) **NOTE:** Each case includes a **break;** statement. If the **break** were to be omitted, the result of the method would be incorrect.

ii) **ALSO NOTE:** A **default case** is included. This may seem redundant because object encapsulation insures that the **monthNumber** field can only changed using the methods of the **Month** class. Nevertheless, it is good programming practice to always include a **default case** when using a **switch** statement. Using redundant data validation operations in a method is referred to as <u>defensive programming</u>.

5) The **toString** method

a) The **toString** method is defined to produce the same result as the **getMonthName** method. The **getMonthName** method invoked to produce the return value of the **toString** method.

6) The **equals** method

a) An **equals** method was demonstrated in the **StockCompare** class.

☞See textbook Section 6.7 and Code Listing 6-18.

i) In the **equals** method of the **Stock** class, an **if-else** statement was used to set the value of a **boolean** status variable.

ii) A more direct way to write this method is to **return** value the value of a **boolean** expression whose value is equivalent to result of the method.

iii) A **Month** object is equal to another **Month** object if the **monthNumber** fields of both objects are equal. If the **monthNumber** fields of two **Month** objects have the same value, then the **Month** objects are equal. Therefore, then equality of **Month** objects is equivalent to the equality of their **monthNumber** fields.

b) The **equals** method returns the value of the **boolean** expression:

```
monthNumber == aMonth.getMonthNumber()
```

7) The **greaterThan** method

a) Using the same reasoning as that given in the **equals** method, the **greaterThan** method returns the value of the **boolean** expression:

```
aMonth.getMonthNumber() < monthNumber
```

i) In mathematics, it is customary to write comparisons with values increasing from left to right.

ii) Another style for writing comparisons is to put the variable being tested on the left hand side of the expression, i.e.

```
monthNumber > aMonth.getMonthNumber
```

iii) For the **greaterThan** method, this expression reads more closely to the method's definition.

iv) Whichever way you chose to write comparison expressions, do so consistently throughout your programs.

8) The **lessThan** method

a) The **lessThan** method returns the value of the **boolean** expression:

```
monthNumber < aMonth.getMonthNumber
```

Code Listing 6 - 4 (Month.java)

```
//*****************************************************
// Written by Myung Kim                               *
// Chapter 6                                          *
// Programming Challenge 5: Month class               *
//*****************************************************

//*****************************************************
//  Write a class named Month. The class should have an *
//  int field named monthNumber which will hold the    *
//  number of the month. For example, January would be *
//  1, February would be 2, etc. In addition, provide  *
//  the following methods:                             *
//  •   A default constructor that sets the monthNumber *
//      field to 1.                                    *
//  •   A constructor that accepts the number of the   *
//      month as an argument. It should set the        *
//      monthNumber field to the value passed as the   *
//      argument. If a value less than 1 or greater than*
//      12 is passed, the constructor should set       *
//      monthNumber to 1.                              *
//  •   A constructor that accepts the name of the     *
//      month, such as "January", "February", etc., as *
//      an argument. It should set the monthNumber     *
//      field to the correct corresponding value.      *
//  •   A setMonthNumber method that accepts an int    *
//      argument, which is assigned to the monthNumber *
//      field. If a value less than 1 or greater than 12*
//      is passed, the method should set monthNumber   *
//      to 1.                                          *
//  •   A getMonthNumber method that returns the value *
//      in the monthNumber field.                      *
//  •   a getMonthName method that returns the name of *
//      the month. For example, if the monthNumber field*
//      contains 1, then this method should return     *
//      "January".                                     *
//  •   A toString method that returns the same value  *
//      as the getMonthName method                     *
//  •   An equals method that accepts a Month object as *
//      an argument. If the argument object holds the  *
//      same data as the calling object, this method   *
//      should return true. Otherwise, it should return *
//      false.                                         *
//  •   A greaterThan method that accepts a Month object*
//      as an argument. If the calling object's        *
//      monthNumber field is greater than the argument's*
//      monthNumber field, this method should return   *
//      true. Otherwise, it should return false.       *
//  •   A lessThan method that accepts a Month object as*
//      an argument. If the calling object's monthNumber*
//      field is less than the argument's monthNumber  *
//      field, this method should return true.         *
//      Otherwise, it should return false.             *
//*****************************************************

//*****************************************************
//  The Month class describes a month of the year as   *
//  an integer.  January is represented as 1, February *
```

```
//  is 2, ... December is 12.                              *
//*********************************************************

public class Month
{
    //*********************************************************
    //  The field monthNumber is the month's sequence         *
    //  number in the year.  Valid values are: 1 for          *
    //  January, 2 for February, ... 12 for December.         *
    //*********************************************************

    private int monthNumber;

    //*********************************************************
    //  Default constructor for Month class - sets month to *
    //  1 for January.                                        *
    //*********************************************************

    public Month()
    {
        monthNumber =   1;
    }

    //*********************************************************
    //  Constructor for Month class - determines whether its*
    //  parameter has a valid value, and sets the field      *
    //  monthNumber to that value.  If the parameter's value*
    //  is not correct, the monthNumber field is set to      *
    //  default value 1, meaning January.                     *
    //*********************************************************

    public Month(int aMonthNumber)
    {
        //  confirm that parameter to constructor
        //  is a valid value for monthNumber
        if ( validMonthNumber( aMonthNumber) )
        {   monthNumber = aMonthNumber; }
        else
            //  parameter has invalid value, set monthNumber
            //  to default value 1 (January)
        {   monthNumber = 1; }
    }

    //*********************************************************
    //  Constructor for Month class that takes a monthName  *
    //  String parameter.  The monthName is compared to the *
    //  names of the months and the monthNumber field is set*
    //  to the number of the month that matches the          *
    //  monthName.  If no match is found for the monthName, *
    //  a default object is created (monthNumber = 1,        *
    //  January).                                             *
    //*********************************************************

    public Month(String monthName)
    {
         //  Compare monthName (case significant) against
         //  the 12 month names.  Set monthNumber to the
         //  number of the matching month.

        if (monthName.equals("January") )
            monthNumber = 1;
        else if ( monthName.equals("February") )
```

```
            monthNumber = 2;
        else if ( monthName.equals("March") )
            monthNumber = 3;
        else if ( monthName.equals("April") )
            monthNumber = 4;
        else if ( monthName.equals("May") )
            monthNumber = 5;
        else if ( monthName.equals("June") )
            monthNumber = 6;
        else if ( monthName.equals("July") )
            monthNumber = 7;
        else if ( monthName.equals("August") )
            monthNumber = 8;
        else if ( monthName.equals("September") )
            monthNumber = 9;
        else if ( monthName.equals("October") )
            monthNumber = 10;
        else if ( monthName.equals("November") )
            monthNumber = 11;
        else if ( monthName.equals("December") )
            monthNumber = 12;

        //  monthName does not match any month's name.
        //  Create a default Month object for January.
        else
            monthNumber = 1;

    }

    //*****************************************************
    //  getMonthNumber method returns the value of the    *
    //  monthNumber field.                                *
    //*****************************************************

   public int getMonthNumber()
    {
        return monthNumber;
    }

    //*****************************************************
    //  setMonthNumber method accepts an integer argument. *
    //  If the argument is valid as a month number, the    *
    //  monthNumber field is set to its value. If the      *
    //  argument's value is not a valid month number, the  *
    //  monthNumber field is set to its default value 1 for *
    //  January                                            *
    //*****************************************************

    public void setMonthNumber(int aMonthNumber)
    {
        //  Demonstrate the ternary conditional expression
        //  operator.
        //  The boolean method validMonthNumber acts
        //  as a "guard" predicate to insure that
        //  monthNumber is given a valid value.

        monthNumber = validMonthNumber(aMonthNumber)
                          ? aMonthNumber
                          : 1;
    }
```

```
//*****************************************************
//  getMonthName method returns the name associated with*
//  this object's month, according to the monthNumber   *
//  field.                                              *
//*****************************************************

public String getMonthName()
{   String monthName;

    //  Performing different actions based
    //  on a limited number of int values is
    //  a natural application of the switch
    //  statement.
    //
    //  Always remember to use a break; statement at
    //  the end of every case.
    //
    //  Also, it is good practice to always include a
    //  default case, so that explicit operations are
    //  included for any value of the switch control
    //  value.

    switch ( monthNumber )
    {
        case 1:
            monthName = "January";
            break;
        case 2:
            monthName = "February";
            break;
        case 3:
            monthName = "March";
            break;
        case 4:
            monthName = "April";
            break;
        case 5:
            monthName = "May";
            break;
        case 6:
            monthName = "June";
            break;
        case 7:
            monthName = "July";
            break;
        case 8:
            monthName = "August";
            break;
        case 9:
            monthName = "September";
            break;
        case 10:
            monthName = "October";
            break;
        case 11:
            monthName = "November";
            break;
        case 12:
            monthName = "December";
            break;

        //  The monthNumber field *should* never have a
```

```
        //  value outside the range of 1 to 12. Class
        //  encapsulation should prevent any values
        //  outside this range to be stored in that
        //  field.
        //
        //  But *never* is a very long time. The default
        //  case of the switch statement insures that a
        //  valid result is given by this method for any
        //  value of the monthNumber field. The default
        //  case also gives the monthNumber field a
        //  correct (default) value.
        //
        //  This style of coding is known as "defensive
        //  programming."  Defensive programming is
        //  commonly used in real time, high
        //  availability systems where programs have to
        //  keep running, no matter what.

        default:
            monthName = "January";

            //  Set monthNumber field to a valid value.

            monthNumber = 1;
            break;
    }

    return monthName;
}

//*********************************************************
//  The toString method returns the name of the month    *
//  that is represented by this object.                  *
//  By definition of the problem, the toString method    *
//  has the same result as the getMonthName method.      *
//*********************************************************

public String toString()
{
    return getMonthName();
}


//********************************************************
//  The equals Method returns true if the month         *
//  represented by the argument object has the same     *
//  value as the month represented by this object.      *
//  if the objects are not equal, the Method returns    *
//  false. Two Month objects are equal if their         *
//  monthNumber fields have the same value.             *
//********************************************************

public boolean equals(Month aMonth)
{
    //  If the monthNumber field of the parameter is
    //  equal to the monthNumber field of this
    //  object, the method returns true.  Otherwise
    //  the value false is returned. The return
    //  value of this method is equivalent to an
    //  equality comparison of the two monthNumber
    //  values.
```

```
        return monthNumber == aMonth.getMonthNumber();
    }

    //*********************************************************
    //  The greaterThan Method returns true if the            *
    //  calling Month object comes later in the year          *
    //  than the parameter Month object.                      *
    //*********************************************************

    public boolean greaterThan(Month aMonth)
    {
        //  A Month object's sequence in the year is
        //  determined by the value of the monthNumber
        //  field.  A Month object is later in the year
        //  if its monthNumber is greater
        //  than another Month's monthNumber.

        return aMonth.getMonthNumber() < monthNumber ;
    }

    //*********************************************************
    //  The lessThan Method returns true if the               *
    //  calling Month object comes earlier in the year        *
    //  than the parameter Month object.                      *
    //*********************************************************

    public boolean lessThan(Month aMonth)
    {
        //  Similar to the greaterThan method except the
        //  order of the values in the < comparison are
        //  reversed.

        return monthNumber < aMonth.getMonthNumber() ;
    }

    //*********************************************************
    //  Private method validMonthNumber determines if its     *
    //  parameter has a valid value, i.e. in the range        *
    //  1 to 12.                                              *
    //*********************************************************

    private boolean validMonthNumber( int aMonthNumber )
    {
        //  One style of coding to test whether a number is within
        //  a given range is to write the expression similar
        //  to the way it would be written in mathematics.
        //
        //      1 <= aMonthNumber <= 12
        //
        //  To write this expression in Java, two comparisons
        //  need to be made, and joined by the logical 'and'
        //  operator.
        //
        //      1 <= aMonthNumber && aMonthNumber <= 12

        //  Some programmers prefer that comparisons be written
        //  this way.
        //    o It is easier to write expressions that are 'true'
        //      when there is no error.
        //    o The comparisons are made using semantically
        //      meaningful values (e.g. 1 for January and
        //      12 for December) vs. values outside the range
```

```
        //      of values (e.g. 0 and 13).
        //    o Keeping the order of values listed in increasing
        //      order, left to right, makes it is easier to
        //      spot typing errors.

        //  The method returns true if the return expression
        //  is satisfied.  Otherwise the value false is returned.

        return 1 <= aMonthNumber && aMonthNumber <= 12 ;
    }
}
```

Solution: The MonthDemonstration Class

Define What The Class Is To Do

Purpose	Demonstrate Capabilities of **Month Class**
Input	None
Process	A collection of **Month** objects are created. All three constructors of the **Month** class are used. Valid and invalid parameters are used for those constructors that require arguments. The objects are displayed on the screen. This shows the results of the constructors. The **setMonthNumber** method is used to change the **monthNumber** field of several **Month** objects. Valid and invalid arguments are used. The objects are again displayed, to show the results of the **setMonthNumber** method. The **equals, lessThan,** and **greaterThan** methods are evaluated using two **Month** objects, with different values. The results of these relationships are displayed. The value of the **Month** objects are set to the same value. The **equals, lessThan,** and **greaterThan** methods are evaluated using these objects. The results of these relationships are displayed.
Output	As described in the Process Section.

Pseudocode for MonthDemonstration Class

1) Create objects of class **Month** using each of the **Month** constructors defined. Use valid and invalid parameters when using these constructors.

2) Display the **Month** objects that were created to see that each of them have valid fields. Use both the **getMonthName** method and the automatically called **toString** method while displaying **Month** objects.

3) Demonstrate the **setMonth** method, using valid and invalid arguments.

4) Display the **Month** objects to show they all have valid fields.

5) Demonstrate the **boolean** comparison methods.

6) Compare an object to itself using:

   a) **equals** method,

   b) **lessThan** method, and

   c) **greatherThan** method.

7) Compare an object with one that is not equal to it using:

   a) **equals** method,

   b) **lessThan** method, and

   c) **greaterThan** method.

8) Reverse the order of comparison of the objects used in the previous steps. Determine their relationship using the:

   a) **equals** method,

   b) **lessThan** method, and

   c) **greaterThan** method.

Code Listing 6 - 5 (MonthDemonstration.java)

```
//*******************************************************
// Written by Myung Kim                                 *
// Chapter 6                                            *
// Programming Challenge 5: Month class                 *
//*******************************************************

//*******************************************************
//  Demonstrate the use of the Month class              *
//*******************************************************

public class MonthDemonstration
{
    public static void main(String[] args)
    {
        //  Construct a collection of Month objects
        //  using each variation of the class' constructors
        //  using good data and bad.

        Month   m0  =   new Month( 0 );
                            // No good. 0 is not a valid month.
                            // m0's monthNumber field should be
                            // set to 1.

        Month   m1  =   new Month();     // good
        Month   m2  =   new Month( 1 ); // good
        Month   m3  =   new Month( 3 ); // good
        Month   m4  =   new Month( 12 );// good
        Month   m5  =   new Month( 42 );
```

```
                        // No good. 42 is not a valid month.
                        // m5's monthNumber field should be
                        // set to 1.

    Month   m6  =   new Month( "April" ); // good
    Month   m7  =   new Month( "MAY" );
                        // No good. Month name parameter is
                        // case sensitive.  m7's monthNumber
                        // field should be set to 1,
                        // "January".

    System.out.println("Month Class Demonstration");
    System.out.println();

    //  Display the Month objects, their monthNumbers, and
    //  the result of the toString and getMonthName methods

    System.out.println("m0: "
        + m0.getMonthNumber() + ": " + m0);
    System.out.println("m1: "
        + m1.getMonthNumber() + ": " + m1);

    //  Use the getMonthName method instead of the
    //  implied toString method.  Result should be the same.

    System.out.println("m2: "
        + m2.getMonthNumber() + ": " + m2.getMonthName());
    System.out.println("m3: "
        + m3.getMonthNumber() + ": " + m3);
    System.out.println("m4: "
        + m4.getMonthNumber() + ": " + m4.getMonthName());
    System.out.println("m5: "
        + m5.getMonthNumber() + ": " + m5);
    System.out.println("m6: "
        + m6.getMonthNumber() + ": " + m6.getMonthName());
    System.out.println("m7: "
        + m7.getMonthNumber() + ": " + m7);
    System.out.println();

    //  Demonstrate setMonthNumber mutator method.

    System.out.println("setMonthNumber Demonstration");
    m0.setMonthNumber( 3 ); // good
    m1.setMonthNumber( 12 );// good
    m2.setMonthNumber( 8 ); // good
    m3.setMonthNumber( 1 ); // good
    m4.setMonthNumber( 42 );
        // No good.  42 is not a valid Month number.
        // m4's monthNumber field should be set to 1.

    //  Display the Month objects again, reflecting
    //  the changes made in the preceding statements.

    System.out.println("m0: "
        + m0.getMonthNumber() + ": " + m0);
    System.out.println("m1: "
        + m1.getMonthNumber() + ": " + m1);

    //  Use the getMonthName method instead of the
    //  implied toString method.  Results should be the same.

    System.out.println("m2: "
```

```
            + m2.getMonthNumber() + ": " + m2.getMonthName());
        System.out.println("m3: "
            + m3.getMonthNumber() + ": " + m3);
        System.out.println("m4: "
            + m4.getMonthNumber() + ": " + m4.getMonthName());
        System.out.println("m5: "
            + m5.getMonthNumber() + ": " + m5);
        System.out.println("m6: "
            + m6.getMonthNumber() + ": " + m6.getMonthName());
        System.out.println("m7: "
            + m7.getMonthNumber() + ": " + m7);
        System.out.println();

        //  Demonstrate the methods for comparing Month objects
        //  using m0 and m1.

        System.out.println("lessThan, equals, and greaterThan "
            + "demonstration");
        System.out.println("m0 : " + m0);
        System.out.println("m1 : " + m1);
        System.out.println();
        //
        //  compare an object with itself
        //
        System.out.println("m0 == m0: " + m0.equals(m0));
            //  true - An object has to be equal to itself.

        System.out.println("m0 <  m0: " + m0.lessThan(m0));
            //  false - An object can't be less than itself.

        System.out.println("m0 >  m0: " + m0.greaterThan(m0));
            //  false - An object can't be greater than itself.
        //
        //  Compare two objects.
        //
        System.out.println("m0 == m1: " + m0.equals(m1));
        System.out.println("m0 <  m1: " + m0.lessThan(m1));
        System.out.println("m0 >  m1: " + m0.greaterThan(m1));
        //
        //  Compare the same two objects, but reversing their
        //  order in the comparison.
        //
        System.out.println("m1 == m0: " + m1.equals(m0));
            // This expression must have the same value
            // as the equals comparison from the previous tests.

        System.out.println("m1 <  m0: " + m1.lessThan(m0));
            //  This expression must have the negation of the
            //  value from the previous less than test.

        System.out.println("m1 >  m0: " + m1.greaterThan(m0));
            //  This expression must have the negation of the
            //  value from the previous greater than test.

        System.out.println();
        System.out.println("Month Class Demonstration Complete.");
    }
}
```

Program Output

```
Month Class Demonstration
```

```
m0: 1: January
m1: 1: January
m2: 1: January
m3: 3: March
m4: 12: December
m5: 1: January
m6: 4: April
m7: 1: January

setMonthNumber Demonstration
m0: 3: March
m1: 12: December
m2: 8: August
m3: 1: January
m4: 1: January
m5: 1: January
m6: 4: April
m7: 1: January

lessThan, equals, and greaterThan demonstration
m0 : March
m1 : December

m0 == m0: true
m0 <  m0: false
m0 >  m0: false
m0 == m1: false
m0 <  m1: true
m0 >  m1: false
m1 == m0: false
m1 <  m0: false
m1 >  m0: true

Month Class Demonstration Complete.
```

Programming Challenge 7: RetailItem Class Modification

Problem Statement:

Modify this chapter's **RetailItem** class (which uses an inner class named **CostData**) to include accessor and mutator methods for getting and setting an item's wholesale and retail cost. Demonstrate the methods in a program.

Solution: RetailItem Class Modification

See Textbook Section 6.11 for a discussion of inner classes. See Textbook Code Listing 6-27 for the RetailItem.java file. See Textbook Code Listing 6-28 for a demonstration of the use of the RetailItem class.

The key to this problem is understanding the properties of an inner class and how it relates to its outer class. An inner class is one that is defined within another class. The inner class must have **private** access and can only be accessed by the class in which it is defined, the outer class. The fields and methods of the inner class are not visible or available to any other class. The inner class may access any field or method, **private** or **public**, of the outer class. The outer class, however, can only access **public** fields and **public** methods of the inner class.

In the **RetailItem** class, the **CostData** inner class is defined. The **CostData** class has a **public** constructor (if the constructor was not **public**, it could not be used by the outer class). The **CostData** constructor takes two **doubles** as arguments: the first for the retail price of an item; the second for the wholesale cost of that item. The **CostData** class has two **public** fields of type **double**: the field wholesale stores the wholesale cost of an item; the field **retail** stores the retail price of an item. Because these fields are **public**, they can be used directly in methods of the **RetailItem** class.

Inner class fields are accessed are shown in this excerpt from Textbook Code Listing 6-33, the **RetailItem** class **toString** method (bold and underline added for emphasis):

```
Str = "Description: " + description
    + "\nItem Number: " + itemNumber
    + "\nWholesale Cost: $"
    + dollar.format(cost.wholesale)
    + "\nRetail Cost: $"
    + dollar.format(cost.retail);
```

Accessor methods let another program retrieve a value from an object. In this problem, **public** methods **getRetailPrice** and **getWholesaleCost** return the values of the retail field and wholesale fields, respectively, from the inner class object **cost**. The values of those fields are retrieved as in the example above.

```
//*******************************************************
```

```
//  CostData inner class accessor method                    *
//  getWholesaleCost.  Returns the wholesale field of       *
//  the RetailItem's cost field.  This method is public *
//  and can be used by any program.                         *
//*******************************************************

public double getWholesaleCost()
{
    return  cost.wholesale;
    // Note ^^^^^^^^^^^^^^ reference to inner class
    // public field.
}

//*******************************************************
//  CostData inner class accessor method                    *
//  getRetailPrice.  Returns the retail field of            *
//  the RetailItem's cost field.  This method is public *
//  and can be used by any program.                         *
//*******************************************************

public double getRetailPrice()
{
    return  cost.retail;
    // Note ^^^^^^^^^^^ reference to inner class
    // public field.
}
```

Mutator methods let a program set the value of a **private** field in an object. In this problem, **public** methods **setRetailPrice** and **setWholesaleCost** take a **double** value as a parameter. The **retail** field and **wholesale** fields, respectively, are set to the values passed to the mutator methods. The **retail** and wholesale **fields** are accessed using the same notation that was used in the accessor methods.

```
//*******************************************************
//  CostData inner class mutator method                     *
//  getWholesaleCost.  Sets the wholesale field of          *
//  the RetailItem's cost field.  This method is public *
//  and can be used by any program.                         *
//*******************************************************

public void setWholesaleCost(double aCost)
{
    cost.wholesale  =   aCost;
    //^^^^^^^^^^^^^     Note reference to inner class public field.
}

//*******************************************************
//  CostData inner class mutator method                     *
//  setRetailPrice.  Sets the retail field of               *
//  the RetailItem's cost field.  This method is public *
//  and can be used by any program.                         *
//*******************************************************

public void setRetailPrice(double aCost)
{
    cost.retail =   aCost;
    //^^^^^^^^^^    Note reference to inner class public field.
}
```

Code Listing 6 - 6 shows the updated **RetailItem** class. Code Listing 6 - 7 shows the class **RetailItemInnerClassDemo** that uses the new methods added to class **RetailItem**. Following that, the program's output is given.

Code Listing 6 - 6 (RetailItem.java)

```
//*****************************************************
//  Written by Jars Jillssen                          *
//  Chapter 6                                         *
//  Programming Challenge 7: RetailItem Class         *
//  Modification                                      *
//*****************************************************

//*****************************************************
//  Modify this chapter's RetailItem class (which uses  *
//  an inner class named CostData) to include accessor  *
//  and mutator methods for getting and setting an    *
//  item's wholesale and retail cost. Demonstrate the  *
//  methods in a program.                             *
//*****************************************************

//*****************************************************
//  Modified Textbook Code Listing 6-27               *
//  (RetailItem.java)                                 *
//                                                    *
//  This class uses an inner class.                   *
//*****************************************************

import java.text.DecimalFormat;

public class RetailItem
{
    private String description;  // Item description
    private int itemNumber;      // Item number
    private CostData cost;       // Item cost
                                 // (using the inner class CostData)

    //*************************************************
    // RetailItem class constructor.                  *
    //*************************************************

    public RetailItem(String desc, int itemNum,
        double wholesale, double retail)
    {
        description = desc;
        itemNumber = itemNum;

        //  use the CostData class constructor to store
        //  the item's wholesale cost and retail price
        //  in the cost field.

        cost = new CostData(wholesale, retail);
    }

    //*************************************************
    // RetailItem class toString method.              *
    //*************************************************

    public String toString()
    {
```

```
        String str;
        DecimalFormat dollar = new DecimalFormat("#,##0.00");

        str = "Description: " + description
            + "\nItem Number: " + itemNumber
            + "\nWholesale Cost: $"
            + dollar.format(cost.wholesale)
            + "\nRetail Price: $"
            + dollar.format(cost.retail);
        return str;
    }

    //*******************************************************
    //                                                      *
    //  -- Modification --                                  *
    //                                                      *
    //  RetailItem class getDescription method.             *
    //  Return a String with the object's description.      *
    //  This method is not required for the problem         *
    //  but it's convenient for use in the demonstration    *
    //  program.                                            *
    //*******************************************************

    public String getDescription()
    {
        return  description;
    }

    //*******************************************************
    //                                                      *
    //  -- Modifications --                                 *
    //                                                      *
    //  Accessor methods for fields in CostData inner class.*
    //  The outer class, RetailItem, can access the public  *
    //  members of its inner class, CostData.               *
    //*******************************************************

    //*******************************************************
    //  CostData inner class accessor method                *
    //  getWholesaleCost.  Returns the wholesale field of   *
    //  the RetailItem's cost field.  This method is public *
    //  and can be used by any program.                     *
    //*******************************************************

    public double getWholesaleCost()
    {
        return  cost.wholesale;
        // Note ^^^^^^^^^^^^^^ reference to inner class
        // public field.
    }

    //*******************************************************
    //  CostData inner class accessor method                *
    //  getRetailPrice.  Returns the retail field of        *
    //  the RetailItem's cost field.  This method is public *
    //  and can be used by any program.                     *
    //*******************************************************

    public double getRetailPrice()
    {
        return  cost.retail;
        // Note ^^^^^^^^^^^ reference to inner class
```

```
    // public field.
}

//*****************************************************
//   -- Modifications --                              *
//   Mutator methods for fields in CostData inner class. *
//   The outer class, RetailItem, can access the public  *
//   members of its inner class, CostData.            *
//*****************************************************

//*****************************************************
//   CostData inner class mutator method              *
//   getWholesaleCost.  Sets the wholesale field of   *
//   the RetailItem's cost field.  This method is public *
//   and can be used by any program.                  *
//*****************************************************

public void setWholesaleCost(double aCost)
{
    cost.wholesale =   aCost;
    //^^^^^^^^^^^^^ Note reference to inner class public field.
}

//*****************************************************
//   CostData inner class mutator method              *
//   setRetailPrice.  Sets the retail field of        *
//   the RetailItem's cost field.  This method is public *
//   and can be used by any program.
//*****************************************************

public void setRetailPrice(double aCost)
{
    cost.retail =   aCost;
    //^^^^^^^^^^ Note reference to inner class public field.
}

//**************************************************
// CostData Inner Class                            *
//                                                 *
// An inner class must be private.  It can only be *
// used by the public enclosing outer class.  There *
// can be only one public class in a Java source   *
// file.                                           *
//**************************************************

private class CostData
{
    //**********************************************
    //  Only public fields of an inner class can be  *
    //  used by the outer class.  But public fields  *
    //  in an inner class can not be used by any     *
    //  other program.                               *
    //**********************************************

    public double
        wholesale,
        retail;

    //  Because they have public access, the wholesale
    //  and retail fields can be used by the outer class.
    //  In the RetailItem class these fields are made
    //  visible to any program by public accessor and
```

```
        //  mutator methods of the public RetailItem class.

        //*********************************************
        // CostData class constructor.                *
        //*********************************************

        public CostData(double w, double r)
        {
            wholesale = w;
            retail = r;
        }
    }
}
```

Solution: RetailItemInnerClassDemo

RetailItemInnerClassDemo Pseudocode

1) Declare local variables.
2) Construct a sample **RetailItem** object named **aCandyItem**.
3) Display **aCandyItem**.
4) Display **aCandyItem's** retail price using the **getRetailPrice** method.
5) Display **aCandyItem's** wholesale cost using the **getWholesaleCost** method.
6) Calculate new retail price and wholesale cost values for **aCandyItem**.
7) Use the mutator methods **setRetailPrice** and **setWholesaleCost** to change the **cost** field of **RetailItem** object **aCandyItem**.
8) Display **aCandyItem**. The new retail price and wholesale cost should be shown.

Code Listing 6 - 7 (RetailItemInnerClassDemo.java)

```
//*****************************************************
//  Written by Jars Jillssen                          *
//                                                    *
//  Chapter 6                                         *
//  Programming Challenge 7:                          *
//  Demonstration of RetailItem Inner Class CostData  *
//  accessor and mutator methods.                     *
//*****************************************************

//*****************************************************
//  Based on Textbook Code Listing 6-28               *
//  (InnerClassDemo.java).                            *
//*****************************************************

public class RetailItemInnerClassDemo
{
    //*************************************************
    //  Demonstrate the accessor and mutator methods for*
    //  the inner class CostData of class RetailItem.   *
    //*************************************************
```

```
public static void main(String[] args)
{
    System.out.println(
        "RetailItem Inner Class Demonstration");
    System.out.println();

    double  newRetailPrice;
    double  newWholesaleCost;

    //  Construct RetailItem object aCandyItem.

    RetailItem aCandyItem
        = new RetailItem(
          "Reese's Cup - 10 Pack", 17789, 0.75, 1.5);

    //  Display aCandyItem.

    System.out.println(aCandyItem);
    System.out.println();

    //  Demonstrate use of accessor methods
    //  for RetailItem inner class.

    System.out.println("Show aCandyItem's contents using "
        + "newly added accessor methods.");

    System.out.println(aCandyItem.getDescription());

    System.out.println("  Retail Price: "
        + aCandyItem.getRetailPrice());

    System.out.println("  Wholesale Cost: "
        + aCandyItem.getWholesaleCost());
    System.out.println();

    //  Demonstrate use of mutator methods
    //  for RetailItem inner class.

    System.out.println("Increase the wholesale cost of "
        + aCandyItem.getDescription() + " by 10%.");
    System.out.println("Increase the retail price of "
        + aCandyItem.getDescription() + " by $0.25.");
    System.out.println();

    //  Revise aCandyItem's wholesale cost and
    //  retail price.

    //  Buy low, sell high.

    //  Increase wholesale cost by 10%.

    newWholesaleCost    = aCandyItem.getWholesaleCost()
        + aCandyItem.getWholesaleCost() * .10;
    aCandyItem.setWholesaleCost( newWholesaleCost );

    //  Increase retail price by 25 cents.

    newRetailPrice      = aCandyItem.getRetailPrice() + 0.25;
    aCandyItem.setRetailPrice( newRetailPrice );

    // Display updated contents of aCandyItem.
```

```
        System.out.println("Updated wholesale cost and "
            + "retail price for " + aCandyItem.getDescription()
            + ".");
        System.out.println(aCandyItem);
        System.out.println();

        System.out.println("Demonstration Complete");
    }
}
```

Program Output

```
RetailItem Inner Class Demonstration

Description: Reese's Cup - 10 Pack
Item Number: 17789
Wholesale Cost: $0.75
Retail Price: $1.50
Show aCandyItem's contents using newly added accessor methods.
Reese's Cup - 10 Pack
  Retail Price: 1.5
  Wholesale Cost: 0.75

Increase the wholesale cost of Reese's Cup - 10 Pack by 10%.
Increase the retail price of Reese's Cup - 10 Pack by $0.25.

Updated wholesale cost and retail price for Reese's Cup - 10 Pack.
Description: Reese's Cup - 10 Pack
Item Number: 17789
Wholesale Cost: $0.82
Retail Price: $1.75
Demonstration Complete
```

CHAPTER 7

Arrays

Solutions

- Programming Challenge 2: Payroll Class
- Programming Challenge 6: Quarterly Sales Statistics
- Programming Challenge 7: Grade Book
- Programming Challenge 8: Grade Book Modification
- Programming Challenge 10: ArrayOperations Class

Programming Challenge 2: Payroll Class

Problem Statement:

Write a Payroll class that uses the following arrays as fields:

- employeeId. An array of seven integers to hold employee identification numbers. The array should be initialized with the following numbers:

  5658845 4520125 7895122 8777541 8451277 1302850 7580489

- hours. An array of seven integers to hold the number of hours worked by each employee
- payRate. An array of seven doubles to hold each employee's hourly pay rate
- wages. An array of seven doubles to hold each employee's gross wages

The class should relate the data in each array through the subscripts. For example, the number in element 0 of the hours array should be the number of hours worked by the employee whose identification number is stored in element 0 of the employeeId array. That same employee's pay rate should be stored in element 0 of the payRate array.

In addition to the appropriate accessor and mutator methods, the class should have a method that accepts an employee's identification number as an argument and returns the gross pay for that employee.

Demonstrate the class in a complete program that displays each employee number and asks the user to enter that employee's hours and pay rate. It should then display each employee's identification number and gross wages.

Input Validation: Do not accept negative values for hours or numbers less than 6.00 for pay rate.

Solution:

Define What The Program Is To Do

Purpose	Describe the payroll of a company.	
Fields	employeeId	An array of seven integers to hold employee identification numbers.
	hours	An array of seven integers to hold the number of hours worked by each employee.
	payRate	An array of seven doubles to hold each employee's gross wages.
	wages	An array of seven doubles to hold each employee's gross wages.
Constructor	Payroll()	Create a payroll object by creating the arrays.

	getEmployeeId	If the index parameter is between 0 and one less than the array length, return the employeeId stored at that index. If the index parameter is not valid, return -1.
	getHours	If the index parameter is between 0 and one less than the array length, return the hours worked for the employee that corresponds to the parameter index. If the index parameter is not valid, return -1.
	getPayRate	If the index parameter is between 0 and one less than the array length, return the pay rate for the employee that corresponds to the parameter index. If the index parameter is not valid, return -1.
	getWages	If the index parameter is between 0 and one less than the array length, return the gross pay for the employee that corresponds to the parameter index. If the index parameter is not valid, return -1.
Methods	setHours	If the number of hours is non-negative and the index is between 0 and one less than the length of the array, set the number of hours for the employee that corresponds to the parameter index to the parameter number of hours.
	setPayRate	If the pay rate is greater than or equal to 6.00 and the index is between 0 and one less than the length of the array, set the pay rate for the employee that corresponds to the parameter index to the parameter pay rate.
	setWages	If the index is between 0 and one less than the length of the array, calculate the wages, including any overtime pay, and set the wages for the employee that corresponds to the parameter index to the wages.
	searchForPay	Return the gross pay for the employee that corresponds to the parameter employee identification number.

High Level Pseudocode for Payroll Class

1) Define Payroll class fields.

   a) The field employeeId represents an array of seven integers to hold employee identification numbers. It is initialized with the following numbers:

      5658845 4520125 7895122 8777541 8451277 1302850 7580489

   b) The field hours represents an array of seven integers to hold the number of hours worked by each employee.

   c) The field payRate represents an array of seven doubles to hold each employee's gross wages.

   d) The field wages represents an array of seven doubles to hold each employee's gross wages.

2) Define Payroll class constructors.

   a) Default constructor (having no arguments).

      i) Create an object of class Payroll having an employeeId array initialized with the employee id numbers, as well as arrays of hours, payRate and wages, all created to the same size as the employeeId array.

3) Define accessor method getEmployeeId.

   a) Validate the method's argument as an index location in the employeeId array, and return the employeeId for that location.

4) Define accessor method getHours.

   a) Validate the method's argument as an index location in the hours array, and return the hours for that location.

5) Define accessor method getPayRate.

   a) Validate the method's argument as an index location in the payRate array, and return the payRate for that location.

6) Define accessor method getWages.

   a) Validate the method's argument as an index location in the wages array, and return the wages for that location.

7) Define mutator method setHours.

   a) Validate the method's first argument as an index location in the hours array, validate the method's second argument as a non-negative number, and change the value of the hours array at that index to the value of the second argument.

8) Define mutator method setPayRate.

   a) Validate the method's first argument as an index location in the payRate array, validate the method's second argument as greater than or equal to 6.00, and change the value of the payRate array at that index to the value of the second argument.

9) Define the mutator method setWages.

   a) Validate the method's argument as an index location in the wages array. If hours are greater than 40, calculate wages by multiplying payRate by 40 and adding the result of multiplying the number of hours over 40 by 1.5 and the payRate. Otherwise, calculate wages by hours times payRate.

10) Define the method searchForPay.

   a) Search for the method's argument in the employeeId array. If it is found, return the wages for the employee, otherwise return -1.

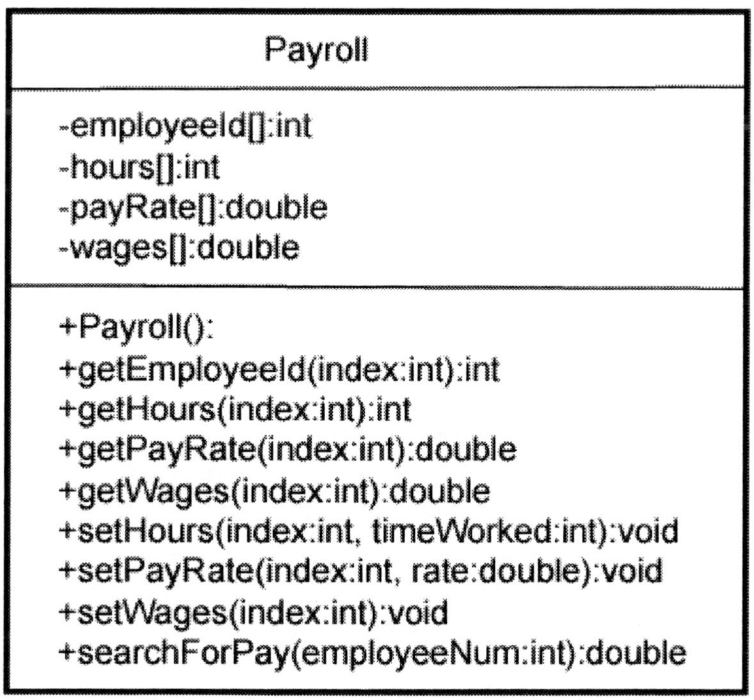

Figure 7-1 UML Drawing for Payroll Class

Low Level Pseudocode for Payroll Class

1) Create employeeId array using initializer list:

```
private int [] employeeId =
   {5658845, 4520125, 7895122, 8777541, 8451277,1302850, 7580489};
```

2) Default constructor creates all other arrays to be of the same size as employeeId array:

```
int numEmployees = employeeId.length;

hours = new int [numEmployees];
```

3) Accessor method getEmployeeId

   a) Validate parameter as a possible index location:

      0 <= index < employee.length

   b) Determine what value to return:

```
if (index >=0 && index <employee.length)
      return employeeId[index];
else
      return -1;
```

NOTE: Other accessor methods similar.

4) Mutator method setHours

   a) Validate index parameter as in accessor methods.

   b) Validate timeWorked parameter as non-negative:

      timeWorked >=0

   c) Assign timeWorked parameter value as the array value at that index:

```
hours[index] = timeWorked;
```

5) Mutator method setRate

   a) Validate index parameter as in accessor methods.

b) Validate rate as no less than 6.00:

```
rate >=6.0
```

c) Assign rate parameter value as the array value at that index:

```
payRate[index] = rate;
```

6) Mutator method setWages

a) Validate index parameter as in accessor methods.

b) Determine how to calculate gross pay:

```
if (hours[index] > 40)
   wages[index] = payRate[index] * 40 +
               payRate[index] * 1.5 * (hours[index] - 40);
else
   wages[index] = hours[index] * payRate[index];
```

7) The searchForPay method

a) Loop through the employeeId array to find a match to the employeeIdNum parameter.

b) Determine if there is a match:

```
if (employeeIdNum == employeeId[index])
      return wages[index];
```

c) Completion of loop without a match:

```
return -1;
```

Code Listing 7-1 (Payroll.java)

```
//***********************************************************
// Written by Diane Christie
// Chapter 7
// Programming Challenge 2:  Payroll Class
//***********************************************************

//***********************************************************
// Write a Payroll class that uses the following arrays
// as fields:
//    employeeId--An array of seven integers to hold
//    employee identification numbers. The array should
//    be initialized with the following numbers:
//    5658845      4520125      7895122      8777541
//    8451277      1302850      7580489
//    hours--An array of seven integers to hold the number
//          of hours worked by each employee
//    payRate--An array of seven doubles to hold each
//          employee's hourly pay rate
//    wages--An array of seven doubles to hold each
//          employee's gross wages
//The class should relate the data in each array through the
//subscripts.  For example, the number in element 0 of the
//hours array should be the number of hours worked by the
//employee whose identification number is stored in element
//0 of the employeeId array.  That same employee's pay rate
//should be stored in element 0 of the payRate array.  In
//addition to the appropriate accessor and mutator methods,
//the class should have a method that accepts an employee's
//identification number as an argument and returns the gross
//pay for that employee.
//Input Validation:  Do not accept negative values for
//hours or numbers less than 6.00 for pay rate.
//***********************************************************
//***********************************************************
//The Payroll class describes a company's payroll.  Each
//employee corresponds to a subscript in the array.  The data
//in each array is related through the subscripts. For
//example, the number in element 0 of the hours array should
//be the number of hours worked by the employee whose
//identification number is stored in element 0 of the
//employeeId array.  That same employee's pay rate should be
//stored in element 0 of the payRate array.
//***********************************************************
public class Payroll
{
      private int [] employeeId =
            {5658845, 4520125, 7895122, 8777541, 8451277,
            1302850, 7580489};
      private int [] hours;
      private double [] payRate;
      private double [] wages;

      //*****************************************************
      //Default constructor creates arrays to the same     *
      //size as the employeeId array.                      *
      //*****************************************************
```

```
public Payroll()
{
      int numEmployees = employeeId.length;
      hours = new int [numEmployees];
      payRate = new double [numEmployees];
      wages = new double [numEmployees];
}

//***************************************************
//If the index parameter is between 0 and one less  *
//than the array length, return the employeeId      *
//stored at that index.  If the index parameter is  *
//not valid, return -1.                             *
//***************************************************
public int getEmployeeId(int index)
{
      if (index >=0 && index < employeeId.length)
            return employeeId[index];
      else
            return -1;
}

//***************************************************
//If the index parameter is between 0 and one less  *
//than the array length, return the hours worked for*
//the employee that corresponds to the parameter    *
//index. If the index parameter is not valid, return*
//-1.                                               *
//***************************************************
public int getHours(int index)
{
      if (index >=0 && index < hours.length)
            return hours[index];
      else
            return -1;
}

//***************************************************
//If the index parameter is between 0 and one less  *
//than the array length, return the pay rate for the*
//employee that corresponds to the parameter index. *
//If the index parameter is not valid, return -1.   *
//***************************************************
public double getPayRate(int index)
{
      if (index >=0 && index < payRate.length)
            return payRate[index];
      else
            return -1;
}

//***************************************************
//If the index parameter is between 0 and one less  *
//than the array length, return the gross pay for   *
//the employee that corresponds to the parameter    *
//index. If the index parameter is not valid, return*
//-1.                                               *
//***************************************************
public double getWages(int index)
```

```
{
      if (index >=0 && index < wages.length)
            return wages[index];
      else
            return -1;
}

//**************************************************
//If the number of hours is non-negative and the    *
//index is between 0 and one less than the length of*
//the array, set the number of hours for the        *
//employee that corresponds to the parameter index  *
//to the parameter number of hours.                 *
//**************************************************
public void setHours(int index, int timeWorked)
{
      if (index >=0 && index < hours.length &&
                        timeWorked >=0)
            hours[index] = timeWorked;
}

//**************************************************
//If the pay rate is greater than or equal to 6.00  *
//and the index is between 0 and one less than the  *
//length of the array, set the pay rate for the     *
//employee that corresponds to the parameter index  *
//to the parameter pay rate.                        *
//**************************************************
public void setPayRate(int index, double rate)
{
      if (index >=0 && index < payRate.length &&
                  rate >=6.0)
            payRate[index] = rate;
}

//**************************************************
//If the index is between 0 and one less than the   *
//length of the array, calculate the wages,         *
//including any overtime pay, and set the wages for *
//the employee that corresponds to the parameter    *
//index to the wages.                               *
//**************************************************
public void setWages(int index)
{
      if (index >=0 && index < wages.length)
      {
            if (hours[index] > 40)
            {
                  wages[index] = payRate[index] * 40 +
                  payRate[index] * 1.5 * (hours[index] - 40);
            }
            else
            {
                  wages[index] = hours[index] * payRate[index];
            }
      }
}

//**************************************************
```

```
    //Return the gross pay for the employee that         *
    //corresponds to the parameter employee              *
    //identification number.                             *
    //****************************************************
    public double searchForPay (int employeeIdNum)
    {
          for (int index = 0; index < employeeId.length; index++)
          {
                if (employeeIdNum == employeeId[index])
                      return wages[index];
          }
          return -1.0;
    }
}
```

Solution: The RunPayroll Class

Define What The Class is To Do

Purpose	**Demonstrate capabilities of the Payroll Class**
Input	**The hours worked and the rate of pay for each employee**
Process	**A Payroll object is created. The program will display each employee number and ask the user to input the employee's hours and pay rate. Each employee's wages are calculated.**
Output	**The employee identification numbers along with the gross wages are displayed.**

Pseudocode for RunPayroll Class

1) Create an object of class Payroll and declare local variables.

2) For each employee:

   a) Display employee number.

   b) Ask user to enter the number of hours worked.

   c) Read in hoursWorked, validate, and set the hours for that employee.

   d) Ask user to enter the hourly pay rate.

   e) Read in rate, validate, and set the pay rate for that employee.

   f) Set the wages for that employee.

3) Get each employee number and use it to search for that employee's wages.

4) Print out a list of employee numbers and corresponding wages.

Code Listing 7-2 (RunPayroll.java)

```
//*****************************************************
// Written by Diane Christie                          *
// Chapter 7                                          *
// Programming Challenge 2:  RunPayroll Class         *
//*****************************************************

//*****************************************************
//Demonstrate the Payroll class in a complete program *
//that displays each employee number and asks the user *
//to enter that employee's hours and pay rate.  It     *
//should then display each employee's identification   *
//number and gross wages.  Uses Keyboard class to read *
//from keyboard.                                       *
//*****************************************************

//*****************************************************
// To format numbers to two decimal places
//*****************************************************
import java.text.DecimalFormat;
import java.util.Scanner;

public class RunPayroll
{
    public static void main (String [] args)
    {
        //Create a Scanner object to read from the keyboard
        Scanner keyboard = new Scanner (System.in);

        //Create an object of type Payroll
        Payroll weeklyPayroll = new Payroll ();
        int hoursWorked;
        double rate;
        int id;

        //repeat for all employees
        for (int index = 0; index < 7; index++)
        {
            System.out.print("Employee Number:  ");
            System.out.println(weeklyPayroll.getEmployeeId(index));

            do    //validate number of hours worked
            {
                System.out.print(
                    "\tEnter the number of hours worked: ");
                hoursWorked = keyboard.nextInt();
            }while(hoursWorked < 0);

                //store the hours for this employee
```

```
            weeklyPayroll.setHours(index, hoursWorked);


            do    //validate hourly rate
            {
                System.out.print("\tEnter the pay rate: ");
                rate = keyboard.nextDouble();
            }while (rate < 6.00);

            //store the payrate for this employee
            weeklyPayroll.setPayRate(index, rate);

            //calculate the pay for this employee
            weeklyPayroll.setWages(index);
        }

        //print out listing of employees and their pay
        System.out.println("\n\n");
        System.out.println("Payroll Information");
        System.out.println(
            "________________________________________");
        for  (int index = 0; index < 7; index++)
        {
            id = weeklyPayroll.getEmployeeId(index);
            DecimalFormat money = new DecimalFormat("0.00");
            System.out.print("Employee number:  " + id);
            System.out.println("\tGross Pay:  $" +
            money.format(weeklyPayroll.searchForPay(id)));
        }
    }
}
```

Program Output

```
    Employee Number:  5658845
            Enter the number of hours worked: 2
            Enter the pay rate: 6
    Employee Number:  4520125
            Enter the number of hours worked: 10
            Enter the pay rate: 6
    Employee Number:  7895122
            Enter the number of hours worked: 20
            Enter the pay rate: 7
    Employee Number:  8777541
            Enter the number of hours worked: 22
            Enter the pay rate: 8
    Employee Number:  8451277
            Enter the number of hours worked: 40
            Enter the pay rate: 10
    Employee Number:  1302850
            Enter the number of hours worked: 41
            Enter the pay rate: 10
    Employee Number:  7580489
            Enter the number of hours worked: 50
            Enter the pay rate: 10
```

```
Payroll Information
______________________________________________________
Employee number:  5658845        Gross Pay:  $12.00
Employee number:  4520125        Gross Pay:  $60.00
Employee number:  7895122        Gross Pay:  $140.00
Employee number:  8777541        Gross Pay:  $176.00
Employee number:  8451277        Gross Pay:  $400.00
Employee number:  1302850        Gross Pay:  $415.00
Employee number:  7580489        Gross Pay:  $550.00
```

Programming Challenge 6: Quarterly Sales Statistics

Problem Statement:

Write a program that lets the user enter four quarterly sales figures for six divisions of a company. The figures should be stored in a two-dimensional array. Once the figures are entered, the program should display the following data for each quarter:

- A list of the sales figures by division
- Each division's increase or decrease from the previous quarter (this will not be displayed for the first quarter)
- The total sales for the quarter
- The company's increase or decrease from the previous quarter (this will not be displayed for the first quarter)
- The average sales for all divisions that quarter
- The division with the highest sales for that quarter

Input Validation: Do not accept negative numbers for sales figures.

Solution:

Define What The Program Is To Do

Purpose	To store quarterly sales figures for six divisions and to print out reports
Input	The quarterly sales figures for each division
Process	Read in sales data

Output

Display:

- A list of the sales figures by division
- Each division's increase or decrease from the previous quarter (this will not be displayed for the first quarter)
- The total sales for the quarter
- The company's increase or decrease from the previous quarter (this will not be displayed for the first quarter)
- The average sales for all divisions that quarter
- The division with the highest sales for that quarter

Pseudocode for Quarterly Sales Statistics

1) Define constants for number of quarters and number of divisions.

2) Create a two-dimensional array with number of division rows and number of quarter columns.

3) Break the tasks into separate methods. The methods are defined as static methods. The method calls go into the main method.

4) Call the method to fill the array.

   a) The method takes a two-dimensional array as a parameter. It prompts user for and reads in sales for each division, for each quarter, and stores them in the correct location in the array.

5) Call the method to list sales figures by division.

   a) The method takes a two-dimensional array as a parameter. It validates the input as non-negative and formats sales figures to two decimal places. It prints out a heading for this report. The each division number is listed followed by the sales for each quarter for that division.

6) Call the method to list each division's increase or decrease from the previous quarter.

   a) The method takes a two-dimensional array as a parameter. It formats sales figures to two decimal places. It prints out a heading for this report. For each division the following is performed. There is nothing displayed for the first quarter. The increase or decrease is found by taking the current quarter sales and subtracting the previous quarter sales.

7) Call the method to calculate total sales for each quarter.

   a) The method takes a two-dimensional array as a parameter. It formats sales figures to two decimal places. It prints out a heading for this report. The sales of all divisions for each quarter are summed and the total is displayed.

8) Call the method to show the company's increase or decrease from the previous quarter.

   a) The method takes a two-dimensional array as a parameter. It formats sales figures to two decimal places. It prints out a heading for this report. There is nothing displayed for the first quarter. The increase or decrease for each division is found and summed. The sum is reported as the increase or decrease.

9) Call the method to show the average sales for all divisions for each quarter.

   a) The method takes a two-dimensional array as a parameter. It formats sales figures to two decimal places. It prints out a heading for this report. For each quarter, all sales are summed. The average is found by dividing the sum by the number of divisions.

10) Call the method to show the division with the highest sales for that quarter.

   a) The method takes a two-dimensional array as a parameter. It formats sales figures to two decimal places. It prints out a heading for this report. For each quarter, the division with the largest sales is reported along with the sales figure.

Detailed Pseudocode for Program

1) The fillArray method

   a) The columns representing quarters are used for the outer loop.

```
for (int qtr = 0; qtr < QUARTERS; qtr++)
```

   b) Prompt the user for the sales for that quarter.

```
System.out.println("Enter sales for quarter " + (qtr + 1) + ":  ");
```

c) The rows representing divisions are used for the inner loop. Each for loop starts at 0 and continues until it is one less than the length of the array.

```
for (int div = 0; div < sales.length; div++)
```

d) Prompt the user for the correct division, and read in the sales. Verify that input is greater than or equal to 0 before storing it into the array. Otherwise, allow the user to type it again.

```
do

{

   System.out.print("\tDivision " + (div + 1) + ":  ");

   quarterSales = Keyboard.readDouble();

}while (quarterSales < 0);
```

e) Store the sales into the correct row and column of the array.

```
sales[div][qtr]= quarterSales;
```

2) The salesByDivision method

a) The rows represent divisions, so are used in the outer loop.

```
for (int div = 0; div < sales.length; div++)
```

b) The sales for each quarter are printed inside the inner loop using the columns for the index.

```
for (int qtr = 0; qtr < sales[div].length; qtr++)

{

   System.out.print("\tQuarter " + (qtr + 1) + ":  $");

   System.out.println(money.format(sales[div][qtr]));

}
```

3) The quarterChangeByDivision method

a) The rows represent divisions, so are used for the outer loop.

b) The index for the inner loop (which represents quarters) begins at 1 instead of 0 so that you do not get an

ArrayOutOfBoundsException when looking at the previous quarter. This does not display a result for the first quarter (index 0).

```
for (int qtr = 1; qtr < sales[div].length; qtr++)
```

c) The difference between the sales of the current quarter and the previous quarter is printed in the inner loop.

```
System.out.print("\tQuarter " + (qtr + 1) + ":  $");

System.out.println(money.format(sales[div][qtr]-sales[div][qtr-1]));
```

4) The totalSalesByQuarter method

a) The columns representing quarters are used for the outer loop.

b) The total is initialized to 0 inside the outer loop.

c) The sales for each division are summed inside the inner loop using rows for the index.

```
total = total + sales[div][qtr];
```

d) The resulting total is printed out after the inner loop, but inside the outer loop.

5) The quarterChange method

a) The columns representing quarters are used for the outer loop and begin with 1 instead of 0 so that you do not get an ArrayOutOfBoundsException when looking at the previous quarter. This does not display a result for the first quarter (index 0).

b) The total is initialized to 0 inside the outer loop.

c) The difference between the sales of the current quarter and the previous quarter is calculated and added to the total inside the inner loop.

d) Rows representing divisions are used as the index for the inner loop.

e) The resulting total is printed out after the inner loop, but inside the outer loop.

6) The averageSales method

a) The columns representing quarters are used for the outer loop.

b) The total is initialized to 0 inside the outer loop.

c) The sales for each division are summed inside the inner loop using the rows for the index.

d) The average is calculated and printed after the inner loop but inside the outer loop, by dividing the total by the number of divisions.

```
System.out.println(money.format(total/sales.length));
```

7) The highestSalesDivisionByQuarter method

a) The columns representing quarters are used for the outer loop.

b) Variables representing the highest sales and the index of the division with the highest sales are initialized to 0 inside the outer loop.

```
double high = 0;

int highRow = 0;
```

c) Rows representing divisions are used as the index for the inner loop.

d) Inside the inner loop, the current sales are compared with the highest sales. If the current sales are greater than the highest sales, the current sales value is assigned to the highest sales and the current index is assigned to the index of the division with the highest sales.

```
if (sales[div][qtr] > high)

{

   highRow = div;

   high = sales[div][qtr];

}
```

e) The highest sales and the division with the highest sales are printed out after the inner loop, but inside the outer loop.

```
System.out.println("Quarter " + (qtr+1) + "\tDivision " +

      (highRow + 1) + "\t$" + money.format(high));
```

Code Listing 7-3 (QuarterlySales.java)

```
//*****************************************************
// Written by Diane Christie
// Chapter 7
// Programming Challenge 6: QuarterlySales
//*****************************************************

//*****************************************************
// Write a program that lets the user enter four quarterly
// sales figures for six divisions of a company.  The
// figures should be stored in a two-dimensional array.
// Once the figures are entered, the program should
// display the following data for each quarter:
// ·  A list of the sales figures by division
// ·  Each division's increase or decrease from the
//      previous quarter (this will not be displayed for
//      the first quarter)
// ·  The total sales for the quarter
// ·  The company's increase or decrease from the
//      previous quarter (this will not be displayed for
//      the first quarter)
// ·  The average sales for all divisions that quarter
// ·  The division with the highest sales for that quarter
// Input Validation:  Do not accept negative numbers for
// sales figures.
//*****************************************************

//*****************************************************
// Class will allow user to enter quarterly sales figures
// six divisions of a company.  The program will then
// display data in various forms.
//*****************************************************

//*****************************************************
// To format numbers to two decimal places
//*****************************************************
import java.text.*;
import java.util.Scanner;

public class QuarterlySales
{
   static final int QUARTERS = 4;
   static final int DIVISIONS = 6;

   public static void main(String [] args)
   {
      double [][] sales = new double[DIVISIONS][QUARTERS];
      System.out.println(
         "Program to enter quarterly sales statistics");

      fillArray(sales);
      salesByDivision(sales);
      quarterChangeByDivision(sales);
      totalSalesByQuarter(sales);
      quarterChange(sales);
      averageSales(sales);
      highestSalesDivisionByQuarter(sales);
```

```
}


//****************************************************
//Enter quarterly sales figures for each division,
//method requires a two-dimensional array as a parameter
//****************************************************
public static void fillArray(double [] [] sales)
{
   double quarterSales;
   Scanner keyboard = new Scanner(System.in);

   for (int qtr = 0; qtr <QUARTERS; qtr++)
   {
      System.out.println("Enter sales for quarter "
         + (qtr + 1) + ":  ");
      for (int div = 0; div < sales.length; div++)
      {
         do
         {
            System.out.print(
               "\tDivision " + (div + 1) + ":  ");
            quarterSales = keyboard.nextDouble();
         }while (quarterSales < 0);
         sales[div] [qtr]= quarterSales;
      }
   }
   System.out.println();
}

//****************************************************
//Print out sales figures by division
//method requires a two-dimensional array as a parameter
//****************************************************
public static void salesByDivision(double [] [] sales)
{
   DecimalFormat money = new DecimalFormat("#,###,##0.00");
   System.out.println();
   System.out.println("Sales figures by Division");
   System.out.println(
      "____________________________________________");
   for (int div = 0; div < sales.length; div++)
   {
      System.out.println("Division " + (div + 1));
      for (int qtr = 0; qtr < sales[div].length; qtr++)
      {
         System.out.print(
            "\tQuarter " + (qtr + 1) + ":  $");
         System.out.println(money.format(sales[div] [qtr]));
      }
   }
}

//*****************************************************
//Print each division's increase or decrease from the
//previous quarter (this will not be displayed for the
//first quarter)method requires a two-dimensional array
//as a parameter.
//*****************************************************
```

```
public static void quarterChangeByDivision(
      double [] [] sales)
{
   DecimalFormat money = new DecimalFormat("#,###,##0.00");
   System.out.println();
   System.out.println(
      "Increase or decrease from previous quarter");
   System.out.println(
      "__________________________________________");
   for (int div = 0; div < sales.length; div++)
   {
      System.out.println("Division " + (div + 1));
      for (int qtr = 1; qtr < sales[div].length; qtr++)
      {
         System.out.print(
            "\tQuarter " + (qtr + 1) + ":  $");
         System.out.println(money.format(
            sales[div][qtr]-sales[div][qtr-1]));
      }
   }
   System.out.println();
}

//*********************************************************
//The total sales for the quarter
//method requires a two-dimensional array as a parameter
//*********************************************************
public static void totalSalesByQuarter(double [] [] sales)
{
   DecimalFormat money = new DecimalFormat("#,###,##0.00");
   System.out.println();
   System.out.println("Total sales");
   System.out.println(
      "__________________________________________");
   for (int qtr = 0; qtr < QUARTERS; qtr++)
   {
      double total = 0;
      for (int div = 0; div < sales.length; div++)
      {
         //sum up the sales for the quarter
         total = total + sales[div][qtr];
      }
      System.out.print("Quarter " + (qtr+1) + ":  $");
      System.out.println(money.format(total));
   }
   System.out.println();
}

//***********************************************************
//The company's increase or decrease from the previous
//quarter (this will not be displayed for the first quarter)
//method requires a two-dimensional array as a parameter
//***********************************************************
public static void quarterChange(double [] [] sales)
{
   DecimalFormat money = new DecimalFormat("#,###,##0.00");
   System.out.println();
   System.out.println();
   System.out.println(
```

```
         "Increase or decrease from previous quarter");
      System.out.println(
         "__________________________________________");
      for (int qtr = 1; qtr < QUARTERS; qtr++)
      {
         double total = 0;

         for (int div = 0; div < sales.length; div++)
         {
            //sum up the differences
            total = total + sales[div][qtr]-sales[div][qtr-1];

         }
         System.out.print("Quarter " + (qtr + 1) + ":  $");
         System.out.println(money.format(total));
      }
      System.out.println();
   }

   //************************************************************
   //The average sales for all divisions that quarter
   //method requires a two-dimensional array as a parameter
   //************************************************************
   public static void averageSales(double[] [] sales)
   {
      DecimalFormat money = new DecimalFormat("#,###,##0.00");
      System.out.println();
      System.out.println("Average sales");
      System.out.println(
         "__________________________________________");
      for (int qtr = 0; qtr < QUARTERS; qtr++)
      {
         double total = 0;
         for (int div = 0; div < sales.length; div++)
         {
            //sum up the sales
            total = total + sales[div][qtr];
         }
         System.out.print("Quarter " + (qtr+1) + ":  $");
         //print calculated average
         System.out.println(money.format(total/sales.length));
      }
      System.out.println();
   }

   //**************************************************************
   //The division with the highest sales for that quarter
   //method requires a two-dimensional array as a parameter
   //**************************************************************
   public static void highestSalesDivisionByQuarter(
         double [] [] sales)
   {
      DecimalFormat money = new DecimalFormat("#,###,##0.00");
      System.out.println();
      System.out.println(
         "Division with highest sales for the quarter");
      System.out.println(
         "__________________________________________");
      for (int qtr = 0; qtr < QUARTERS; qtr++)
```

```
        {
           double high = 0;
           int highRow = 0;
           for (int div = 0; div < sales.length; div++)
           {
              //compare sales against high
              if (sales[div][qtr] > high)
              {
                 //replace with higher sales value and location
                 highRow = div;
                 high = sales[div][qtr];
              }
           }

           System.out.println("Quarter " + (qtr+1) +
              "\tDivision " + (highRow + 1) + "\t$" +
              money.format(high));
        }
        System.out.println();
     }
  }
```

Program Output

```
Program to enter quarterly sales statistics
Enter sales for quarter 1:
        Division 1:  59773.30
        Division 2:  73734.04
        Division 3:  48445.18
        Division 4:  40158.91
        Division 5:  75839.21
        Division 6:  53220.09
Enter sales for quarter 2:
        Division 1:  74322.33
        Division 2:  81470.76
        Division 3:  74802.52
        Division 4:  78354.25
        Division 5:  82891.48
        Division 6:  87604.88
Enter sales for quarter 3:
        Division 1:  90703.84
        Division 2:  95085.82
        Division 3:  92381.82
        Division 4:  77082.27
        Division 5:  91194.84
        Division 6:  79624.45
Enter sales for quarter 4:
        Division 1:  82178.44
        Division 2:  93163.32
        Division 3:  88940.43
        Division 4:  80490.67
        Division 5:  113838.68
        Division 6:  101454.00


Sales figures by Division
___________________________________________
Division 1
```

```
            Quarter 1:  $59,773.30
            Quarter 2:  $74,322.33
            Quarter 3:  $90,703.84
            Quarter 4:  $82,178.44
Division 2
            Quarter 1:  $73,734.04
            Quarter 2:  $81,470.76
            Quarter 3:  $95,085.82
            Quarter 4:  $93,163.32
Division 3
            Quarter 1:  $48,445.18
            Quarter 2:  $74,802.52
            Quarter 3:  $92,381.82
            Quarter 4:  $88,940.43
Division 4
            Quarter 1:  $40,158.91
            Quarter 2:  $78,354.25
            Quarter 3:  $77,082.27
            Quarter 4:  $80,490.67
Division 5
            Quarter 1:  $75,839.21
            Quarter 2:  $82,891.48
            Quarter 3:  $91,194.84
            Quarter 4:  $113,838.68
Division 6
            Quarter 1:  $53,220.09
            Quarter 2:  $87,604.88
            Quarter 3:  $79,624.45
            Quarter 4:  $101,454.00

Increase or decrease from previous quarter
__________________________________________
Division 1
            Quarter 2:  $14,549.03
            Quarter 3:  $16,381.51
            Quarter 4:  $-8,525.40
Division 2
            Quarter 2:  $7,736.72
            Quarter 3:  $13,615.06
            Quarter 4:  $-1,922.50
Division 3
            Quarter 2:  $26,357.34
            Quarter 3:  $17,579.30
            Quarter 4:  $-3,441.39
Division 4
            Quarter 2:  $38,195.34
            Quarter 3:  $-1,271.98
            Quarter 4:  $3,408.40
Division 5
            Quarter 2:  $7,052.27
            Quarter 3:  $8,303.36
            Quarter 4:  $22,643.84
Division 6
            Quarter 2:  $34,384.79
            Quarter 3:  $-7,980.43
            Quarter 4:  $21,829.55


Total sales
```

```
________________________________________
Quarter 1:  $351,170.73
Quarter 2:  $479,446.22
Quarter 3:  $526,073.04
Quarter 4:  $560,065.54


Increase or decrease from previous quarter
________________________________________
Quarter 2:  $128,275.49
Quarter 3:  $46,626.82
Quarter 4:  $33,992.50

Average sales
________________________________________
Quarter 1:  $58,528.45
Quarter 2:  $79,907.70
Quarter 3:  $87,678.84
Quarter 4:  $93,344.26

Division with highest sales for the quarter
________________________________________
Quarter 1       Division 5      $75,839.21
Quarter 2       Division 6      $87,604.88
Quarter 3       Division 2      $95,085.82
Quarter 4       Division 5      $113,838.68
```

Programming Challenge 7: Grade Book

Problem Statement:

A teacher has five students who have taken four tests. The teacher uses the following grading scale to assign a letter grade to a student, based on the average of his or her four test scores.

Test Score	Letter Grade
90-100	A
80-89	B
70-79	C
60-69	D
0-59	F

Write a class that uses a String array to hold the five students' names, an array of five characters to hold the five students' letter grades, and the five arrays of four doubles each to hold each student's test scores. The class should have methods that return a specific student's name, average test score, and a letter grade based on the average.

Demonstrate the class in a program that allows the user to enter each student's name and his or her four test scores. It should then display each student's average test score and letter grade.

Input validation: Do not accept test scores less than zero or greater than 100.

Solution:

Define What The Program Is To Do

Purpose	**Describe a grade book consisting of 5 students and 4 tests.**

Fields	studentName	An array of Strings to hold names of students. It is of size NUM_STUDENTS.
	letterGrade	An array of characters to hold the final letter grade of each student. It is of size NUM_TESTS.
	testScore	A two-dimensional array of doubles consisting of test scores for each student. It is of size NUM_STUDENTS by NUM_TESTS.
	NUM_STUDENTS	A public constant containing the number of students.
	NUM_TESTS	A public constant containing the number of test scores.
Constructor	GradeBook()	Create a gradeBook object by creating. Initialization of the arrays is accomplished by calling the private methods fillGradeBook and assignGrades.
Methods	fillGradeBook	Uses Keyboard class to enter student names and grades from the keyboard.
	assignGrades	Calculates the average score and assigns a letter grade as follows: A 90-100 B 80-89 C 70-79 D 60-69 F 0-59
	getStudentAverage	Returns an average score if the parameter is a valid index number. Returns -1 otherwise.
	getStudentName	Returns the student name if the parameter is a valid index number. Returns "Not a valid index" otherwise.
	getLetterGrade	Returns the letter grade if the parameter is a valid index number. Returns a blank otherwise.

Psuedocode for GradeBook Class

1) Define GradeBook Class fields

   a) The field studentName represents an array of Strings to hold names of students. It is of size NUM_STUDENTS.

   b) The field letterGrade represents an array of characters to hold the final letter grade of each student. It is of size NUM_STUDENTS.

   c) The field testScore represents a two-dimensional array of doubles consisting of test scores for each student. It is of size NUM_STUDENTS by NUM_TESTS.

   d) The field NUM_STUDENTS is a public constant that represents the number of students that are used in the GradeBook.

   e) The field NUM_TESTS is a public constant that represents the number of tests that each student takes.

2) Define the GradeBook class constructors.

   a) Default constructor (having no arguments).

      i) Create an object of class GradeBook by creating arrays of studentName, letterGrade, and testScore. It then calls the private methods fillGradeBook and assignGrades.

3) Define method fillGradeBook.

   a) Use the Keyboard class to read in a student name and four test scores. Each test score is validated to be between 0 and 100. This is repeated for each of five students.

4) Define method assignGrades.

   a) Calls the method getStudentAverage and assigns the letter grade according to the defined grading scale:

      A 90-100

      B 80-89

      C 70-79

      D 60-69

      E 0-59

5) Define method getStudentAverage

a) Validates the parameter as a valid index for a student. It returns the calculated average score for that student, rounded to the nearest whole number if it is a valid index. It returns -1 if it is not a valid index.

6) Define method getStudentName

a) Validates the parameter as a valid index for a student. It returns the student's name if it is a valid index, otherwise it returns "Not a valid index".

7) Define method getLetterGrade

a) Validates the parameter as a valid index for a student. It returns a letter grade corresponding to that student if it is valid. It returns a blank otherwise.

GradeBook
-studentName[]: String -letterGrade[]: char -testScore[][]: double +NUM_STUDENTS: int +NUM_TESTS: int
+GradeBook(): -fillGradeBook(): void -assignGrades(): void +getStudentAverage(i:int):int +getStudentName(i:int):String +getLetterGrade(i:int):char

Figure 7-2 UML Drawing for GradeBook Class

Detailed Pseudocode for GradeBook Class

1) Default constructor.

a) Create letterGrade array of size NUM_STUDENTS.

b) Create studentName array of size NUM_STUDENTS.

c) Create testScore array of size NUM_STUDENTS by NUM_TESTS.

d) Call fillGradeBook method.

e) Call assignGrades method.

2) The fillGradeBook method.

a) The rows representing each student are used for the outer loop.

b) The student name is read in from the keyboard.

c) The columns representing each test are used for the inner loop.

d) A test score is read in from the keyboard and validated. If the score is not between 0 and 100, a message is printed and the loop allows the user to enter that score again.

```
do

{

        score = Keyboard.readDouble();

        if (score < 0 || score > 100)

        System.out.println("Invalid Entry:  " +

               "Test score must be between 0 and 100");

}while (score < 0 || score > 100);
```

3) The assignGrades method

a) The rows representing each student are used for the loop.

b) The average is obtained by calling the getStudentAverage for that student.

c) A nested if-else is used to determine correct grade to assign.

```
        if (average >= 90)

        letterGrade[i] = 'A';

    else if (average >= 80)

        letterGrade[i] = 'B';

    else if (average >= 70)

        letterGrade[i] = 'C';
```

```
else if (average >= 60)

   letterGrade[i] = 'D';

else

   letterGrade[i] = 'F';
```

4) The getStudentAverage method

   a) Validates the parameter as a valid index for a student.

   ```
   if (i >=0 && i < NUM_STUDENTS)
   ```

   b) If the parameter is valid, a total is initialized to 0, and the scores for that student are summed using a loop.

   ```
   for (int j = 0; j < NUM_TESTS; j++)

   {

         total = total + testScore[i][j];

   }
   ```

   c) The average is calculated and rounded to the nearest whole number and returned.

   ```
   return (int) (total/NUM_TESTS + 0.5);
   ```

   d) If the parameter is not valid, return -1.

5) The getStudentName method.

   a) Validate the parameter as a valid index for a student.

   b) If the parameter is valid, return the studentName for that student, otherwise return "Not a valid index".

6) The getLetterGrade method.

   a) Validate the parameter as a valid index for a student.

   b) If the parameter is valid, return the letterGrade for that student, otherwise return a blank.

Code Listing 7-4 (GradeBook.java)

```
//*****************************************************
// Written by Diane Christie
// Chapter 7
```

```
// Programming Challenge 7: GradeBook class
//*********************************************************

//*********************************************************
// A teacher has five students who have taken four tests.
// The teacher uses the following grading scale to assign
// a letter grade to a student, based on the average of
// his or her four test scores.
// Test Score  Letter Grade
// 90-100         A
// 80-89       B
// 70-79       C
// 60-69       D
// 0-59        F
// Write a class that uses a String array to hold the five
// students' names, an array of five characters to hold
// the five students' letter grades, and the five arrays
// of four doubles each to hold each student's test scores.
// The class should have methods that return a specific
// student's name, average test score, and a letter grade
// based on the average.
// Demonstrate the class in a program that allows the user
// to enter each student's name and his or her four test
// scores.  It should then display each student's average
// test score and letter grade.
// Input validation:  Do not accept test scores less than
// zero or greater than 100.
//*********************************************************

//*********************************************************
// The GradeBook class describes a teacher's grade book.
// Each student corresponds to a subscript in the arrays.
// There is an array to store student names, an array to
// store student letter grades, and a two-dimensional array
// to store test scores for all students. Requires use of
// the Keyboard class.
//*********************************************************

import java.util.Scanner;

public class GradeBook
{
   private String[] studentName;
   private char[] letterGrade;
   private double [] [] testScore;
   public final int NUM_STUDENTS = 5;
   public final int NUM_TESTS = 4;


   //*****************************************************
   // Constructor creates the arrays then calls the methods
   // fillGradeBook and assignGrades in order to initialize
   // all elements of the arrays.
   //*****************************************************
   public GradeBook()
   {
      letterGrade = new char[NUM_STUDENTS];
      studentName = new String[NUM_STUDENTS];
      testScore = new double[NUM_STUDENTS][NUM_TESTS];
```

```
    fillGradeBook();
    assignGrades();
}

//*****************************************************
// Uses Keyboard class to enter student names and
// grades from the keyboard.
//*****************************************************
private void fillGradeBook()
{
    Scanner keyboard = new Scanner(System.in);

    for (int i = 0; i <NUM_STUDENTS; i++)
    {
        double score;
        System.out.print("Enter student number " +
            (i+1) + "'s name:  ");
        studentName[i] = keyboard.next();
        for (int j = 0; j < NUM_TESTS; j++)
        {
            System.out.print("Enter test score " +
                (j + 1) + ":  ");
            //validate that the scores are between
            //0 and 100
            do
            {
                score = keyboard.nextDouble();
                if (score < 0 || score > 100)
                    System.out.println("Invalid Entry:"
                        +  "  Test score must be " +
                        "between 0 and 100");
            }while (score < 0 || score > 100);
            testScore [i][j] = score;
        }
        System.out.println();
    }
}

//*****************************************************
// Calculates the average score and assigns a letter
// grade as follows:
// A   90-100
// B   80-89
// C   70-79
// D   60-69
// F   0-59
//*****************************************************
private void assignGrades()
{
    for (int i = 0; i < NUM_STUDENTS; i++)
    {
        double average = getStudentAverage(i);
        if (average >= 90)
            letterGrade[i] = 'A';
        else if (average >= 80)
            letterGrade[i] = 'B';
        else if (average >= 70)
            letterGrade[i] = 'C';
        else if (average >= 60)
```

```
            letterGrade[i] = 'D';
         else
            letterGrade[i] = 'F';
      }
   }

   //*****************************************************
   // Returns an average score if the parameter is a valid
   // index number.  Returns -1 otherwise.
   //*****************************************************
   public int getStudentAverage(int i)
   {
      if (i >=0 && i < NUM_STUDENTS)
      {
         double total = 0;
         for (int j = 0; j < NUM_TESTS; j++)
         {
            total = total + testScore[i][j];
         }
         return (int) (total/NUM_TESTS + 0.5);
      }
      else
         return -1;
   }

   //*****************************************************
   // Returns the student name if the parameter is a valid
   // index number.  Returns "Not a valid index" otherwise.
   //*****************************************************
   public String getStudentName (int i)
   {
      if (i >=0 && i < NUM_STUDENTS)
         return studentName[i];
      else
         return "Not a valid index";
   }
   //*****************************************************
   // Returns the letter grade if the parameter is a valid
   // index number.  Returns a blank otherwise.
   //*****************************************************
   public char getLetterGrade (int i)
   {
      if (i >=0 && i < NUM_STUDENTS)
         return letterGrade[i];
      else
         return ' ';
   }
}
```

Solution: The GradeBookDemo Class

Define What The Class is To Do

Purpose	**Demonstrate capabilities of the GradeBook Class**
Input	**The name and test scores for each student**

Process	**A GradeBook object is created. The user will be prompted for each student name and test scores. Each student's grades are calculated.**
Output	**The student names, average score, and letter grade are displayed.**

Pseudocode for GradeBookDemo Class

1) Create an object of class GradeBook.

2) Print column titles for grade report

3) Print out the student name, average score, and letter grade for each student by calling the appropriate accessor methods.

Code Listing 7-5 (GradeBookDemo.java)

```
//*****************************************************
// Written by Diane Christie                          *
// Chapter 7                                          *
// Programming Challenge 7:  GradeBookDemo Class      *
//*****************************************************

//*****************************************************
//Demonstrate the GradeBook class in a complete program *
//that allows the user to enter each student's name and *
//his or her four test scores.  It should then display  *
//each student's average test score and letter grade.   *
//Uses Keyboard class to read from the keyboard.        *
//*****************************************************
public class GradeBookDemo
{
   public static void main (String [] args)
   {
      //Create an object of type GradeBook
      GradeBook cs144fall03 = new GradeBook ();

      //Print out column headings
      System.out.println("Student Name\tAverage\tGrade");

      //Print a line for each student's information
      for (int i = 0; i < cs144fall03.NUM_STUDENTS; i++)
      {
         System.out.println(cs144fall03.getStudentName(i) +
             "\t" + cs144fall03.getStudentAverage(i) +
             "\t" + cs144fall03.getLetterGrade(i));
      }
   }
}
```

Program Output

```
Enter student number 1's name:  Joe Brown
Enter test score 1:  55
Enter test score 2:  60
Enter test score 3:  58
Enter test score 4:  52

Enter student number 2's name:  Charlie Jones
Enter test score 1:  71
Enter test score 2:  60
Enter test score 3:  65
Enter test score 4:  68

Enter student number 3's name:  Sue Cantwell
Enter test score 1:  79
Enter test score 2:  75
Enter test score 3:  77
Enter test score 4:  77

Enter student number 4's name:  Erica Maxwell
Enter test score 1:  83
Enter test score 2:  88
Enter test score 3:  85
Enter test score 4:  82

Enter student number 5's name:  Andrew Jenkins
Enter test score 1:  99
Enter test score 2:  92
Enter test score 3:  94
Enter test score 4:  97

Student Name    Average Grade
Joe Brown       56      F
Charlie Jones   66      D
Sue Cantwell    77      C
Erica Maxwell   85      B
Andrew Jenkins  96      A
```

Programming Challenge 8: Grade Book Modification

Problem Statement:

Modify the grade book application in Programming Challenge 7 so that it drops each student's lowest score when determining the test score averages and letter grades.

Solution:

The only modification is in the average score calculation. The program must find the lowest score as the sum of the scores is being performed. The lowest score can then be subtracted out and the average is then calculated by dividing by one less score.

Pseudocode for modified getStudentAverage method

1) A variable to hold the lowest score must be initialized. Since we will be comparing it to other scores and looking for the lowest, we want to initialize it to the highest possible value, 100.

2) When the scores are being summed, each score should be compared to the low. If the score is smaller than the low, its value is assigned to the low.

3) After summing is complete, the modified total is found by subtracting the low.

4) The average is found by dividing by one less than in the original method.

Code Listing 7-6 (modified getStudentAverage method of Gradebook2.java)

```
public int getStudentAverage(int i)
{
   if (i >=0 && i < NUM_STUDENTS)
   {
      double total = 0;
      double low = 100;
      for (int j = 0; j < NUM_TESTS; j++)
      {
         if (testScore[i][j] < low)
            low = testScore[i][j];
         total = total + testScore[i][j];
      }
      total = total - low;
      return (int) (total/(NUM_TESTS-1) + 0.5);
   }
   else
      return -1;
```

```
}
```

Program Output

```
Enter student number 1's name:  Joe Brown
Enter test score 1:  55
Enter test score 2:  60
Enter test score 3:  58
Enter test score 4:  52

Enter student number 2's name:  Charlie Jones
Enter test score 1:  71
Enter test score 2:  60
Enter test score 3:  65
Enter test score 4:  68

Enter student number 3's name:  Sue Cantwell
Enter test score 1:  79
Enter test score 2:  75
Enter test score 3:  77
Enter test score 4:  77

Enter student number 4's name:  Erica Maxwell
Enter test score 1:  83
Enter test score 2:  88
Enter test score 3:  85
Enter test score 4:  82

Enter student number 5's name:  Andrew Jenkins
Enter test score 1:  99
Enter test score 2:  92
Enter test score 3:  94
Enter test score 4:  97

Student Name    Average Grade
Joe Brown       58      F
Charlie Jones   68      D
Sue Cantwell    78      C
Erica Maxwell   85      B
Andrew Jenkins  97      A
```

Programming Challenge 10: ArrayOperations Class

Problem Statement:

Write a class name ArrayOperations with the following static methods:

- getTotal. This method should accept a one-dimensional array as its argument and return the total of the values in the array. Write overloaded versions of this method that work with int, float, double, and long arrays.
- getAverage. This method should accept a one-dimensional array as its argument and return the average of the values in the array. Write overloaded versions of this method that work with int, float, double, and long arrays.
- getHighest. This method should accept a one-dimensional array as its argument and return the highest value in the array. Write overloaded versions of this method that work with int, float, double, and long arrays.
- getLowest. This method should accept a one-dimensional array as its argument and return the lowest value in the array. Write overloaded versions of this method that work with int, float, double, and long arrays.

Demonstrate the class in a complete program with test data stored in arrays of various data types.

Solution:

Define What The Program Is To Do

Purpose	To perform operations on one-dimensional arrays
Input	None
Process	• Total the values in an array • Average the values in an array • Find the highest value in an array • Find the lowest value in an array

Output

- The total of the values in an array
- The average of the values in an array
- The highest value in an array
- The lowest value in an array

Pseudocode for ArrayOperations Class

1) Define the getTotal method

   a) The values from the array parameter are summed. The method returns a value which represents the total of all values in the array.

   b) There are four versions of this method. One version which takes an int array parameter and returns an int value, a second version using double values, a third version using float, and a fourth version using long values.

2) Define the getAverage method

   a) The values from the array parameter are averaged. The method returns a value which represents the average of all values in the array.

   b) There are four versions of this method. One version which takes an int array parameter and returns an int value, a second version using double values, a third version using float, and a fourth version using long values.

3) Define the getHighest method

   a) The values from the array parameter are searched for the highest value. The method returns a value which represents the highest of all values in the array.

   b) There are four versions of this method. One version which takes an int array parameter and returns an int value, a second version using double values, a third version using float, and a fourth version using long values.

4) Define the getLowest method

   a) The values from the array parameter are searched for the lowest value. The method returns a value which represents the lowest of all values in the array.

   b) There are four versions of this method. One version which takes an int array parameter and returns an int value, a second version using double values, a third version using float, and a fourth version using long values.

5) Define a main method

   a) Declare an array of int values using an initialization list.

   b) Declare an array of double values using an initialization list.

   c) Declare an array of float values using an initialization list.

   d) Declare an array of long values using an initialization list.

   e) Obtain the total for the first array by passing it to the getTotal method.

   f) Obtain the average for the first array by passing it to the getAverage method.

   g) Obtain the highest value in the first array by passing it to the getHighest method.

   h) Obtain the lowest value in the first array by passing it to the getLowest method.

   i) Do the same for the other arrays.

   j) Print out all results.

Code Listing 7-7 (ArrayOperations.java)

```
//***********************************************************
// Written by Diane Christie
// Chapter 7
// Programming Challenge 10:  ArrayOperations Class
//***********************************************************

//***********************************************************
// The ArrayOperations class performs operations on different
// types of one-dimensional array.  Array types include int,
// double, float, and long.  Operations include totalling the
// values in the array, averaging the values in the array,
// finding the highest value in the array, and finding the
// lowest value in the array.
//***********************************************************

public class ArrayOperations
{
   public static void main(String [] args)
   {
      int [] wholeNumbers = {1,2,3,4,5,6};
      double [] fractions = {0.5, 1.5, 2.5, 3.5};
      float [] fractions2 = {0.5F, 1.5F, 2.5F};
      long [] bigNumbers = {1L, 2L, 3L, 4L, 5L};
```

```
int wholeNumberTotal = getTotal(wholeNumbers);
int wholeNumberAverage = getAverage(wholeNumbers);
int wholeNumberHighest = getHighest(wholeNumbers);
int wholeNumberLowest = getLowest(wholeNumbers);
double fractionTotal = getTotal(fractions);
double fractionAverage = getAverage(fractions);
double fractionHighest = getHighest(fractions);
double fractionLowest = getLowest(fractions);
float fraction2Total = getTotal(fractions2);
float fraction2Average = getAverage(fractions2);
float fraction2Highest = getHighest(fractions2);
float fraction2Lowest = getLowest(fractions2);
long bigNumberTotal = getTotal(bigNumbers);
long bigNumberAverage = getAverage(bigNumbers);
long bigNumberHighest = getHighest(bigNumbers);
long bigNumberLowest = getLowest(bigNumbers);


System.out.println(
   "The numbers in the array are 1, 2, 3, 4, 5, 6");
System.out.println("The total is " + wholeNumberTotal);
System.out.println(
   "The average is " + wholeNumberAverage);
System.out.println(
   "The highest value is " + wholeNumberHighest);
System.out.println(
   "The lowest value is " + wholeNumberLowest);
System.out.println();

System.out.println(
   "The numbers in the array are 0.5, 1.5, 2.5, 3.5");
System.out.println("The total is " + fractionTotal);
System.out.println("The average is " + fractionAverage);
System.out.println(
   "The highest value is " + fractionHighest);
System.out.println(
   "The lowest value is " + fractionLowest);
System.out.println();

System.out.println(
   "The numbers in the array are 0.5, 1.5, 2.5");
System.out.println("The total is " + fraction2Total);
System.out.println(
   "The average is " + fraction2Average);
System.out.println(
   "The highest value is " + fraction2Highest);
System.out.println(
   "The lowest value is " + fraction2Lowest);
System.out.println();

System.out.println(
   "The numbers in the array are 1, 2, 3, 4, 5");
System.out.println("The total is " + bigNumberTotal);
System.out.println(
   "The average is " + bigNumberAverage);
System.out.println(
   "The highest value is " + bigNumberHighest);
System.out.println(
   "The lowest value is " + bigNumberLowest);
```

```
   System.out.println();
}

//******************************************************
// This method takes a one-dimensional array as its
//parameter and returns the total of the values in the
//array.
//*******************************************************
public static int getTotal (int [] data)
{
   int total = 0;

   for (int i = 0; i < data.length; i++)
   {
      total += data[i];
   }

   return total;
}

//*******************************************************
// This method takes a one-dimensional array as its
// parameter
// and returns the total of the values in the array.
//*******************************************************
public static double getTotal (double [] data)
{
   double total = 0;

   for (int i = 0; i < data.length; i++)
   {
      total += data[i];
   }

   return total;
}

//*******************************************************
// This method takes a one-dimensional array as its
//parameter and returns the total of the values in the
//array.
//*******************************************************
public static float getTotal (float [] data)
{
   float total = 0;

   for (int i = 0; i < data.length; i++)
   {
      total += data[i];
   }

   return total;
}

//*******************************************************
// This method takes a one-dimensional array as its
//parameter and returns the total of the values in the
//array.
//*******************************************************
```

```
public static long getTotal (long [] data)
{
   long total = 0;

   for (int i = 0; i < data.length; i++)
   {
      total += data[i];
   }

   return total;
}

//**********************************************************
// This method takes a one-dimensional array as its
//parameter and returns the average of the values in the
//array.
//**********************************************************
public static int getAverage (int [] data)
{
   int total = 0;

   for (int i = 0; i < data.length; i++)
   {
      total += data[i];
   }

   return total/data.length;
}

//**********************************************************
// This method takes a one-dimensional array as its
//parameter and returns the average of the values in the
//array.
//**********************************************************
public static double getAverage (double [] data)
{
   double total = 0;

   for (int i = 0; i < data.length; i++)
   {
      total += data[i];
   }

   return total/data.length;
}

//**********************************************************
// This method takes a one-dimensional array as its
// parameter and returns the average of the values in the
// array.
//**********************************************************
public static float getAverage (float [] data)
{
   float total = 0;

   for (int i = 0; i < data.length; i++)
   {
      total += data[i];
   }
```

```
   return total/data.length;
}

//*****************************************************
// This method takes a one-dimensional array as its
// parameter and returns the average of the values in the
//array.
//*****************************************************
public static long getAverage (long [] data)
{
   long total = 0;

   for (int i = 0; i < data.length; i++)
   {
      total += data[i];
   }

   return total/data.length;
}

//*****************************************************
// This method takes a one-dimensional array as its
// parameter
// and returns the highest of the values in the array.
//*****************************************************
public static int getHighest (int [] data)
{
   int high = data[0];

   for (int i = 1; i < data.length; i++)
   {
      if (data[i] > high)
      high = data[i];

   }

   return high;
}

//*****************************************************
// This method takes a one-dimensional array as its
// parameter and returns the highest of the values in the
// array.
//*****************************************************
public static double getHighest (double [] data)
{
   double high = data[0];

   for (int i = 1; i < data.length; i++)
   {
      if (data[i] > high)
         high = data[i];

   }

   return high;
}
```

```
//*****************************************************
// This method takes a one-dimensional array as its
// parameter and returns the highest of the values in the
//array.
//*****************************************************
public static float getHighest (float [] data)
{
   float high = data[0];

   for (int i = 1; i < data.length; i++)
   {
      if (data[i] > high)
         high = data[i];

   }

   return high;
}

//*****************************************************
// This method takes a one-dimensional array as its
// parameter and returns the highest of the values in the
// array.
//*****************************************************
public static long getHighest (long [] data)
{
   long high = data[0];

   for (int i = 1; i < data.length; i++)
   {
      if (data[i] > high)
         high = data[i];

   }

   return high;
}

//*****************************************************
// This method takes a one-dimensional array as its
// parameter and returns the lowest of the values in the
// array.
//*****************************************************
public static int getLowest (int [] data)
{
   int low = data[0];

   for (int i = 1; i < data.length; i++)
   {
      if (data[i] < low)
         low = data[i];

   }

   return low;
}

//*****************************************************
// This method takes a one-dimensional array as its
```

```
   // parameter and returns the lowest of the values in the
   // array.
   //*********************************************************
   public static double getLowest (double [] data)
   {
      double low = data[0];

      for (int i = 1; i < data.length; i++)
      {
         if (data[i] < low)
            low = data[i];

      }

      return low;
   }

   //*********************************************************
   // This method takes a one-dimensional array as its
   // parameter and returns the lowest of the values in the
   // array.
   //*********************************************************
   public static float getLowest (float [] data)
   {
      float low = data[0];

      for (int i = 1; i < data.length; i++)
      {
         if (data[i] < low)
            low = data[i];

      }

      return low;
   }

   //*********************************************************
   // This method takes a one-dimensional array as its
   // parameter and returns the lowest of the values in the
   // array.
   //*********************************************************
   public static long getLowest (long [] data)
   {
      long low = data[0];

      for (int i = 1; i < data.length; i++)
      {
         if (data[i] < low)
            low = data[i];

      }

      return low;
   }
}
```

Program Output

```
The numbers in the array are 1, 2, 3, 4, 5, 6
The total is 21
The average is 3
The highest value is 6
The lowest value is 1

The numbers in the array are 0.5, 1.5, 2.5, 3.5
The total is 8.0
The average is 2.0
The highest value is 3.5
The lowest value is 0.5

The numbers in the array are 0.5, 1.5, 2.5
The total is 4.5
The average is 1.5
The highest value is 2.5
The lowest value is 0.5

The numbers in the array are 1, 2, 3, 4, 5
The total is 15
The average is 3
The highest value is 5
The lowest value is 1
```

CHAPTER 8

Text Processing and Wrapper Classes

Solutions

- Programming Challenge 2: Word Counter
- Programming Challenge 6: Phone Number List
- Programming Challenge 10: Word Counter

Programming Challenge 2: Word Counter

Problem Statement:

Write a method that accepts a String object as an argument and returns the number of words it contains. For instance, if the argument is "Four score and seven years ago" the method should return the number 6. Demonstrate the method in a program that asks the user to input a string and then passes it to the method. The number of words in the string should be displayed on the screen.

Solution:Define What The Program Is To Do

Purpose	**To count the number of words typed in by the user.**
Input	**A string**
Process	**The program tokenizes the input.**
Output	**The number of words.**

Pseudocode for WordCounter Class

1) Create a wordCount method.
   a) Initialize a counter
   b) Create an object of StringTokenizer.
   c) While the StringTokenizer object has more tokens,
      i) Get the next token
      ii) Increment the counter
   d) Return the value of the counter
2) Create a main method
   a) Get a phrase or sentence from the user.
   b) Count the number of words.
   c) Print out the results.

Code Listing 8-1 (WordCounter.java)

```
//*******************************************************
// Written by Diane Christie
// Chapter 8
// Programming Challenge 2:  Word Counter
//*******************************************************

//*******************************************************
// Write a method that accepts a String object as an argument
// and returns the number of words it contains.  For instance,
// if the argument is "Four score and seven years ago" the
// method should return the number 6.  Demonstrate the method
// in a program that asks the user to input a string and then
// passes it to the method.  The number of words in the
// string should be displayed on the screen.
//*******************************************************

//*******************************************************
// The WordCounter class reads a string from the keyboard
// and returns the number of words in that string.  It uses
// the Keyboard class to get input.
//*******************************************************

import java.util.Scanner;
import java.util.StringTokenizer;

public class WordCounter
{
   //***************************************************
   // The wordCount method accepts any string and returns
   // the number of words it contains.
   //***************************************************
   public static int wordCount (String phrase)
   {
      int count = 0;      // To count the number of words
      String wordToken;   // To hold a word token

      // Tokenize the string
      StringTokenizer tokenizer = new StringTokenizer (phrase);

      // Count the number of tokens
      while (tokenizer.hasMoreTokens())
      {
         wordToken = tokenizer.nextToken();
         count++;
      }

      // Return the number of tokens or words
      return count;
   }

   public static void main (String [] args)
   {
      // Create a scanner object to read from the keyboard.
      Scanner keyboard = new Scanner (System.in);

      // Get a string from the user
      System.out.print("Enter a phrase or sentence:  ");
      String line = keyboard.nextLine();
```

```
        // Count the number of words
        int number = wordCount(line);

        System.out.println("There are " + number + " words in \"" + line +
"\"");
    }
}
```

Program Output

```
Enter a phrase or sentence:  Four score and seven years ago
There are 6 words in "Four score and seven years ago"
```

Programming Challenge 6: Phone Number List

Problem Statement:

Write a program that has two parallel arrays of String objects. One of the arrays should hold people's names and the other should hold their phone numbers. Here are example contents of both arrays.

Name Array Example Contents	Phone Array Example Contents
"Harrison, Rose"	"555-2234"
"James, Jean"	"555-9098"
"Smith, William"	"555-1785"
"Smith, Brad"	"555-9224"

The program should ask the user to enter the name or the first few characters of a name to search for it in the array. The program should display all of the names that match the user's input and their corresponding phone numbers. For example, if the user enters "Smith," the program should display the following names and phone numbers from the list:

Smith, William: 555-1785

Smith, Brad: 555-9224

Solution:

Define What The Program Is To Do

Purpose	To find the names and phone numbers from the list that match the user's input.
Input	A name or first few characters of a name.
Process	Search though the list of names for those that start with the user input.
Output	Display the names and phone numbers from the list that match the user's input.

Pseudocode for PhoneNumberList

1) Create an array containing a list of names.

2) Create an array containing a list of phone numbers corresponding to the names.

3) Get a name to search for from the user.

4) Loop through the name array.

   a) If the name in the name array starts with the user input, print it out along with the corresponding phone number.

Code Listing 8-2 (PhoneNumberList.java)

```
//***********************************************************
// Written by Diane Christie
// Chapter 8
// Programming Challenge 6:  Phone Number List
//***********************************************************

//***********************************************************
// Write a program that has two parallel arrays of String
// objects.  One of the arrays should hold people's names
// and the other should hold their phone numbers.  Here
// are example contents of both arrays.
//Name Array Example Contents    Phone Array Example Contents
//"Harrison, Rose"               "555-2234"
//"James, Jean"                  "555-9098"
//"Smith, William"               "555-1785"
//"Smith, Brad"                  "555-9224"
// The program should ask the user to enter the name or
// the first few characters of a name to search for it in
// the array.  The program should display all of the names
// that match the user's input and their corresponding phone
// numbers.  For example, if the user enters "Smith," the
// program should display the following names and phone
// numbers from the list:
// Smith, William:  555-1785
// Smith, Brad:  555-9224
//***********************************************************

//***********************************************************
// The PhoneNumberList class allows the user to search for
// the phone number of a person on the list by entering
// the name or first few characters of a name.  It displays
// the names and phone numbers of all matches from the list.
//***********************************************************

import java.util.Scanner;

public class PhoneNumberList
{
   public static void main(String [] args)
   {
      // Create a scanner object to read from the keyboard.
      Scanner keyboard = new Scanner(System.in);

      // Create the lists of names and phone numbers
      String [] name = {"Harrison, Rose", "James, Jean",
         "Smith, William", "Smith, Brad"};
      String [] phone = {"555-2234", "555-9098", "555-1785",
         "555-9224"};

      // Get the name from the user
      System.out.print("Enter a name:  ");
```

```
      String str = keyboard.nextLine();

      // loop through the array
      for (int i = 0; i < name.length; i++)
      {
         // print if the name starts with the user input
         if (name[i].startsWith(str))
            System.out.println (name[i] + ":  " + phone[i]);
      }
   }
}
```

Program Output

```
Enter a name:  Smith
Smith, William:  555-1785
Smith, Brad:  555-9224
```

Programming Challenge 10: Word Counter

Problem Statement:

Write a program that asks the user for the name of a file. The program should display the number of words that the file contains.

Solution:

Purpose	**To count the number of words contained in a file.**
Input	**The name of the file.**
Process	**The file is read in one line at a time. The line is tokenized and the number of tokens are counted. The number of words of each line are summed.**
Output	**The total number of words for the file.**

Pseudocode for WordCounter2 Class

1) Modify the main method from WordCount

   a) Initialize the total number of words to 0.

   b) Get the file name.

   c) Read the first line of the file.

   d) While there is more to read in the file,

      i) Use the wordCount method to count the number of words in that line and add it to the total number of words.

      ii) Read another line of the file.

   e) Close the file.

Code Listing 8-3 (WordCounter2.java)

```
//*****************************************************************
// Written by Diane Christie
// Chapter 8
// Programming Challenge 10:  Word Counter
//*****************************************************************

//*****************************************************************
// Write a program that asks the user for the name of a file.
// The program should display the number of words that the
// file contains.
//*****************************************************************
```

```
//*********************************************************
// The WordCounter2 class is a modified version of
// WordCounter from Programming Challenge 2.
//*********************************************************

import java.io.*;
import java.util.Scanner;
import java.util.StringTokenizer;

public class WordCounter2
{
   //*****************************************************
   // The wordCount method accepts any string and returns
   // the number of words it contains.
   //*****************************************************
   public static int wordCount (String phrase)
   {
      int count = 0;    // To count the number of words
      String wordToken;        // To hold a word token
      StringTokenizer tokenizer; //to hold a tokenized string

      // Tokenize the string
      tokenizer = new StringTokenizer (phrase);

      // Count the number of tokens
      while (tokenizer.hasMoreTokens())
      {
         wordToken = tokenizer.nextToken();
         count++;
      }

      // Return the number of tokens or words
      return count;
   }

   public static void main (String [] args) throws IOException
   {
      FileReader input;     //to be able to read from a file
      BufferedReader in;    //to be able to read a line at a time
      String filename;      //to hold the name of the file
      String line;          //to hold one line of the file
      int totalWords = 0;   //to hold the number of words

      // Create a Scanner object to read from the keyboard
      Scanner keyboard = new Scanner (System.in);

      // Get the file name
      System.out.print("Enter the file name:  ");
      filename = keyboard.nextLine();

      // Create objects to be able read from the file
      input = new FileReader (filename);
      in = new BufferedReader(input);

      // Read the first line of the file
      line = in.readLine();

      while (line != null)//continue until the file is empty
      {
         // add the number of words in that line
```

```
            totalWords += wordCount(line);
            // read next line of file
            line = in.readLine();
        }

        // close file
        in.close();

        // display results
        System.out.println(
            "The file contains " + totalWords + " words.");
    }
}
```

Listing of Input file used: Preamble.txt

```
We the people of the United States, in order to form a
more perfect union, establish justice, insure domestic
tranquility, provide for the common defense, promote
the general welfare, and secure the blessings of
liberty to ourselves and our posterity, do ordain and
establish this Constitution for the United States of
America.
```

Program Output

```
Enter the file name:  Preamble.txt
The file contains 52 words.
```

CHAPTER 9

Inheritance

Solutions

- Programming Challenge 4: Essay Class
- Programming Challenge 7: Person and Customer Classes
- Programming Challenge 8: PreferredCustomer Class

Programming Challenge 4: Essay Class

Problem Statement:

Design an Essay class that is derived from the GradedActivity class presented in this chapter. The Essay class should determine the grade a student receives on an essay. The student's essay score can be up to 100 and is determined in the following manner:

Grammar: 30 points

Spelling: 20 points

Correct Length: 20 points

Content: 30 points

Demonstrate the class in a simple program.

Solution:

Define What The Program Is To Do

Purpose	Describe an essay which is a graded activity.	
Fields	grammar	The number of points out of 30 that the student earns for grammar in the essay.
	spelling	The number of points out of 20 that the student earns for spelling in the essay.
	correctLength	The number of points out of 20 that the student earns for the correct length of the essay.
	content	The number of points out of 20 that the student earns for the content of the essay.
Constructor	Essay(double, double, double, double)	Create an Essay object with points assigned for grammar, spelling, correctLength, and content. Total points are assigned to the inherited field score.

Methods	**getGrammar**	**Returns the points earned for grammar in the essay.**
	getSpelling	**Returns the points earned for spelling in the essay.**
	getCorrectLength	**Returns the points earned for the correct length of the essay.**
	getContent	**Returns the points earned for the content of the essay.**

Pseudocode for Essay Class

1) Extend the GradedActivity class. This allows the Essay class to inherit fields and methods of GradedActivity.

   a) The score field which represents a value out of 100 points possible.

   b) The accessor method getScore which returns the value of score.

   c) The mutator method setScore which stores its argument in the score field.

   d) The getGrade method which returns a letter grade based on the scale:

A	90-100
B	80-89
C	70-79
D	60-69
F	0-59

2) Declare the fields.

   a) grammar represents the number of points out of 30 that the student earns for grammar in the essay.

   b) spelling represents the number of points out of 20 that the student earns for spelling in the essay.

   c) correctLength represents the number of points out of 20 that the student earns for the correct length of the essay.

   d) content represents the number of points out of 30 that the student earns for the content of the essay.

3) Define a constructor which accepts four double arguments for grammar, spelling, correctLength, and content, in that order.

   a) Store each argument in the corresponding field.

   b) Call the inherited accessor method setScore to store the sum of the arguments in the inherited field score.

4) Define accessor methods.

   a) getGrammar returns the points earned for grammar in the essay.

   b) getSpelling returns the points earned for spelling in the essay.

   c) getCorrectLength returns the points earned for the correct length of the essay.

   d) getContent returns the points earned for the content of the essay.

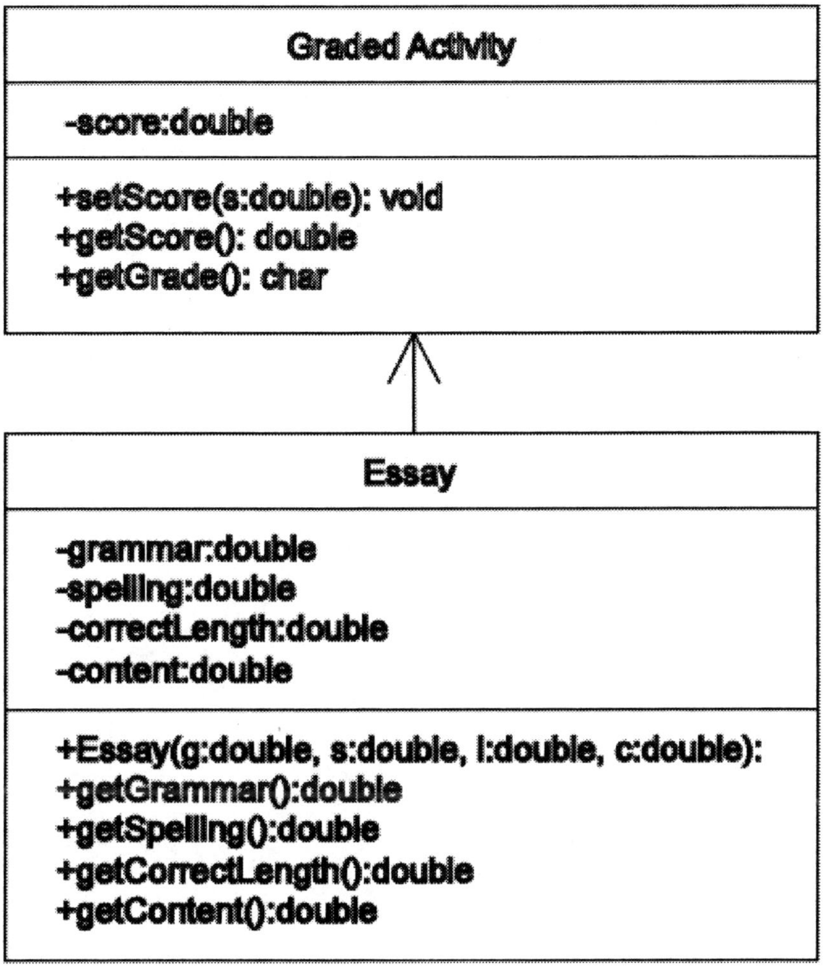

Figure 9-1 UML Drawing for Essay Class

Code Listing 9-1 (Essay.java)

```
//***********************************************************
// Written by Diane Christie
// Chapter 9
// Programming Challenge 4:  Essay Class
//***********************************************************

//***********************************************************
// Design an Essay class that is derived from the
// GradedActivity class presented in this chapter.  The
// Essay class should determine the grade a student receives
// on an essay.  The student's essay score can be up to 100
// and is determined in the following manner:
```

```
// Grammar:  30 points
// Spelling:  20 points
// Correct Length: 20 points
// Content:  30 points
//*******************************************************

//*******************************************************
// The Essay class is a GradedActivity that allows points
// to be assigned for grammar, spelling, correct length,
// and content.
//*******************************************************

public class Essay extends GradedActivity
{
   private double grammar;     //up to 30 points for grammar
   private double spelling;    //up to 20 points for spelling
   private double correctLength;//up to 20 points for length
   private double content;     //up to 30 points for content

   //****************************************************
   // Constructor assigns points for grammar, spelling,
   // correctLength, and content. Total points are assigned
   // to the inherited field score.
   //****************************************************
   public Essay(double g, double s, double l, double c)
   {
      grammar = g;
      spelling = s;
      correctLength = l;
      content = c;
      setScore (grammar + spelling + correctLength + content);
   }

   //****************************************************
   // The getGrammar method returns the points for grammar.
   //****************************************************
   public double getGrammar()
   {
      return grammar;
   }

   //****************************************************
   // The getSpelling method returns the points for spelling.
   //****************************************************
   public double getSpelling()
   {
      return spelling;
   }

   //****************************************************
   // The getCorrectLength method returns the points for
   // the correctLength.
   //****************************************************
      public double getCorrectLength()
   {
      return correctLength;
   }

   //****************************************************
```

```
        // The getContent method returns the points for content.
        //*****************************************************
        public double getContent()
        {
           return content;
        }
     }
```

Solution The EssayDemo Class

Define What The Program Is To Do

Purpose	**To demonstrate the Essay class which is derived from the GradedActivity class**
Input	**The points earned for grammar, spelling, correct length, and content.**
Process	**The points for each component are summed and a grade is assigned.**
Output	**The total number of points and the letter grade.**

Pseudocode for EssayDemo Class

1) Get the points for grammar, spelling, correct length, and content.

2) Create an Essay object.

3) Display results.

Code Listing 9-2 (EssayDemo.java)

```
//*****************************************************
// Written by Diane Christie
// Chapter 9
// Programming Challenge 4:  Essay Class
//*****************************************************

//*****************************************************
// The EssayDemo class demonstrates the Essay class which
// is derived from the GradedActivity class.
//*****************************************************

import java.util.Scanner;

public class EssayDemo
{
   public static void main (String [] args)
   {
      double grammar;      //points for grammar
```

```
      double spelling;  //points for spelling
      double length;    //points for correct length
      double content;      //points for content
      Essay paper;

      //Create a scanner object to read from the keyboard
      Scanner keyboard = new Scanner (System.in);

      //Get points for each component of the student's grade
      System.out.println("How many points did the student earn for");
      System.out.print("     grammar?  ");
      grammar = keyboard.nextDouble();
      System.out.print("     spelling?  ");
      spelling = keyboard.nextDouble();
      System.out.print("     correct length?  ");
      length = keyboard.nextDouble();
      System.out.print("     content?  ");
      content = keyboard.nextDouble();

      //Create an Essay object
      paper = new Essay(grammar, spelling, length, content);

      //Display the results
      System.out.println("The total score is " + paper.getScore());
      System.out.println("The essay grade is " + paper.getGrade());
   }
}
```

Program Output

```
How many points did the student earn for
     grammar?  25
     spelling?  18
     correct length?  20
     content?  23
The total score is 86.0
The essay grade is B
```

Programming Challenge 7: Person and Customer Classes

Problem Statement:

Design a class named Person with fields for holding a person's name, address, and telephone number. Write one or more constructors and the appropriate mutator and accessor methods for the class's fields.

Next, design a class named Customer, which is derived from the Person class. The Customer class should have a field for a customer number and aBoolean field indicating whether the customer wishes to be on a mailing list. Write one or more constructors and the appropriate mutator and accessor methods for the class's fields. Demonstrate an object of the Customer class in a simple program.

Solution The Person Class:

Describe what the program is to do

Purpose	**Describe a person.**	
Fields	**name**	**The name of the person.**
	address	**The address of the person.**
	phone	**The telephone number of the person.**
Constructor	**Person()**	**Create a Person object.**
	Person(String)	**Create a Person object with a name.**
	Person(String, String)	**Create a Person object with a name and address.**
	Person(String, String, String)	**Create a Person object with a name, address, and phone number.**

Methods	getName	Returns the person's name.
	getAddress	Returns the person's address.
	getPhone	Returns the person's phone number.
	setName	Stores the argument in the name field.
	setAddress	Stores the argument in the address field.
	setPhone	Stores the argument in the phone field.

Pseudocode for the Person Class

1) Define constructors.

   a) Default constructor does nothing.

   b) Constructor with one parameter accepts a name.

   c) Constructor with two parameters accepts a name and address.

   d) Constructor with three parameters accepts a name, address, and phone number.

2) Define accessor methods.

   a) The getName method returns the name.

   b) The getAddress method returns the address.

   c) The getPhone method returns the phone.

3) Define mutator methods.

   a) The setName method stores the argument in the name field.

   b) The setAddress method stores the argument in the address field.

   c) The setPhone method stores the argument in the phone field.

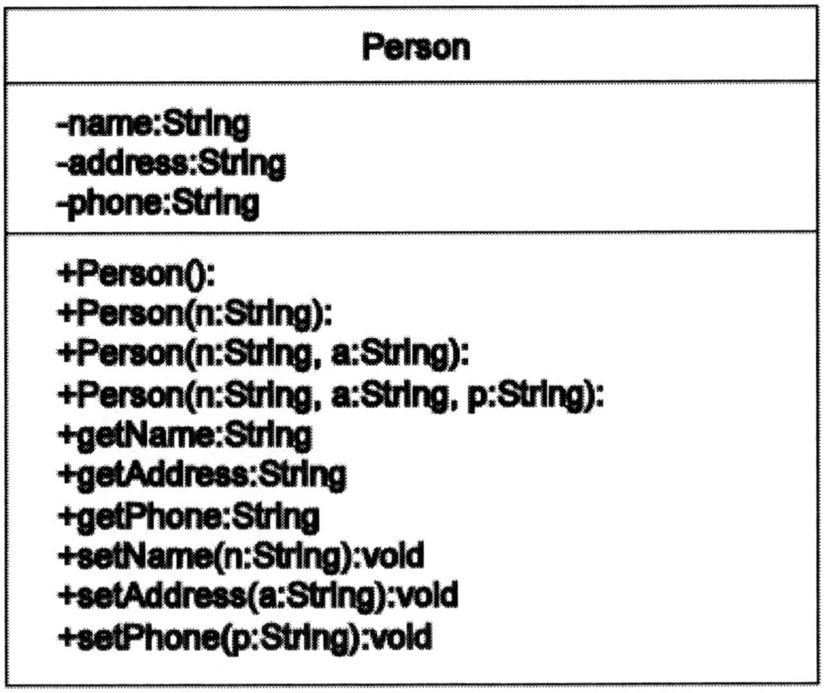

Figure 9-2 UML Drawing for Person Class

Code Listing 9-3 (Person.java)

```
//************************************************************
// Written by Diane Christie
// Chapter 9
// Programming Challenge 7:  Person and Customer Classes
// ***********************************************************

//************************************************************
// Design a class name Person with fields for holding a
// person's name, address, and telephone number.  Write one
// or more constructors and the appropriate mutator and
// accessor methods for the class's fields.
//************************************************************

//************************************************************
// The Person class represents a person by using their
// name, address, and telephone number.
//************************************************************

public class Person
{
   private String name; // The full name
   private String address; // The mailing address
```

```
private String phone;   // The telephone number

//*******************************************************
// Default constructor does nothing
//*******************************************************
public Person ()
{
   ;               // Does nothing
}

//*******************************************************
// Constructor accepts a person's name as an argument.
//*******************************************************
public Person(String n)
{
   name = n;
}

//*******************************************************
// Constructor accepts as arguments the name and address
// of a person, in that order.
//*******************************************************
public Person(String n, String a)
{
   name = n;
   address = a;
}

//*******************************************************
// Constructor accepts as arguments the name, address,
// and phone number of the person, in that order.
//*******************************************************
public Person(String n, String a, String p)
{
   name = n;
   address = a;
   phone = p;
}

//******************************************************
// The getName method returns the name of the person.
//******************************************************
public String getName()
{
   return name;
}

//******************************************************
// The getAddress method returns the address of the person.
//******************************************************
public String getAddress()
{
   return address;
}

//******************************************************
// The getPhone method returns the phone number of the
// person.
//******************************************************
```

```
   public String getPhone()
   {
      return phone;
   }

   //*****************************************************
   // The setName method stores its argument in the name
   // field.
   //*****************************************************
   public void setName (String n)
   {
      name = n;
   }

   //*****************************************************
   // The setAddress method stores its argument in the
   // address field.
   //*****************************************************
   public void setAddress (String a)
   {
      address = a;
   }

   //*****************************************************
   // The setPhone method stores its argument in the phone
   // field.
   //*****************************************************
   public void setPhone (String p)
   {
      phone = p;
   }

}
```

Solution The Customer Class

Describe what the program is to do

Purpose	**Describe a customer.**	
Fields	**currentNumber**	**A static variable initialized to 1, that will count the number of customers, thereby allowing each customer to have a different number.**
	customerNumber	**The unique number for a customer.**
	onMailingList	**True if the customer is on the mailing list, false if the customer is not.**

Constructor	**Customer()**	**Create a Customer object. Customer will not be on the mailing list.**
	Customer(String)	**Create a Customer object with a name. Customer will not be on the mailing list.**
	Customer(String,String)	**Create a Customer object with a name and address. Customer will be on the mailing list.**
	Customer(String, String, String)	**Create a Customer object with a name, address, and phone number. Customer will be on the mailing list.**
	Customer(String, String, String, boolean)	**Create a Customer object with a name, address, phone number, and mailing list option.**
Methods	**getCustomerNumber**	**Returns the customer's unique number.**
	getOnMailingList	**Returns true if the customer is on the mailing list, false if not.**
	changeOnMailingList	**allows the user to be removed from the mailing list if he or she is currently on it, or to be added to the mailing list, if he or she is not currently on it.**

Pseudocode for the Customer Class

1) Extend the Person Class. This allows the Customer class to inherit the fields and methods of the Person Class.

   a) The name field represents a customer's full name.

   b) The address field represents the customer's address.

   c) The phone field represents the customer's phone number.

   d) The accessor methods, getName, getAddress, and getPhone return the value stored in the corresponding field.

   e) The mutator methods, setName, setAddress, and setPhone, store the argument in the corresponding field.

2) Declare fields.

a) currentNumber is a static variable that counts the number of customers, thereby allowing each customer to have a unique number.

b) customerNumber is the unique number assigned to each customer.

c) onMailingList is true if the customer is on the mailing list, false if not.

3) Define constructors.

a) Default constructor Customer()

i) Calls the default super constructor.

ii) Sets onMailingList to false.

iii) Assigns the currentNumber to the customerNumber.

iv) Increments currentNumber since the number has already been used.

b) Constructor Customer(String)

i) Passes its argument on to the super constructor to store the customer's name.

ii) Sets onMailingList to false since there is no address.

iii) Assigns the currentNumber to the customerNumber.

iv) Increments currentNumber since the number has already been used.

c) Constructor Customer(String, String)

i) Passes its arguments on to the super constructor to store the customer's name and address.

ii) Sets onMailingList to true since there is an address.

iii) Assigns the currentNumber to the customerNumber.

iv) Increments currentNumber since the number has already been used.

d) Constructor Customer(String, String, String)

i) Passes its arguments on to the super constructor to store the customer's name, address, and phone number.

ii) Sets onMailingList to true since there is an address.

iii) Assigns the currentNumber to the customerNumber.

iv) Increments currentNumber since the number has already been used.

e) Constructor Customer(String, String, String, boolean)

i) Passes its first three arguments on to the super constructor to store the customer's name, address, and phone number.

ii) Sets onMailingList to the last argument.

iii) Assigns the currentNumber to the customerNumber.

iv) Increments currentNumber since the number has already been used.

f) Accessor Methods

i) getCustomerNumber returns the customer's unique number.

ii) getOnMailingList returns true if the customer is on the mailing list, false if not.

g) Mutator Methods

i) changeOnMailingList uses the NOT operator ! to swap the state of onMailingList.

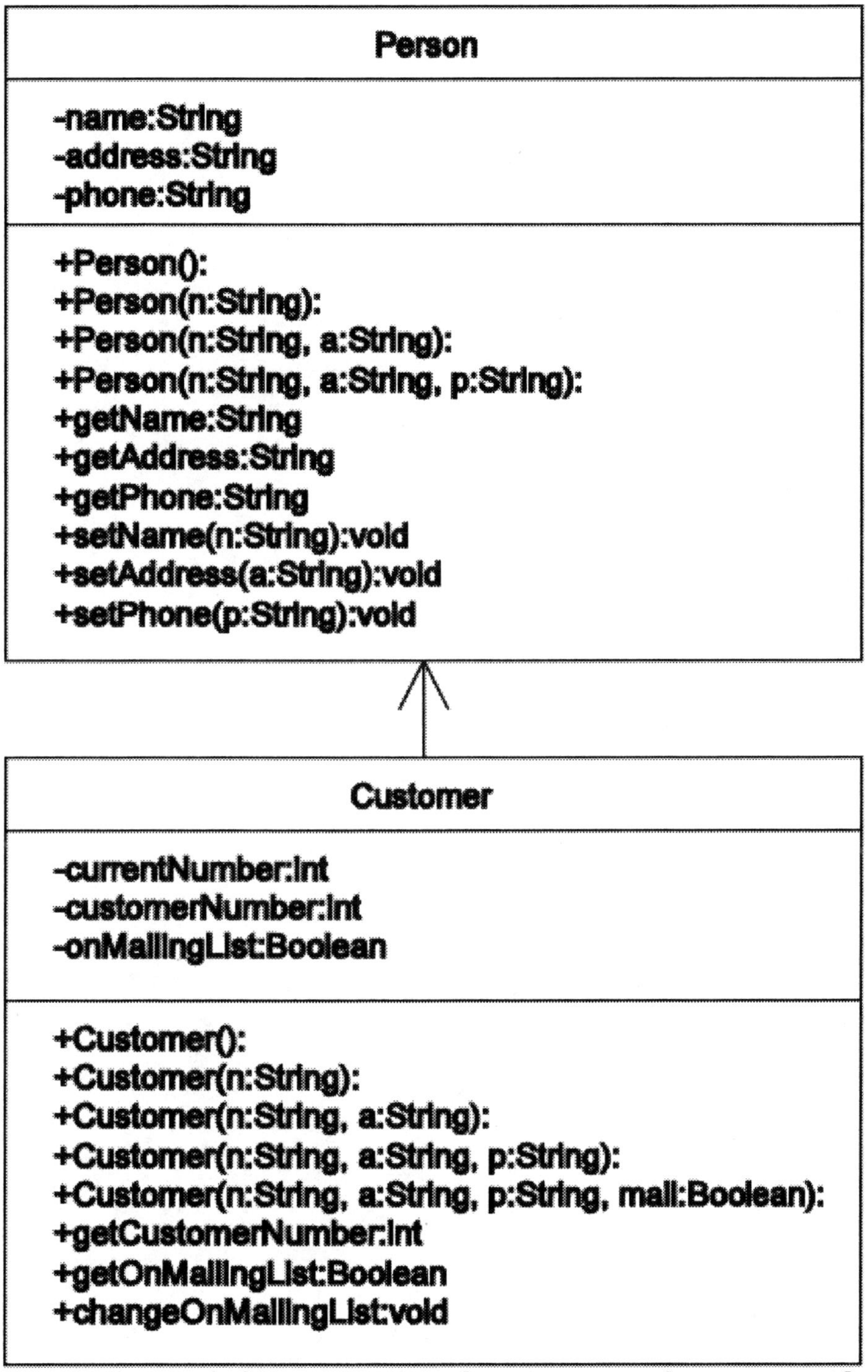

Figure 9-3 UML Drawing for Person and Customer Classes

Code Listing 9-4 (Customer.java)

```
//***********************************************************
// Written by Diane Christie
// Chapter 9
// Programming Challenge 7:  Person and Customer Classes
// **********************************************************

//***********************************************************
// Design a class named Customer, which is derived from the
// Person class.  The Customer class should have a field for
// a customer number and aBoolean filed indicating whether
// the customer is wishes to be on a mailing list.  Write one
// or more constructors and the appropriate mutator and
// accessor methods for the class's fields.
//***********************************************************

//***********************************************************
// The Customer class is derived from the Person class.  It
// represents a customer by assigning them a customer number
// and allowing them to be on a mailing list.
//***********************************************************

public class Customer extends Person
{
   //class variable assures that each customer is counted
   //each customer should have a different customer number.
   private static int currentNumber = 1;

   //this customer's individual customer number
   private int customerNumber;

   //true if customer wants to be on the mailing list
   private boolean onMailingList;

   //******************************************************
   // Default constructor assigns a customer number only.
   //******************************************************
   public Customer()
   {
      super();
      onMailingList = false;
      customerNumber = currentNumber;
      currentNumber++;
   }

   //******************************************************
   // Constructor accepts a person's name as an argument.
   //******************************************************
   public Customer (String n)
   {
      super (n);
      onMailingList = false;
      customerNumber = currentNumber;
      currentNumber++;
   }

   //******************************************************
```

```
// Constructor accepts as arguments the name and address
// of a person, in that order.
//*****************************************************
public Customer (String n, String a)
{
   super(n,a);
   onMailingList = true;
   customerNumber = currentNumber;
   currentNumber++;
}

//*****************************************************
// Constructor accepts as arguments the name, address,
// and phone number of the person, in that order.
//*****************************************************
public Customer(String n, String a, String p)
{
   super(n, a, p);
   onMailingList = true;
   customerNumber = currentNumber;
   currentNumber++;
}

//*****************************************************
// Constructor accepts as arguments the name, address,
// and phone number of the person, in that order, followed
// by a choice to be added to the mailing list or not.
//*****************************************************
public Customer(String n, String a, String p, boolean m)
{
   super(n, a, p);
   onMailingList = m;
   customerNumber = currentNumber;
   currentNumber++;
}

//*****************************************************
// The getCustomerNumber method returns the unique number
// for that customer.
//*****************************************************
public int getCustomerNumber()
{
   return customerNumber;
}

//*****************************************************
// The getOnMailingList method returns true if the
// customer's name is on the mailing list, false if it is
// not.
//*****************************************************
public boolean getOnMailingList()
{
   return onMailingList;
}

//*****************************************************
// The changeOnMailingList method allows the user to be
// removed from the mailing list if he/she is currently
// on it, or to be added to the mailing list, if he/she
```

```
        // is not currently on it.
        //*****************************************************
        public void changeOnMailingList()
        {
           onMailingList = !onMailingList;
        }
    }
```

Solution The CustomerDemo Class:

Define What The Program Is To Do

Purpose	Demonstrate the Customer class
Input	None.
Process	Create several customers and use accessor and mutator methods.
Output	Display the customer information.

Pseudocode for CustomerDemo class

1) Create a customer using the default constructor.

2) Use the mutator methods to store the name, address, and phone number.

3) Display all customer information.

4) Create another customer using the constructor that takes a name, address, and phone number.

5) Display all customer information.

6) Use the mutator method to remove this customer from the mailing list.

7) Display mailing list information.

8) Create another customer using the contructor that takes a name, address, phone number, and mailing list option.

9) Display all customer information.

Code Listing 9-5 (CustomerDemo.java)

```
//**********************************************************
// Written by Diane Christie
// Chapter 9
// Programming Challenge 7:  Person and Customer Classes
// *********************************************************

//**********************************************************
// Demonstrate the Customer class.
//**********************************************************

public class CustomerDemo
{
   public static void main(String [] args)
   {
      //Create a customer
      Customer customer1 = new Customer ();
      customer1.setName("John Brown");
      customer1.setAddress("465 Maple Dr., New York, NY");
      customer1.setPhone("555-1234");

      //Display customer information
      System.out.println("Customer number " +
            Customer1.getCustomerNumber());
      System.out.println(customer1.getName());
      System.out.println(customer1.getAddress());
      System.out.println(customer1.getPhone());
      if (customer1.getOnMailingList())
         System.out.println("Customer number " +
            customer1.getCustomerNumber() +
            " is on the mailing list");
      else
         System.out.println("Customer number " +
            customer1.getCustomerNumber() +
            " is not on the mailing list");
      System.out.println();


      //Create another customer
      Customer customer2 = new Customer("Sue Green",
         "9005 Pine Lane, Los Angeles, CA", "765-4444");

      //Display customer information
      System.out.println("Customer number " +
            customer2.getCustomerNumber());
      System.out.println(customer2.getName());
      System.out.println(customer2.getAddress());
      System.out.println(customer2.getPhone());
      if (customer2.getOnMailingList())
         System.out.println("Customer number " +
            customer2.getCustomerNumber() +
            " is on the mailing list");
      else
         System.out.println("Customer number " +
            customer2.getCustomerNumber() +
            " is not on the mailing list");
      System.out.println();
```

```
            //Take customer2 off the mailing list.
            customer2.changeOnMailingList();
            System.out.println("Removing from the mailing list");
            System.out.println();

            //Display change
            if (customer2.getOnMailingList())
               System.out.println("Customer number " +
                  customer2.getCustomerNumber() +
                  " is on the mailing list");
            else
               System.out.println("Customer number " +
                  customer2.getCustomerNumber() +
            " is not on the mailing list");
            System.out.println();

            //Create another customer
            Customer customer3 = new Customer("Paul Jones",
               "123 Oak Rd., Allentown, PA", "123-4567", false);

            //Display customer information
            System.out.println("Customer number " +
                  customer3.getCustomerNumber());
            System.out.println(customer3.getName());
            System.out.println(customer3.getAddress());
            System.out.println(customer3.getPhone());
            if (customer3.getOnMailingList())
               System.out.println("Customer number " +
                  customer3.getCustomerNumber() +
                  " is on the mailing list");
            else
               System.out.println("Customer number " +
                  customer3.getCustomerNumber() +
                  " is not on the mailing list");
            System.out.println();
      }
   }
```

Program Output

```
Customer number 1
John Brown
465 Maple Dr., New York, NY
555-1234
Customer number 1 is not on the mailing list

Customer number 2
Sue Green
9005 Pine Lane, Los Angeles, CA
765-4444
Customer number 2 is on the mailing list

Removing from the mailing list

Customer number 2 is not on the mailing list

Customer number 3
Paul Jones
123 Oak Rd., Allentown, PA
123-4567
Customer number 3 is not on the mailing list
```

Programming Challenge 8: PreferredCustomer Class

Problem Statement:

A retail store has a preferred customer plan where customers can earn discounts on all their purchases. The amount of a customer's discount is determined by the amount of the customer's cumulative purchases in the store, as follows:

- When a preferred customer spends $500, he or she gets a 5% discount on all future purchases.
- When a preferred customer spends $1,000, he or she gets a 6% discount on all future purchases.
- When a preferred customer spends $1,500, he or she gets a 7% discount on all future purchases.
- When a preferred customer spends $2,000 or more, he or she gets a 10% discount on all future purchases.

Design a class named Preferred Customer, which is derived from the Customer class you created in Programming Challenge 7. The PreferredCustomer class should have fields for the amount of the customer's purchases and the customer's discount level. Write one or more constructors and the appropriate mutator and accessor methods for the class's fields. Demonstrate the class in a simple program.

Solution PreferredCustomer Class

Define What The Program Is To Do

Purpose	**Describe a preferred customer.**	
Fields	**purchases**	**The cumulative purchases made by the customer in the store.**
	discountRate	**The discount rate the customer has earned.**

Constructor	PreferredCustomer( )	Create a PreferredCustomer object. This customer is not on the mailing list.
	PreferredCustomer(String)	Create a PreferredCustomer object with a name. This customer is not on the mailing list.
	PreferredCustomer(String,String)	Create a PreferredCustomer object with a name and address. This customer is on the mailing list.
	PreferredCustomer(String, String, String)	Create a PreferredCustomer object with a name, address, and phone number. This customer is on the mailing list.
	PreferredCustomer(String, String, String, boolean)	Create a PreferredCustomer object with a name, address, phone number, and mailing list option.
Methods	getPurchases	Returns the amount of purchases.
	getDiscountRate	Returns the discountRate the customer receives on all future purchases

Pseudocode for the PreferredCustomer Class

1) Extend the Customer Class. This allows the PreferredCustomer class to inherit the fields and methods of the Customer Class and the Person class.

   a) The name field represents a customer's full name.

   b) The address field represents the customer's address.

   c) The phone field represents the customer's phone number.

   d) The currentNumber field is a static variable that counts the number of customers, thereby allowing each customer to have a unique number.

   e) The customerNumber field is the unique number assigned to each customer.

   f) The onMailingList field is true if the customer is on the mailing list, false if not.

   g) The accessor methods, getName, getAddress, getPhone, getCusotmerNumber, and getOnMailingList return the value stored in the corresponding field.

h) The mutator methods, setName, setAddress, and setPhone, store the argument in the corresponding field. The mutator method changeOnMailingList uses the NOT operator ! to swap the state of onMailingList.

2) Declare fields.

a) purchases represents the customer's cumulative purchases in the store.

b) discountRate represents the percent discount the customer receives on all future purchases.

3) Define constructors.

a) Default constructor PreferredCustomer()

i) Calls the default super constructor. The default super constructor is the default constructor of the Customer class, which then calls the default constructor of the Person class.

ii) Initializes purchases and discountRate to 0.

b) Constructor Customer(String)

i) Passes its argument on to the super constructor to store the customer's name. The super constructor is the constructor of the Customer class, which then calls the constructor of the Person class.

ii) Initializes purchases and discountRate to 0.

c) Constructor Customer(String, String)

i) Passes its arguments on to the super constructor to store the customer's name and address. The super constructor is the constructor of the Customer class, which then calls the constructor of the Person class.

ii) Initializes purchases and discountRate to 0.

d) Constructor Customer(String, String, String)

i) Passes its arguments on to the super constructor to store the customer's name, address, and phone number. The super constructor is the constructor of the Customer class, which then calls the constructor of the Person class.

ii) Initializes purchases and discountRate to 0.

e) Constructor Customer(String, String, String, boolean)

i) Passes its first three arguments on to the super constructor to store the customer's name, address, and phone number. The super constructor is the constructor of the Customer class, which then calls the constructor of the Person class.

ii) Initializes purchases and discountRate to 0.

4) Accessor Methods

i) getPurchases returns the customer's cumulative in store purchases.

ii) getDiscountRate returns the customer's discount percentage on all future purchases.

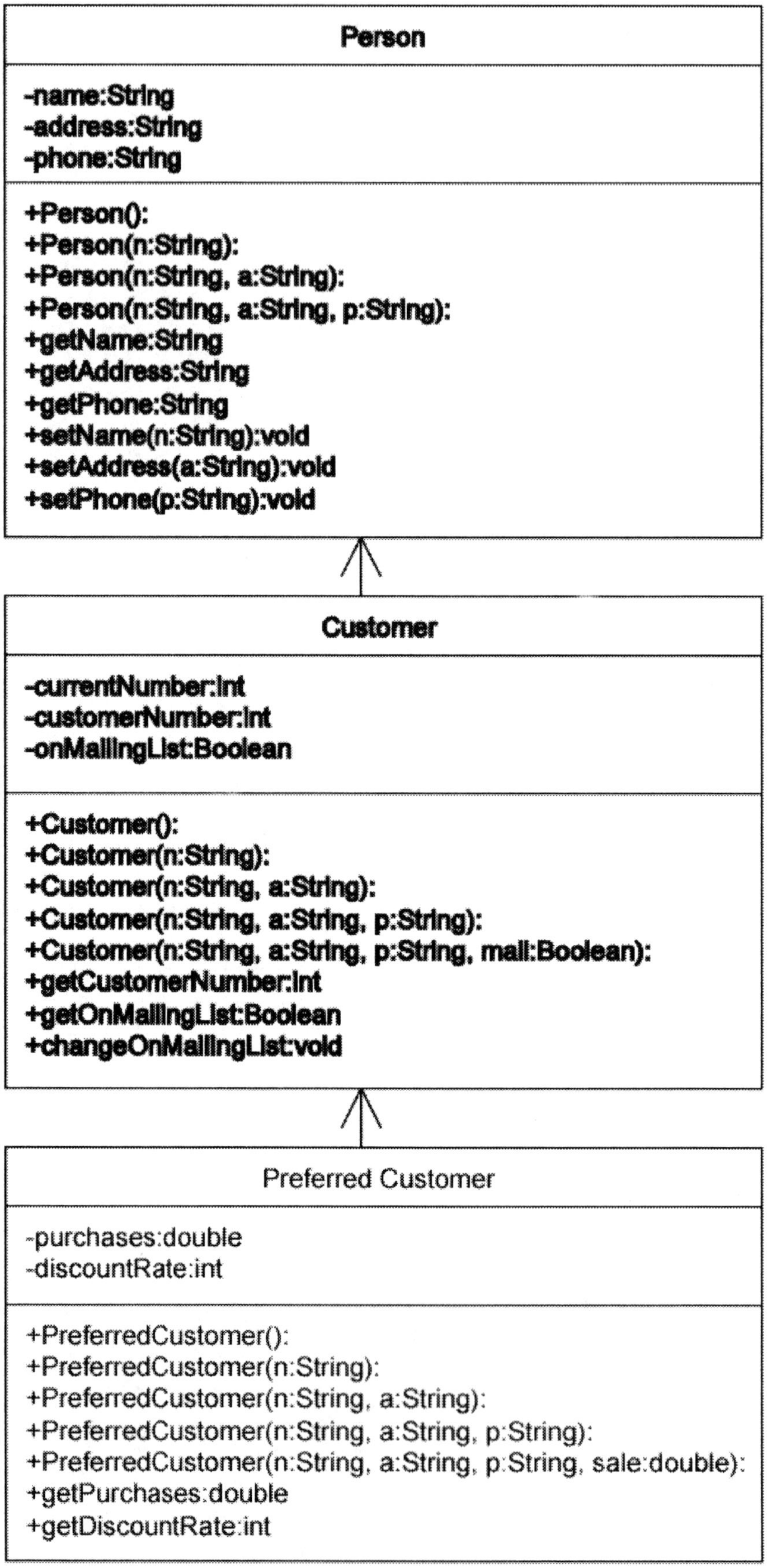
Person
-name:String
-address:String
-phone:String
+Person():
+Person(n:String):
+Person(n:String, a:String):
+Person(n:String, a:String, p:String):
+getName:String
+getAddress:String
+getPhone:String
+setName(n:String):void
+setAddress(a:String):void
+setPhone(p:String):void
Customer
-currentNumber:int
-customerNumber:int
-onMailingList:Boolean
+Customer():
+Customer(n:String):
+Customer(n:String, a:String):
+Customer(n:String, a:String, p:String):
+Customer(n:String, a:String, p:String, mail:Boolean):
+getCustomerNumber:int
+getOnMailingList:Boolean
+changeOnMailingList:void
Preferred Customer
-purchases:double
-discountRate:int
+PreferredCustomer():
+PreferredCustomer(n:String):
+PreferredCustomer(n:String, a:String):
+PreferredCustomer(n:String, a:String, p:String):
+PreferredCustomer(n:String, a:String, p:String, sale:double):
+getPurchases:double
+getDiscountRate:int

Figure 9-4 UML Drawing for Preferred Customer Class

Code Listing 9-6 (PreferredCustomer.java)

```
//***********************************************************
// Written by Diane Christie
// Chapter 9
// Programming Challenge 8:  PreferredCustomer Class
// **********************************************************

//***********************************************************
// A retail store has a preferred customer plan where
// customers can earn discounts on all their purchases.  The
// amount of a customer's discount is determined by the amount
// of the customer's cumulative purchases in the store, as
// follows:
// ·  When a preferred customer spends $500, he or she gets
//    a 5% discount on all future purchases.
// ·  When a preferred customer spends $1,000, he or she
//    gets a 6% discount on all future purchases.
// ·  When a preferred customer spends $1,500, he or she gets
//    a 7% discount on all future purchases.
// ·  When a preferred customer spends $2,000 or more, he or
// she gets a 10% discount on all future purchases.
// Design a class named Preferred Customer, which is derived
// from the Customer class you created in Programming
// Challenge 7. The PreferredCustomer class should have fields
// for the amount of the customer's purchases and the
// customer's discount level.  Write one or more constructors
// and the appropriate mutator and accessor methods for the
// class's fields.  Demonstrate the class in a simple program.
//***********************************************************

//***********************************************************
// The PreferredCustomer class is derived from the Customer
// class.  It represents a preferred customer by assigning
// them a discount percentage based on cumulative purchases.
//***********************************************************

public class PreferredCustomer extends Customer
{
   //cumulative in store purchases
   private double purchases;
   //percentage discount on future purchases;
   private int discountRate;


   //********************************************************
   // Default constructor assigns a customer number only.
   //********************************************************
   public PreferredCustomer()
   {
      super();
      purchases = 0;
      discountRate = 0;
   }
```

```
//*****************************************************
// Constructor accepts a person's name as an argument.
//*****************************************************
public PreferredCustomer (String n)
{
   super (n);
   purchases = 0;
   discountRate = 0;
}

//*****************************************************
// Constructor accepts as arguments the name and address
// of a person, in that order.
//*****************************************************
public PreferredCustomer (String n, String a)
{
   super(n,a);
   purchases = 0;
   discountRate = 0;
}

//*****************************************************
// Constructor accepts as arguments the name, address,
// and phone number of the person, in that order.
//*****************************************************
public PreferredCustomer(String n, String a, String p)
{
   super(n, a, p);
   purchases = 0;
   discountRate = 0;
}

//*****************************************************
// Constructor accepts as arguments the name, address,
// and phone number of the person, in that order, followed
// by a choice to be added to the mailing list or not.
//*****************************************************
public PreferredCustomer(String n, String a, String p,
   boolean m)
{
   super(n, a, p);
   purchases = 0;
   discountRate = 0;
}

//*****************************************************
// Constructor accepts as arguments the name, address,
// and phone number of the person, in that order, followed
// by the amount of purchases.
//*****************************************************
public PreferredCustomer(String n, String a, String p,
   double amount)
{
   super(n, a, p, true); //automatically on mailing list
   purchases = amount;
   //discountRate according to preferred customer plan
   if (purchases <500)
      discountRate = 0;
```

```
      else if (purchases < 1000)
         discountRate = 5;
      else if (purchases < 1500)
         discountRate = 6;
      else if (purchases < 2000)
         discountRate = 7;
      else
         discountRate = 10;
   }

   //*****************************************************
   // The getPurchases method returns the cumulative amount
   // of in store purchases.
   //*****************************************************
   public double getPurchases()
   {
      return purchases;
   }

   //*****************************************************
   // The getDiscountRate method returns the discount rate
   // on all future purchases..
   //*****************************************************
   public int getDiscountRate()
   {
      return discountRate;
   }

}
```

Solution The PreferredCustomerDemo Class:

Define what the program is to do

Purpose	**To demonstrate the PreferredCustomer class.**
Input	**None.**
Process	**Create several customers at different purchase levels.**
Output	**Display customer information.**

Pseudocode for PreferredCustomerDemo Class

10) Create a DecimalFormat object to be used to display purchases to look like money.

11) Create a PreferredCustomer using constructor which takes in name, address, phone number, and amount of purchases.

12) Display information on that customer using accessor methods.

13) Create other PreferredCustomers with the same process, but at different purchase levels.

14) Display information about these customers.

Code Listing 9-7 (PreferredCustomerDemo.java)

```
//***********************************************************
// Written by Diane Christie
// Chapter 9
// Programming Challenge 8:  PreferredCustomer Class
// **********************************************************

//***********************************************************
// Demonstrate the PreferredCustomer class.
//***********************************************************
import java.text.DecimalFormat;

public class PreferredCustomerDemo
{
   public static void main(String [] args)
   {
      //Declare a DecimalFormat object to look like money.
      DecimalFormat money = new DecimalFormat("#,##0.00");

      //Create a customer
      PreferredCustomer customer1;
      customer1 = new PreferredCustomer ("John Brown",
         "465 Maple Dr.,New York, NY", "555-1234", 1555.25);
      //Display customer information
      System.out.println(customer1.getName());
      System.out.println(customer1.getAddress());
      System.out.println(customer1.getPhone());
      System.out.println("Cumulative purchases:  $" +
         money.format(customer1.getPurchases()));
      System.out.println("DiscountRate:  " +
         customer1.getDiscountRate()  + "%");
      if (customer1.getOnMailingList())
         System.out.println("Customer number " +
            customer1.getCustomerNumber() +
            " is on the mailing list");
      else
         System.out.println("Customer number " +
            customer1.getCustomerNumber() +
            " is not on the mailing list");
      System.out.println();

      PreferredCustomer customer2;
      customer2 = new PreferredCustomer ("Sue Green",
         "9005 Pine Lane, Los Angeles, CA", "765-4444", 500);

      //Display customer information
      System.out.println(customer2.getName());
      System.out.println(customer2.getAddress());
      System.out.println(customer2.getPhone());
```

```
        System.out.println("Cumulative purchases:  $" +
           money.format(customer2.getPurchases()));
        System.out.println("DiscountRate:  " +
           customer2.getDiscountRate()  + "%");
        if (customer2.getOnMailingList())
           System.out.println("Customer number " +
              customer2.getCustomerNumber() +
              " is on the mailing list");
        else
           System.out.println("Customer number " +
              customer2.getCustomerNumber() +
              " is not on the mailing list");
        System.out.println();

        //Create another customer
        PreferredCustomer customer3;
        customer3= new PreferredCustomer("Paul Jones",
           "123 Oak Rd., Allentown, PA", "123-4567", 1489.75);

        //Display customer information
        System.out.println("Customer number " +
              customer3.getCustomerNumber());
        System.out.println(customer3.getName());
        System.out.println(customer3.getAddress());
        System.out.println(customer3.getPhone());
        System.out.println("Cumulative purchases:  $" +
           money.format(customer3.getPurchases()));
        System.out.println("DiscountRate:  " +
           customer3.getDiscountRate() + "%");
        if (customer3.getOnMailingList())
           System.out.println("Customer number " +
              customer3.getCustomerNumber() +
              " is on the mailing list");
        else
           System.out.println("Customer number " +
              customer3.getCustomerNumber() +
              " is not on the mailing list");
        System.out.println();
    }
}
```

Program Output

```
John Brown
465 Maple Dr.,New York, NY
555-1234
Cumulative purchases:  $1,555.25
DiscountRate:  7%
Customer number 1 is on the mailing list

Sue Green
9005 Pine Lane, Los Angeles, CA
765-4444
Cumulative purchases:  $500.00
DiscountRate:  5%
Customer number 2 is on the mailing list

Customer number 3
Paul Jones
123 Oak Rd., Allentown, PA
123-4567
Cumulative purchases:  $1,489.75
DiscountRate:  6%
Customer number 3 is on the mailing list
```

CHAPTER 10

Exceptions and More about Stream I/O

Solutions

- Programming Challenge 1: TestScores Class
- Programming Challenge 2: TestScores Class Custom Exception
- Programming Challenge 4: Month Class Exceptions
- Programming Challenge 7: File Encryption Filter
- Programming Challenge 8: File Decryption Filter

Programming Challenge 1: TestScores Class

Problem Statement:

Write a class named TestScores. The class constructor should accept an array of test scores as its argument. The class should have a method that returns the average of the test scores. If any test score in the array is negative or greater than 100, the class should throw an IllegalArgumentException. Demonstrate the class in a program.

Solution The TestScores Class:

Define What The Program Is To Do

Purpose	**Find the average of a list of valid test scores.**	
Fields	**average**	**The arithmetic average of the scores in the array passed to the constructor.**
Constructor	**TestScores(double[])**	**Create a TestScores object by calculating the average of the scores in the array argument if they are valid.**
Methods	**getAverage**	**Returns the average.**

Pseudocode for TestScores Class

1) Declare the field named average .

2) Define a constructor

   a) It accepts an array of doubles.

   b) As it is looping through the array, it should validate each score. If the score is invalid, it should throw an IllegalArgumentException. Else, add it to the total.

   c) Calculate and store the average.

3) Define accessor methods.

   a) getAverage returns the average.

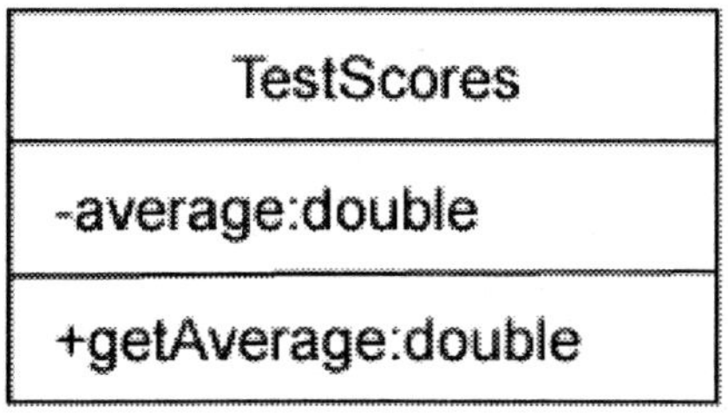

Figure 10-1 UML Drawing for TestScores Class

Code Listing 10-1 (TestScores.java)

```
//**********************************************************
// Written by Diane Christie
// Chapter 10
// Programming Challenge 1:  TestScores Class
//**********************************************************

//**********************************************************
// Write a class named TestScores.  The class constructor
// should accept an array of test scores as its argument.
// The class should have a method that returns the average
// of the test scores.  If any test score in the array is
// negative or greater than 100, the class should throw an
// IllegalArgumentException.  Demonstrate the class in a
// program.
//**********************************************************

//**********************************************************
// The TestScores class throws an IllegalArgumentException
// if a test score is not between 0 and 100, otherwise it
// calculates the average of a set of test scores.
//**********************************************************

public class TestScores
{
   private double average; //the average of the scores
                     //in the array passed into
                     //the constructor
   //******************************************************
   // Constructor accepts an array of test scores.  Each
   // test score in the array is checked for validity.  A
   // valid test score is between 0 and 100.  If the score
   // is valid, it is added to the total.  When all scores
   // are summed, the average is calculated.
   //******************************************************
   public TestScores(double [] data)
   {
      double total = 0;
      for (int i = 0; i < data.length; i++)
      {
         if (data[i] < 0 || data[i] > 100)
         {
```

```
                  throw new IllegalArgumentException("Invalid "
                     + "test score.  Scores must be between "
                     + "0 and 100");
               }
               else //if score is valid, add to sum
               {
                  total += data[i];
               }
            }
            average = total/data.length;
         }

         //*************************************************
         // The getAverage method returns the average of the
         // test scores in the array.
         //*************************************************
         public double getAverage()
         {
            return average;
         }
      }
```

Solution The TestScoresDemo Class

Define What The Program Is To Do

Purpose	**To demonstrate the TestScores class.**
Input	**None.**
Process	**Validate scores and calculate the average if all scores are valid.**
Output	**The scores and the average.**

Pseudocode for TestScoresDemo Class

1) Create an array with valid data.

2) Create an array with a negative score.

3) Create an array with a score over 100.

4) Print the scores from the first array.

5) Try

   a) Create a TestScores object with the first array. This may generate an exception if the scores in the array are not valid.

   b) Print the average.

6) Catch any IllegalArgumentExceptions generated.

7) Print the scores from the second array.

8) Try

   a) Create a TestScores object with the second array. This may generate an exception if the scores in the array are not valid.

   b) Print the average.

9) Catch any IllegalArgumentExceptions generated.

10) Print the scores from the third array.

11) Try

   a) Create a TestScores object with the third array. This may generate an exception if the scores in the array are not valid.

   b) Print the average.

12) Catch any IllegalArgumentExceptions generated.

Code Listing 10-2 (TestScoresDemo.java)

```
//*********************************************************
// Written by Diane Christie
// Chapter 10
// Programming Challenge 1:  TestScores Class
//*********************************************************

//*********************************************************
// Write a class named TestScores.  The class constructor
// should accept an array of test scores as its argument.
// The class should have a method that returns the average
// of the test scores.  If any test score in the array is
// negative or greater than 100, the class should throw an
// IllegalArgumentException.  Demonstrate the class in a
// program.
//*********************************************************

//*********************************************************
// TestScoresDemo demonstrates the TestScores class.
//*********************************************************

import java.text.DecimalFormat;

public class TestScoresDemo
{
   public static void main(String [] args)
   {
      double [] cs1 = {75,88,99,83,94,100,93};
      double [] cs2 = {85,-9, 73,98};
      double [] cs3 = {99, 100, 101};
      double ave;
      DecimalFormat oneDecimal = new DecimalFormat("0.0");
```

```
//*************************************
// Print out test scores from first group
//*************************************
for (int i = 0; i < cs1.length; i++)
{
   System.out.print(cs1[i]);
   //put commas between numbers if more are left
   if(i < cs1.length - 1)
      System.out.print(", ");
}
System.out.println();

//This may generate an exception if a score is
//negative or greater than 100.
try
{
   TestScores test1 = new TestScores(cs1);
   ave = test1.getAverage();
   System.out.println("The average score is "+
       oneDecimal.format(ave));
   System.out.println();
}
catch(IllegalArgumentException e)
{
   System.out.println(e.getMessage());
   System.out.println();
}

//**************************************
// Print out test scores from second group
//**************************************
for (int i = 0; i < cs2.length; i++)
{
   System.out.print(cs2[i]);
   //put commas between numbers if more are left
   if(i < cs2.length - 1)
      System.out.print(", ");
}
System.out.println();
//This may generate an exception if a score is
//negative or greater than 100.
try
{
   TestScores test1 = new TestScores(cs2);
   ave = test1.getAverage();
   System.out.println("The average score is "+
       oneDecimal.format(ave));
   System.out.println();
}
catch(IllegalArgumentException e)
{
   System.out.println(e.getMessage());
   System.out.println();
}

//**************************************
// Print out test scores from third group
//**************************************
```

```
      for (int i = 0; i < cs3.length; i++)
      {
         System.out.print(cs3[i]);
         //put commas between numbers if more are left
         if(i < cs3.length - 1)
            System.out.print(", ");
      }
      System.out.println();
      //This may generate an exception if a score is
      //negative or greater than 100.
      try
      {
         TestScores test1 = new TestScores(cs3);
         ave = test1.getAverage();
         System.out.println("The average score is "+
             oneDecimal.format(ave));
         System.out.println();
      }
      catch(IllegalArgumentException e)
      {
         System.out.println(e.getMessage());
         System.out.println();
      }
   }
}
```

Program Output

```
75.0, 88.0, 99.0, 83.0, 94.0, 100.0, 93.0
The average score is 90.3

85.0, 73.0, 98.0, -4.0
Invalid test score.  Scores must be between 0 and 100

99.0, 100.0, 101.0
Invalid test score.  Scores must be between 0 and 100
```

Programming Challenge 2: TestScores Class Custom Exception

Problem Statement:

Write an exception class named InvalidTestScore. Modify the TestScores class you wrote in Programming Challenge 1 so it throws and InvalidTestScore exception if any of the test scores in the array are invalid.

Solution The InvalidTestScore Class:

Describe what the program is to do

Purpose	**Describe an InvalidTestScore which is an Exception class.**	
Fields	**None (message field is inherited from Exception).**	
Constructor	**InvalidTestScore ()**	**Create an InvalidTestScore object.**
Methods	**None (getMessage is inherited from Exception).**	

Pseudocode for the InvalidTestScore Class

1) Define a default constructor that calls the super constructor.

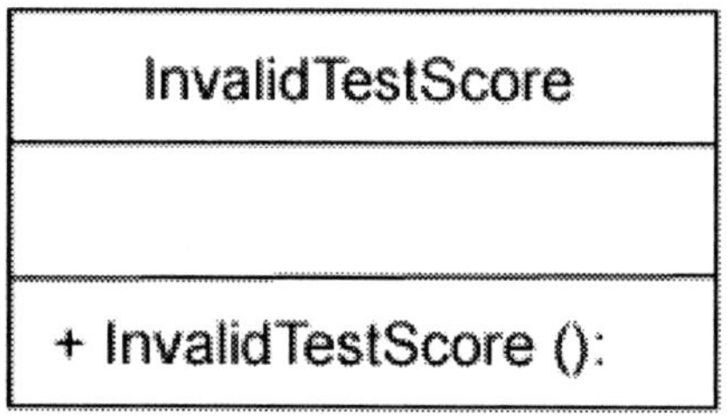

Figure 10-2 UML Drawing for InvalidTestScore Class

Code Listing 10-3 (InvalidTestScore.java)

```
//************************************************************
// Written by Diane Christie
// Chapter 10
// Programming Challenge 2:  TestScores Class Custom Exception
//************************************************************

//************************************************************
// Write an exception class named InvalidTestScore.  Modify
// the TestScores class you wrote in Programming Challenge 1
```

```
// so it throws and InvalidTestScore exception if any of the
// test scores in the array are invalid.
//**********************************************************

//**********************************************************
// The InvalidTestScore exceptions are thrown by the
// TestScores class when a test score is negative or
// greater than 100.
//**********************************************************

public class InvalidTestScore extends Exception
{
   public InvalidTestScore ()
   {
      super("Score is negative or greater than 100");
   }
}
```

Pseudocode for the TestScore2 Class modified from the TestScore Class

1) Modify the constructor.

   a) Change the exception generated to an InvalidTestScore exception.

   b) Add a throws clause to the method heading.

Code Listing 10-4 (TestScores2.java)

```
//**********************************************************
// Written by Diane Christie
// Chapter 10
// Programming Challenge 2:  TestScores Class Custom Exception
//**********************************************************

//**********************************************************
// Write an exception class named InvalidTestScore.  Modify
// the TestScores class you wrote in Programming Challenge 1
// so it throws and InvalidTestScore exception if any of the
// test scores in the array are invalid.
//**********************************************************

//**********************************************************
// The TestScores2 class is modified from TestScores .
// It throws a custom exception called InvalidTestScore
// if a test score is not between 0 and 100, otherwise it
// calculates the average of a set of test scores.
//**********************************************************

public class TestScores2
{
   private double average; //the average of the scores
                          //in the array passed into
                          //the constructor
```

```
    //******************************************************
    // Constructor accepts an array of test scores.  Each
    // test score in the array is checked for validity.  A
    // valid test score is between 0 and 100.  If the score
    // is valid, it is added to the total.  When all scores
    // are summed, the average is calculated.
    // Modification--change exception generation to
    // an InvalidTestScore exception and add throws clause to
    // method heading.
    //******************************************************
    public TestScores2(double [] data) throws InvalidTestScore
    {
       double total = 0;
       for (int i = 0; i < data.length; i++)
       {
          if (data[i] < 0 || data[i] > 100)
          {
             //generate the exception
             throw new InvalidTestScore();
          }
          else //if score is valid, add to sum
          {
             total += data[i];
          }
       }
       average = total/data.length;
    }

    //******************************************************
    // The getAverage method returns the average of the
    // test scores in the array.
    //******************************************************
    public double getAverage()
    {
       return average;
    }
 }
```

Program Output using TestScoresDemo.java with TestScore2 gives same output.

Programming Challenge 4: Month Class Exceptions

Problem Statement:

Programming Challenge 6 of Chapter 6 required you to write a Month class that holds information about the month. Write exception classes for the following error conditions:

- A number less than 1 or greater than 12 is given for the month number.

- An invalid string is given for the name of the month.

Modify the Month class so it throws the appropriate exception when either of these errors occurs. Demonstrate the classes in a program.

Solution The InvalidMonthNumberClass

Define What The Program Is To Do

Purpose	**Describe an InvalidMonthNumber which is an Exception class.**	
Fields	**None (message field is inherited from Exception).**	
Constructor	**InvalidMonthNumber()**	**Create an InvalidMonthNumber object.**
Methods	**None (getMessage is inherited from the Exception class.**	

Pseudocode for the InvalidMonthNumber Class

1) Define a default constructor that calls the super constructor.

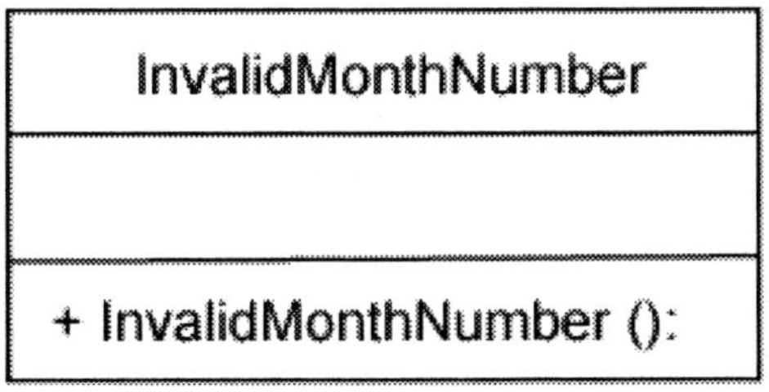

Figure 10-3 UML Drawing for InvalidMonthNumber Class

Code Listing 10-5 (InvalidMonthNumber.java)

```
//*********************************************************
// Written by Diane Christie
// Chapter 10
// Programming Challenge 4:  Month Class Custom Exception
//*********************************************************

//******************************************************
// Programming Challenge 5 of Chapter 6 required you to
// write a Month class that holds information about the
// month.  Write exception classes for the following
// error conditions:
// ·  A number less than 1 or greater than 12 is given
// for the month number.
// ·  An invalid string is given for the name of the
// month.
// Modify the Month class so it throws the appropriate
// exception when either of these errors occurs.
// Demonstrate the classes in a program.
//******************************************************

//*********************************************************
// The InvalidMonthNumber exceptions are thrown by the
// Month class when a month number is less than 1 or more
// than 12..
//*********************************************************

public class InvalidMonthNumber extends Exception
{
   public InvalidMonthNumber()
   {
      super("Month number must be between 1 and 12.");
   }
}
```

Solution The InvalidMonthNameClass

Define What The Program Is To Do

Purpose	**Describe an InvalidMonthName which is an Exception class.**	
Fields	**None (message field is inherited from Exception).**	
Constructor	**InvalidMonthNamd();**	**Create an InvalidMonthName object.**
Methods	**None (getMessage is inherited from the Exception class.**	

Pseudocode for the InvalidMonthName Class

Define a default constructor that calls the super constructor.

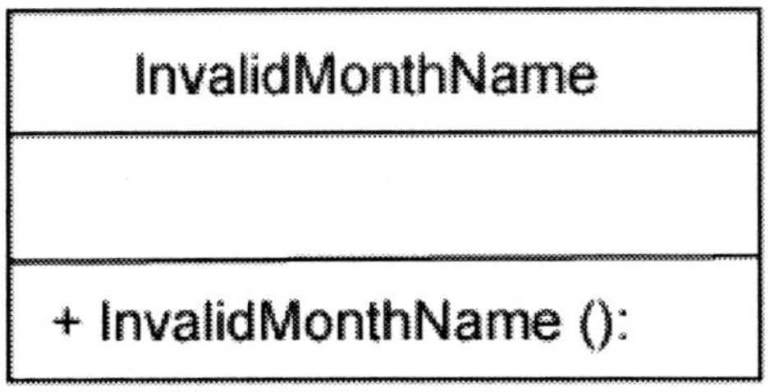

Figure 10-4 UML Drawing for InvalidMonthName Class

Solution The Month Class:

Modify the constructors to throw an exception instead of setting a default value.

Pseudocode for modification of constructors

1. Modify constructors
   a. Month (int)
      i. Insert throws clause in method heading
      ii. Change else branch to throw new InvalidMonthNumber exception.
   b. Month (String)
      i. Insert throws clause in method heading
      ii. Change else branch to throw new InvalidMonthName exception.

Code Listing 10-6 (modifications to Month.java)

```
//*****************************************************
//  Constructor for Month class - determines whether its*
//  parameter has a valid value, and sets the field     *
//  monthNumber to that value.  If the parameter's value*
//  is not correct, an InvalidMonthNumber exception is  *
//  thrown.                                        *
//*****************************************************

public Month(int aMonthNumber) throws InvalidMonthNumber
{
    //  confirm that parameter to constructor
    //  is a valid value for monthNumber
    if ( 1 <=aMonthNumber && aMonthNumber <=12)
    {
     monthNumber = aMonthNumber;
  }
    else//throw an InvalidMonthNumber exception
```

```
        {
          throw new InvalidMonthNumber();
        }
    }

    //*****************************************************
    //  Constructor for Month class that takes a monthName  *
    //  String parameter.  The monthName is compared to the *
    //  names of the months and the monthNumber field is set*
    //  to the number of the month that matches the         *
    //  monthName.  If no match is found for the monthName, *
    //  an InvalidMonthName is thrown.                      *
    //*****************************************************

    public Month(String monthName) throws InvalidMonthName
    {
         //  Compare monthName (case significant) against
         //  the 12 month names.  Set monthNumber to the
         //  number of the matching month.

        if (monthName.equals("January") )
            monthNumber = 1;
        else if ( monthName.equals("February") )
            monthNumber = 2;
        else if ( monthName.equals("March") )
            monthNumber = 3;
        else if ( monthName.equals("April") )
            monthNumber = 4;
        else if ( monthName.equals("May") )
            monthNumber = 5;
        else if ( monthName.equals("June") )
            monthNumber = 6;
        else if ( monthName.equals("July") )
            monthNumber = 7;
        else if ( monthName.equals("August") )
            monthNumber = 8;
        else if ( monthName.equals("September") )
            monthNumber = 9;
        else if ( monthName.equals("October") )
            monthNumber = 10;
        else if ( monthName.equals("November") )
            monthNumber = 11;
        else if ( monthName.equals("December") )
            monthNumber = 12;

        //  monthName does not match any month's name.
        else
            throw new InvalidMonthName();
    }
```

Solution The MonthDemo Class:

Define what the program is to do

Purpose	**To demonstrate the Month class exceptions.**
Input	**None.**
Process	**Create several month objects.**

Output **Display information.**

Pseudocode for MonthDemo Class

13) Create a try-catch block. Try to create a month with a month number less than 1. Catch the InvalidMonthNumber exception.

14) Create a try-catch block. Try to create a month with a month number greater than 12. Catch the InvalidMonthNumber exception.

15) Create a try-catch block. Try to create a month with a month name with incorrect spelling. Catch the InvalidMonthName exception.

16) Create a try-catch block. Try to create a month with a month name with incorrect capitalization (parameter in constructor is case sensitive). Catch the InvalidMonthName exception.

Code Listing 10-7 (MonthDemo.java)

```
//******************************************************
// Written by Diane Christie
// Chapter 10
// Programming Challenge 4:  Month Class Exceptions
//******************************************************

//******************************************************
//  Demonstrate the use of the Month class exceptions   *
//******************************************************

public class MonthDemo
{

    public static void main(String[] args)
    {
      //  Construct a collection of Month objects
      //  using bad data.
      int monthNum = 0; // bad month number
      String monthName = "Merch"; //bad month name
      try
      {
        Month    m0   =    new Month( monthNum );
                           // No good. 0 is not a valid month.
      }
      catch(InvalidMonthNumber e)
      {
         System.out.println("Input month number is " + monthNum);
         System.out.println(e.getMessage());
         System.out.println();
      }

      monthNum = 13;     //try another bad month number
      try
        {
         Month    m1   =    new Month( monthNum );
                               // No good. 13 is not a valid month.
```

```
        }
      catch(InvalidMonthNumber e)
      {
         System.out.println("Input month number is " + monthNum);
         System.out.println(e.getMessage());
         System.out.println();
      }

      try
      {
         Month   m2  =   new Month( monthName);
            // No good. Incorrect spelling of March
      }
      catch(InvalidMonthName e)
      {
         System.out.println("Input month name is " + monthName);
         System.out.println(e.getMessage());
         System.out.println();
      }

      monthName = "MAY";
        try
        {
         Month   m3  =   new Month( monthName );
              // No good. Month name parameter is
              // case sensitive.  m7's monthNumber
              // field should be set to 1,
              // "January".
        }
      catch(InvalidMonthName e)
      {
         System.out.println("Input month name is " + monthName);
         System.out.println(e.getMessage());
         System.out.println();
      }

    }
}
```

Program Output

```
Input month number is 0
Month number must be between 1 and 12.

Input month number is 13
Month number must be between 1 and 12.

Input month name is Merch
String does not represent a month's name.

Input month name is MAY
String does not represent a month's name.
```

Programming Challenge 7: File Encryption Filter

Problem Statement:

File encryption is the science of writing the contents of a file in a secret code. Your encryption program should work like a filter, reading the contents of one file, modifying the data into a code, and then writing the coded contents out to a second file. The second file will be a version of the first file, but written in a secret code.

Although there are complex encryption techniques, you should come up with a simple one of your own. For example, you could read the first file one character at a time, and add 10 to the character code of each character before it is written to the second file.

Solution The Encryption Class:

Define what the program is to do

Purpose	**Read input from the keyboard and store it in a char array.**	
Fields	**symbol**	**Original symbol read in**
	codedSymbol	**Symbol after encryption**
	rotate	**Number which defines how many places to move each letter**
Constructors	**Encryption(char, int)**	**Create an Encryption object by calling the encrypt method.**
Methods	**getCodedSymbol**	**Returns the encrypted character**
	encrypt	**Encrypts the character by moving all alphabet letters to a different position in the alphabet indicated by the rotate field. All capital letters remain capital, and all non-alphabet letters remain unchanged.**

Pseudocode for the Encryption Class

1) Declare fields for symbol, codedSymbol, and rotate.

2) Define a constructor

   a) It accepts and stores a character that is to be encrypted and an integer indicating how many places in the alphabet to rotate this letter.

   b) Call the encrypt method.

3) Define accessor method.

   a) getCodedSymbol returns the encrypted character.

4) Define the encrypt method.

   a) All manipulation is done mathematically, so characters must be cast into integers. When the manipulation is complete, the result must be cast back to a character and stored into codedSymbol.

   b) The algorithm for capital letters is as follows

      i) Subtract 'A' from the symbol

      ii) Add the number of places to rotate to that result

      iii) Take the **remainder** of the result divided by 26 (to wrap around)

      iv) Add 'A' back to the result

   c) If the character is a lower case letter the same algorithm applies, but substitute 'a' for 'A'.

   d) If the character is any other symbol, no encryption is needed.

Code Listing 10-8 (Encryption.java)

```
//*************************************************************
// Written by Diane Christie
// Chapter 10
// Programming Challenge 7:  File Encryption Filter
//*************************************************************

//*************************************************************
//File encryption is the science of writing the contents of
//a file in a secret code. Your encryption program should
//work like a filter, reading the contents of one file,
//modifying the data into a code, and then writing the coded
//contents out to a second file.  The second file will be a
//version of the first file, but written in a secret code.
//
//Although there are complex encryption techniques, you
//should come up with a simple one of your own.  For example,
//you could read the first file one character at a time, and
//add 10 to the character code of each character before it
//is written to the second file.
//*************************************************************

public class Encryption
{
```

```
private int rotate;        //number of places to move
private char symbol;       //symbol to be encrypted
private char codedSymbol;  //symbol after encryption

//***************************************************
// Constructor takes in the character to be encoded
//***************************************************
public Encryption(char old_symbol, int move)
{
   rotate = move;
   symbol = old_symbol;
   codedSymbol = ' ';
   encrypt();//call the method that changes the letter
}

//***************************************************
//getCodedSymbol method returns the encrypted character
//***************************************************
public char getCodedSymbol()
{
   return codedSymbol;
}

//***************************************************
//encrypt method converts each letter to a letter
//which is rotated a number of places, but other symbols
//are not converted
//***************************************************
public void encrypt()
{
   if (symbol >= 'A' && symbol <= 'Z')
   {
      int temp;

      //lets A = 0
      temp = (int)symbol - (int)'A';

      //moves letter rotate number of places
      temp = temp + rotate;

      //wraps letters past Z around to A.
      temp = temp % 26;

      //gets back correct unicode conversion
      temp = temp + (int)'A';

      //changes back to a character
      codedSymbol = (char)temp;
   }
   else if (symbol >= 'a' && symbol <= 'z')
   {
      int temp;

      //lets a = 0
      temp = (int)symbol - (int)'a';

      //moves letter rotate number of places
      temp = temp + rotate;
```

```
            //wraps letters past z around to a.
            temp = temp % 26;

            //gets back correct unicode conversion
            temp = temp + (int)'a';

            //changes back to a character
            codedSymbol = (char)temp;
         }
         else //characters that are not letters
         {
            codedSymbol = symbol;
         }
      }
}
```

Solution The EncryptDemo Class:

Define what the program is to do

Purpose	**To encrypt a file.**
Input	**A file to be encrypted.**
Process	**Read one character at a time, encrypting each character by creating an Encryption object, then writing the resulting character to a file.**
Output	**The encrypted file.**

Pseudocode for the EncryptDemo Class

1) Create a FileReader object and a FileWriter object.

2) Read a character from the input file

3) While it is not the end of the input file

   a) Create an Encryption object with the character and the number of places to move the letters.

   b) Retrieve the resulting encrypted character and write it to a file.

   c) Read another character from the input file.

4) Close the files.

Contents of inputfile.txt

```
Roses are red,
Violets are blue,
Sugar is sweet,
and so are you!
```

Code Listing 10-9 (EncryptDemo.java)

```
//*******************************************************
// Written by Diane Christie
// Chapter 10
// Programming Challenge 7:  File Encryption Filter
//*******************************************************

//*******************************************************
//File encryption is the science of writing the contents of
//a file in a secret code. Your encryption program should
//work like a filter, reading the contents of one file,
//modifying the data into a code, and then writing the coded
//contents out to a second file.  The second file will be a
//version of the first file, but written in a secret code.
//
//Although there are complex encryption techniques, you
//should come up with a simple one of your own.  For example,
//you could read the first file one character at a time, and
//add 10 to the character code of each character before it
//is written to the second file.
//*******************************************************

import java.io.*;

public class EncryptDemo
{
   public static void main(String[]args) throws IOException
   {
      String fileNameIn = "inputFile.txt";
      String fileNameOut = "encrypted.txt";
      char letter;
      int inputValue;

      FileReader inStream = new FileReader(fileNameIn);
      FileWriter outStream = new FileWriter(fileNameOut);

      inputValue = inStream.read();

      while(inputValue != -1)
      {
         letter = (char) inputValue;
         Encryption encryptor = new Encryption(letter);
         outStream.write(encryptor.getCodedSymbol());
         inputValue = inStream.read();
      }

      System.out.println(
         "Encryption complete, filename is encrypted.txt");
      inStream.close();
      outStream.close();
   }
}
```

Contents of encrypted.txt

```
Bycoc kbo bon,
Fsyvodc kbo lveo,
Ceqkb sc cgood,
kxn cy kbo iye!
```

Programming Challenge 8: File Decryption Filter

Problem Statement:

Write a program that decrypts the file produced by the program in Programming Challenge 7. The decryption program should read the contents of the coded file, restore the data to its original state, and write it to another file.

Solution The DecryptDemo Class:

Since decrypting the file will require the same process as encrypting the file, the Encryption class from Programming Challenge 7 will be reused. The DecryptDemo class is a modified EncryptDemo class. The names of the input and output files, and the number of places to move the letters during the encryption have been modified.

Define what the program is to do

Purpose	**To decrypt a file.**
Input	**A file to be decrypted.**
Process	**Read one character at a time, decrypting each character by creating an Encryption object, then writing the resulting character to a file.**
Output	**The decrypted file.**

Pseudocode for the DecryptDemo Class

1) Create a FileReader object and a FileWriter object.

2) Read a character from the encrypted file

3) While it is not the end of the encrypted file

   a) Create an Encryption object with the character and the number of places to move the letters. Note: The number of places to move the letter in the decryption file should be 26 (number of letters in the alphabet) minus the number of places used for the encryption of the file.

   b) Retrieve the resulting decrypted character and write it to a file.

   c) Read another character from the encrypted file.

4) Close the files.

Code Listing 10-10 (DecryptDemo.java)

```
//***********************************************************
```

```
// Written by Diane Christie
// Chapter 10
// Programming Challenge 8:  File Decryption Filter
//**********************************************************

//**********************************************************
//Write a program that decrypts the file produced by the
//program in Programming Challenge 7.  The decryption
//program should read the contents of the coded file,
//restore the data to its original state, and write it to
//another file.
//**********************************************************

import java.io.*;

public class DecryptDemo
{
   public static void main(String[]args) throws IOException
   {
      String fileNameIn = "encrypted.txt";
      String fileNameOut = "decrypted.txt";
      char letter;
      int inputValue;

      //Number to add to character code to undo encryption.
      //Since encryption was done by moving 10, we need to
      //move it 16 more to get it back to its original position.
      //The number of moves in the encrypting and decrypting
      //should add to 26 since there are 26 letters in the alphabet.
      int move = 16;

      FileReader inStream = new FileReader(fileNameIn);
      FileWriter outStream = new FileWriter(fileNameOut);

      inputValue = inStream.read();

      while(inputValue != -1)
      {
         letter = (char) inputValue;
         Encryption decryptor = new Encryption(letter, move);
         outStream.write(decryptor.getCodedSymbol());
         inputValue = inStream.read();
      }

      System.out.println(
         "Decryption complete, filename is decrypted.txt");
      inStream.close();
      outStream.close();
   }
}
```

Contents of decrypted.txt

```
Roses are red,
Violets are blue,
Sugar is sweet,
and so are you!
```

NOTES

CHAPTER 11

GUI Applications—Part 1

Solutions

- Programming Challenge 2: Monthly Sales Tax
- Programming Challenge 6: Joe's Automotive

Programming Challenge 2: Monthly Sales Tax

Problem Statement:

A retail company must file a monthly sales tax report listing the total sales for the month, and the amount of state and county sales tax collected. The state sales tax rate is 4% and the county sales tax rate is 2%. Create a GUI application that allows the user to enter the total sales for the month into a text field. From this figure, the application should calculate and display the following:

- The amount of county sales tax
- The amount of state sales tax
- The total sales tax (county plus state)

In the application's code, represent the county sales tax rate (0.02) and the state tax rate (0.04) as named constants.

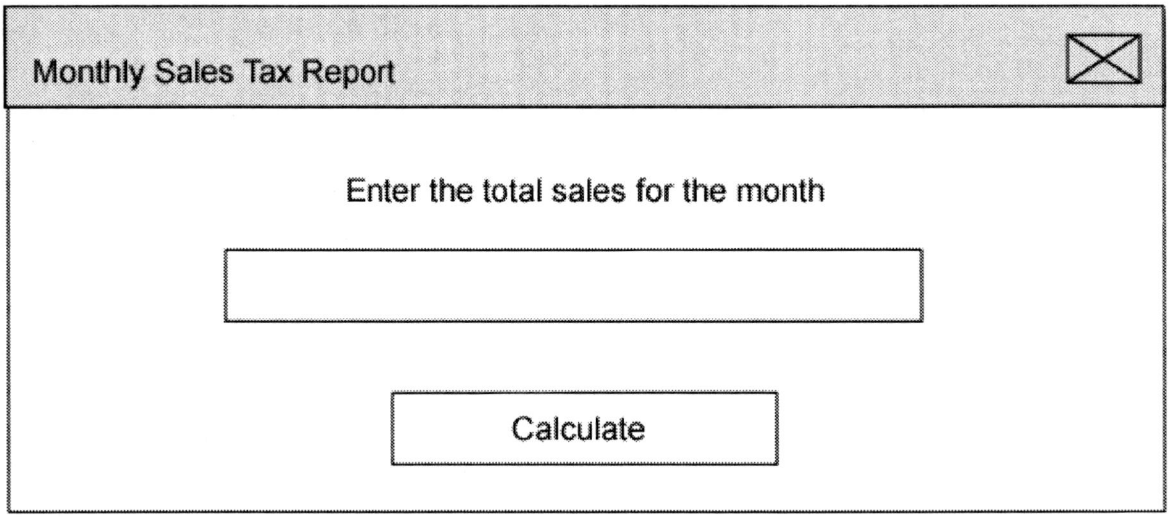

Figure 11-1 Sketch of the Monthly Sales Tax Report Window

Solution The SalesTaxWindow Class:

Define What The Program Is To Do

Purpose	To create window requesting the monthly sales from the user and displaying a tax report listing the total sales for the month and the amount of sales tax (county and state) collected.		
Fields	panel	A panel to hold components	
	contentPane	A reference to the contentPane	
	message	A message to the user	
	totalSales	To hold the user input	
	calcButton	Calculates the taxes collected	
	WINDOW_WIDTH	The width of the window created	
	WINDOW_HEIGHT	The height of the window created	
Constructor	SalesTaxWindow()	Create a SalesTaxWindow object	
Methods	buildPanel	Adds a label, textfield, and a button to a panel and connects the button with the event listener	
Private Inner Class	CalcButtonListener	handles the event when the user clicks the button	
	Fields	COUNTY_RATE	County tax rate
		STATE_RATE	State tax rate
	Methods	actionPerformed	Takes user input, calculates state and county taxes, and displays all information in a message box

Pseudocode for SalesTaxWindow Class

1) This class will extend JFrame.

2) Declare fields for window objects and constants for window size.

3) Constructor.

   a) Create a window with a title by calling the super constructor and passing it the title.

   b) Set the size of the window.

c) Specify what happens when the close button is clicked.

d) Display the window.

4) The buildPanel method.

a) Create label, textfield, and button components.

b) Connect the button to the event listener.

c) Create a panel and add components to it.

5) The private inner class CalcButtonListener.

a) This class will implement ActionListener.

b) The actionPerformed method.

i) Get the user input from the textfield totalSales.

ii) Convert the input string into a double.

iii) Calculate the amount of sales before tax by dividing by 1 plus the total tax rates.

iv) Calculate the amount of county tax by multiplying the sales before tax by the county tax rate.

v) Calculate the amount of state tax by multiplying the sales before tax by the state tax rate.

vi) Create and display a message box with the results.

Code Listing 11-1 (SalesTaxWindow.java)

```
//***********************************************************
// Written by Diane Christie
// Chapter 11
// Programming Challenge 2:  Monthly Sales Tax
//***********************************************************

//***********************************************************
// A retail company must file a monthly sales tax report
// listing the total sales for the month, and the amount of
// state and county sales tax collected.  The state sales tax
// rate is 4% and the county sales tax rate is 2%.  Create a
// GUI application that allows the user to enter the total
// sales for the month into a text field.  From this figure,
// the application should calculate and display the following:
// ·  The amount of county sales tax
// ·  The amount of state sales tax
```

```
// ·  The total sales tax (county plus state)
// In the application's code, represent the county sales tax
// rate (0.02) and the state tax rate (0.04) as named
// constants.
//**************************************************************

//**************************************************************
// The SalesTaxWindow class creates window which allows the
// user to input the total sales for the month, and displays
// the state and county sales tax collected.
//**************************************************************

import java.awt.*;
import java.awt.event.*;
import javax.swing.*;
import java.text.DecimalFormat;

public class SalesTaxWindow extends JFrame
{
   private JPanel panel;       // A panel to hold components
   private Container contentPane;//Reference to contentPane
   private JLabel message;     //A message to the user
   private JTextField totalSales;//To hold the user input
   private JButton calcButton;//Calculates the taxes collected
   private final int WINDOW_WIDTH = 300;//Window width
   private final int WINDOW_HEIGHT = 150;//Window height

   //***********************************************************
   // Constructor creates a window
   //***********************************************************
   public SalesTaxWindow()
   {
      super("Monthly Sales Tax Report");
      setSize(WINDOW_WIDTH, WINDOW_HEIGHT);
      setDefaultCloseOperation(JFrame.EXIT_ON_CLOSE);
      buildPanel();
      contentPane = getContentPane();
      contentPane.add(panel);
      setVisible(true);
   }

   //********************************************************
   // The buildPanel method adds a label, textfield, and a
   // button to a panel and connects the button with the
   // event listener.
   //********************************************************
   private void buildPanel()
   {
      //Create window objects
      message = new JLabel (
            "Enter the total sales for the month");
      totalSales = new JTextField (20);
      calcButton = new JButton ("Calculate");

      //Connect the action listner to the button.
      calcButton.addActionListener(new CalcButtonListener());

      //Create a panel and add the components to it.
      panel = new JPanel();
```

```
      panel.add(message);
      panel.add(totalSales);
      panel.add(calcButton);
   }

   //*****************************************************
   // The CalcButtonListener class is a private inner class
   // that handles the event when the user clicks the button.
   //*****************************************************
   private class CalcButtonListener implements ActionListener
   {
      private final double COUNTY_RATE = 0.02;
      private final double STATE_RATE = 0.04;

      //*************************************************
      // The actionPerformed method calculates state and
      // county taxes, and displays all information in a
      // message box.
      //*************************************************
      public void actionPerformed(ActionEvent e)
      {
         String str;
         double salesWithTax;
         double countyTax;
         double stateTax;
         double salesBeforeTax;
         DecimalFormat money;
         money = new DecimalFormat("#,###,##0.00");

         str = totalSales.getText();
         salesWithTax = Double.parseDouble(str);

         salesBeforeTax = salesWithTax/
            (1 + COUNTY_RATE + STATE_RATE);
         countyTax = salesBeforeTax * COUNTY_RATE;
         stateTax = salesBeforeTax * STATE_RATE;

         //Create and display a message box with results.
         JOptionPane.showMessageDialog(null, "In $" +
            money.format(salesWithTax) + " total sales: " +
            "\nState tax collected is $" +
            money.format(stateTax)+
            "\nCounty tax collected is $" +
            money.format(countyTax)
            +"\nTotal tax collected is $" +
            money.format(stateTax + countyTax));
      }
   }

   public static void main(String [] args)
   {
      SalesTaxWindow stw = new SalesTaxWindow();
   }
}
```

Program Output (user will type in the number)

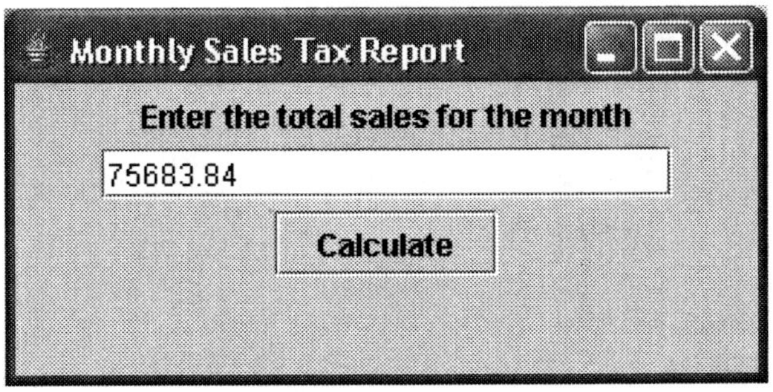

When user enters 75683.84 in the text field and clicks the Calculate button, this window will be displayed.

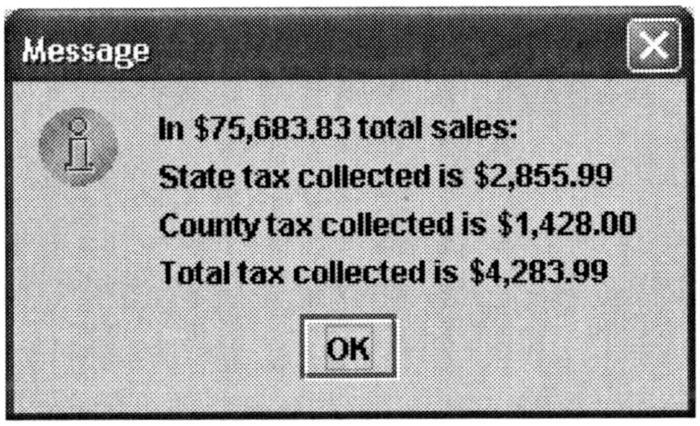

Programming Challenge 6: Joe's Automotive

Problem Statement:

Joe's Automotive performs the following routine maintenance services:

- Oil change--$26.00
- Lube job--$18.00
- Radiator flush--$30.00
- Transmission flush--$80.00
- Inspection--$15.00
- Muffler replacement--$100.00
- Tire rotation--$20.00

Joe also performs other nonroutine services and charges for parts and for labor ($20 per hour). Create a GUI application that displays the total for a customer's visit to Joe's.

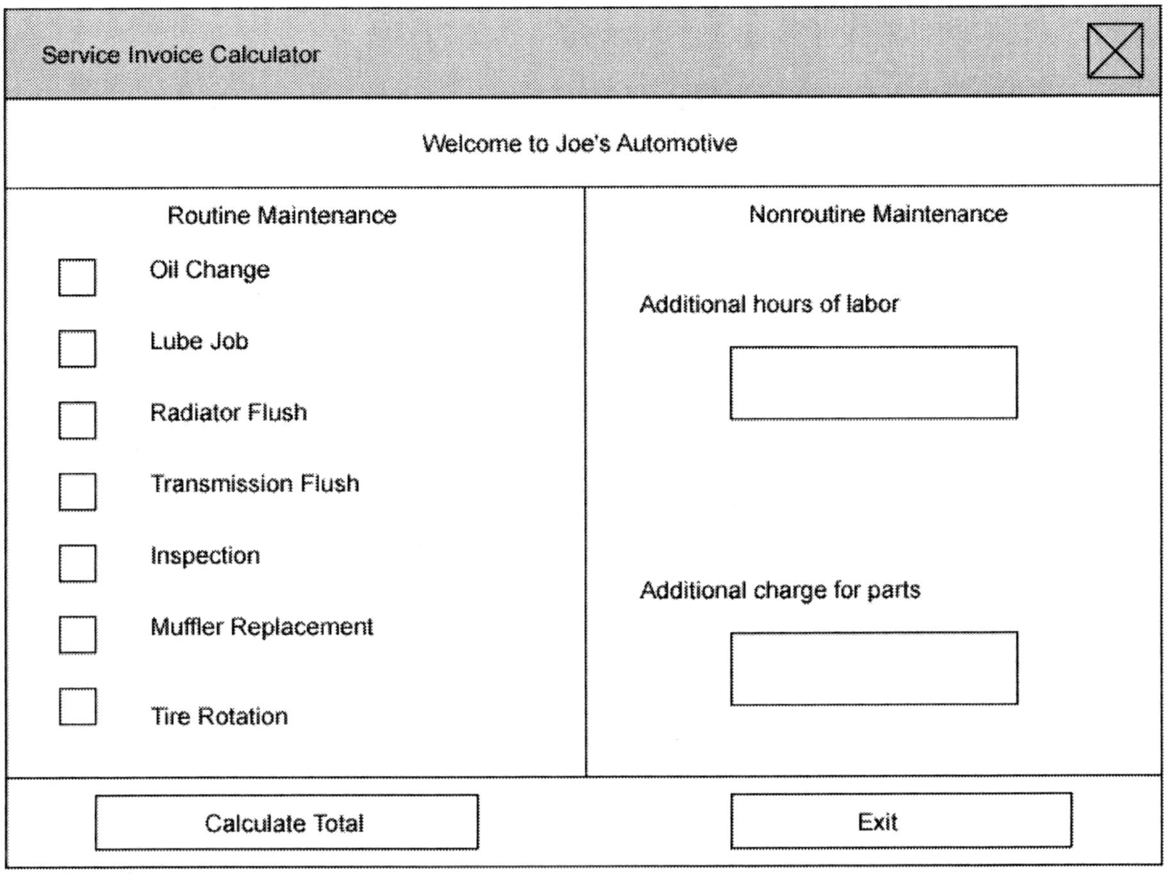

Figure 11-2 Sketch of Joe's Automotive Invoice Window

Solution:

The desired layout can be achieved by using a BorderLayout manager with the AutomotiveInvoiceWindow's content pane. Each panel can be created separately and added to the content pane. We will need the following panels:

- GreetingPanel. This panel contains the label that appears in the window's north region.
- RoutineCheckBoxPanel. This panel contains the check boxes for the routine services.
- NonRoutinePanel. This panel contains the textfields to enter the number of hours of labor and cost of parts.

The GreetingPanel Class

Purpose	To create a greeting panel.	
Fields	greeting	A Jlabel containing a message.
Constructor	GreetingPanel()	Creates a panel.
Methods	None.	

Pseudocode for the GreetingPanelClass

1) This class extends Jpanel.

2) Define Jlabel field.

3) Constructor.

   a) Create a label.

   b) Add the label to the panel.

Code Listing 11-2 (GreetingPanel.java)

```
//*******************************************************
// Written by Diane Christie
// Chapter 11
// Programming Challenge 6: Joe's Automotive
//*******************************************************

//*******************************************************
// Joe's Automotive performs the following routine
// maintenance services:
// ·  Oil change--$26.00
// ·  Lube job--$18.00
// ·  Radiator flush--$30.00
// ·  Transmission flush--$80.00
// ·  Inspection--$15.00
// ·  Muffler replacement--$100.00
// ·  Tire rotation--$20.00
// Joe also performs other nonroutine services and
// charges for parts and for labor ($20 per hour).
// Create a GUI application that displays the total for
// a customer's visit to Joe's.
//*******************************************************

//*******************************************************
// The GreetingPanel class displays a greeting in a panel.
//*******************************************************
```

```
import javax.swing.*;

public class GreetingPanel extends JPanel
{
   private JLabel greeting;

   //***********************************************
   // Constructor
   //***********************************************

   public GreetingPanel()
   {
      //Create the label.
      greeting = new JLabel(
         "Welcome to Joe's Automotive");
      //Add the label to the panel
      add(greeting);
   }
}
```

The RoutineCheckBoxPanel class

Purpose	To create a panel that allows the user to select the routine maintenance services.	
Fields	oil	Check box for an oil change
	lube	Check box for a lube job
	radiator	Check box for a radiator flush
	transmission	Check box for a transmission flush
	inspection	Check box for an inspection
	muffler	Check box for a muffler replacement
	tire	Check box for a tire rotation
	OIL	Constant representing the cost of an oil change
	LUBE	Constant representing the cost of a lube job
	RADIATOR	Constant representing the cost of a radiator flush

	TRANSMISSION	Constant representing the cost of a transmission flush
	INSPECTION	Constant representing the cost of an inspection
	MUFFLER	Constant representing the cost of a muffler replacement
	TIRE	Constant representing the cost of a tire rotation
Constructor	RoutineCheckBoxPanel()	Creates a panel with a titled border and a grid layout.
Methods	getRoutineCost	Returns the total cost of routine services selected.

Pseudocode for RoutineCheckBoxPanel class

1) This class extends Jpanel.

2) Define fields.

3) Constructor

   a) Panel should use a grid layout and a titled border

   b) Create all check boxes.

   c) Add check boxes to panel.

4) The getRoutineCost method.

   a) Initialize the total to 0.

   b) For each check box, if it is selected, then add the corresponding cost constant to the total.

   c) Return the total cost.

Code Listing 11-3 (RoutineCheckBoxPanel.java)

```
//*******************************************************
// Written by Diane Christie
// Chapter 11
// Programming Challenge 6: Joe's Automotive
//*******************************************************

//*******************************************************
// Joe's Automotive performs the following routine
// maintenance services:
// ·  Oil change--$26.00
// ·  Lube job--$18.00
// ·  Radiator flush--$30.00
// ·  Transmission flush--$80.00
// ·  Inspection--$15.00
// ·  Muffler replacement--$100.00
// ·  Tire rotation--$20.00
// Joe also performs other nonroutine services and
// charges for parts and for labor ($20 per hour).
// Create a GUI application that displays the total for
// a customer's visit to Joe's.
//*******************************************************

//******************************************************
// The RoutineCheckBoxPanel class creates a panel that
// allows the user to select the routine maintenance
// services.
//******************************************************

import java.awt.*;
import javax.swing.*;

public class RoutineCheckBoxPanel extends JPanel
{
   // Costs for each routine maintenance service
   public final double OIL = 26.00;
   public final double LUBE = 18.00;
   public final double RADIATOR = 30.00;
   public final double TRANSMISSION = 80.00;
   public final double INSPECTION = 15.00;
   public final double MUFFLER = 100.00;
   public final double TIRE = 20.00;

   // to select each routine maintenance service
   private JCheckBox oil;
   private JCheckBox lube;
   private JCheckBox radiator;
   private JCheckBox transmission;
   private JCheckBox inspection;
   private JCheckBox muffler;
   private JCheckBox tire;

   //*******************************************
   // Constructor
   //*******************************************
```

```
    public RoutineCheckBoxPanel ()
    {
       //Create a GridLayout manager with
       //seven rows and no columns
       setLayout(new GridLayout(7,0));

       //Create the check boxes.
       oil = new JCheckBox("Oil change");
       lube = new JCheckBox("Lube job");
       radiator = new JCheckBox("Radiator flush");
       transmission = new JCheckBox("Transmission flush");
       inspection = new JCheckBox ("Inspection");
       muffler = new JCheckBox ("Muffler replacement");
       tire = new JCheckBox ("Tire rotation");

       //Add a border around the panel
       setBorder(BorderFactory.createTitledBorder(
          "Routine maintenance"));

       //Add the check boxes to the panel.
       add(oil);
       add(lube);
       add(radiator);
       add(transmission);
       add(inspection);
       add(muffler);
       add(tire);
    }

    //****************************************************
    // The getRoutineCost method returns the total cost
    // of all routine maintenance services selected.
    //****************************************************
    public double getRoutineCost()
    {
       double routineCost = 0.0;

       if (oil.isSelected())
          routineCost += OIL;
       if(lube.isSelected())
          routineCost += LUBE;
       if(radiator.isSelected())
          routineCost += RADIATOR;
       if(transmission.isSelected())
          routineCost += TRANSMISSION;
       if(inspection.isSelected())
          routineCost += INSPECTION;
       if(muffler.isSelected())
          routineCost += MUFFLER;
       if(tire.isSelected())
          routineCost += TIRE;

       return routineCost;
    }
}
```

The NonRoutinePanel class

Purpose	To allow the user to enter the number of hours of labor and the total amount for parts.	
Fields	laborLabel	A JLabel for hours of labor.
	partsLabel	A Jlabel for parts.
	laborHours	A JTextField to hold number of hours of labor.
	parts	A JtextField to hold cost of parts.
	LABOR_RATE	A constant field containing the labor charge per hour.
Constructor	NonRoutinePanel()	Creates a panel with a grid layout and titled border.
Methods	getNonRoutineCost	Returns the total cost of nonroutine services based on parts and labor.

Pseudocode for the NonRoutinePanel class

1) This class extends JPanel.

2) Define fields.

3) Constructor.

   a) Panel should use a grid layout and a titled border

   b) Create all JLabels and JTextFields.

   c) Add labels and textfields to the panel.

4) The getNonRoutineCost method.

   a) Initialize the total to 0.

   b) Calculate total by adding labor costs (hours times rate) to parts.

Code Listing 11-4 (NonRoutinePanel.java)

```
//*****************************************************
// Written by Diane Christie
// Chapter 11
// Programming Challenge 6: Joe's Automotive
//*****************************************************

//*****************************************************
// Joe's Automotive performs the following routine
// maintenance services:
// ·  Oil change--$26.00
// ·  Lube job--$18.00
// ·  Radiator flush--$30.00
// ·  Transmission flush--$80.00
// ·  Inspection--$15.00
// ·  Muffler replacement--$100.00
// ·  Tire rotation--$20.00
// Joe also performs other nonroutine services and
// charges for parts and for labor ($20 per hour).
// Create a GUI application that displays the total for
// a customer's visit to Joe's.
//*****************************************************

//*****************************************************
// The NonRoutinePanel class allows the user to enter the
// number of hours of labor and the total amount for
// parts.
//*****************************************************

import java.awt.*;
import javax.swing.*;

public class NonRoutinePanel extends JPanel
{
   private JLabel laborLabel;//label for labor textfield
   private JLabel partsLabel;//label for parts textfield
   private JTextField laborHours;//To hold the user input
            // for hours of labor
   private JTextField parts;//Total charge for parts
   public final double LABOR_RATE = 20.00;
            // labor charge per hour

   //*****************************************************
   // Constructor
   //*****************************************************
   public NonRoutinePanel()
   {
      //Create labels
      laborLabel = new JLabel ("Additional hours of labor");
      partsLabel = new JLabel ("Additional charge for parts");

      //Create textfields with a default value of 0
      laborHours = new JTextField ("0");
      parts = new JTextField("0");

      //Layout uses 4 rows
      setLayout(new GridLayout(4,0));
```

```
      //Put a titled border around the panel
      setBorder(BorderFactory.createTitledBorder(
            "NonRoutine Work"));

      // add components
      add(laborLabel);
      add(laborHours);
      add(partsLabel);
      add(parts);
   }

   //*****************************************************
   // The getNonRoutineCost method returns the total cost
   // of parts and labor for any nonroutine service performed.
   //*****************************************************
   public double getNonRoutineCost()
   {
      double totalCost = 0.0;
      String str1;
      String str2;
      double partsCost;
      double hours;

      //retrieve user input and convert it to numbers
      str1 = parts.getText();
      partsCost = Double.parseDouble(str1);
      str2 = laborHours.getText();
      hours = Double.parseDouble(str2);

      totalCost  = hours * LABOR_RATE + partsCost;

      return totalCost;
   }
}
```

The AutomotiveInvoiceWindow class

Purpose	To create a GUI for an application at Joe's Automotive to calculate the total bill for their customers.		
Fields	routinePanel		A RoutineCheckBoxPanel
	greet		A GreetingPanel
	extraPanel		A NonRoutinePanel
	contentPane		A reference to the content pane
	buttonPanel		A JPanel to contain the buttons
	calcButton		Calculates the total cost of routine and nonroutine maintenance
	exitButton		Exits the program
	TAX_RATE		A constant representing the sales tax rate.
Constructor	AutomotiveInvoiceWindow		Creates a window
Methods	buildButtonPanel		Builds the button panel
Private Inner Class	CalcButtonListener		Handles the event when the user clicks the calculate button
	Methods	actionPerformed	Calculate total charges and display results
Private Inner Class	ExitButtonListener		Handles the event when the user clicks the exit button
	Methods	actionPerformed	Exit the program

Pseudocode for the AutomotiveInvoiceWindow class

1) This class extends JFrame.

2) Declare fields.

3) Constructor.

a) Create a window with a title by calling the super constructor and passing it the title.

b) Specify what happens when the close button is clicked.

c) Set the layout to Border layout.

d) Create custom panels.

e) Create a button panel.

f) Add the panels to the window.

g) Pack contents of the window and display it.

2) The buildButtonPanel method.

a) Create a panel.

b) Create buttons.

c) Connect the event listeners with the correct buttons.

d) Add the buttons to the panel.

3) The private inner class CalcButtonListener .

a) This class implements ActionListener.

b) The actionPerformed method.

i) Calculate the subtotal, tax, and total.

ii) Display results.

4) The private inner class ExitButtonListener.

a) This class implements ActionListener.

b) The actionPerformed method.

i) Exit the program.

Code Listing 11-5 (AutomotiveInvoiceWindow.java)

```
//*******************************************************
// Written by Diane Christie
// Chapter 11
// Programming Challenge 6: Joe's Automotive
//*******************************************************
```

```
//*******************************************************
// Joe's Automotive performs the following routine
// maintenance services:
// ·  Oil change--$26.00
// ·  Lube job--$18.00
// ·  Radiator flush--$30.00
// ·  Transmission flush--$80.00
// ·  Inspection--$15.00
// ·  Muffler replacement--$100.00
// ·  Tire rotation--$20.00
// Joe also performs other nonroutine services and
// charges for parts and for labor ($20 per hour).
// Create a GUI application that displays the total for
// a customer's visit to Joe's.
//*******************************************************

//*******************************************************
// The AutomotiveInvoiceWindow class creates a GUI for
// an application at Joe's Automotive to calculate the
// total bill for their customers.
//*******************************************************

import java.awt.*;
import java.awt.event.*;
import javax.swing.*;
import java.text.DecimalFormat;

public class AutomotiveInvoiceWindow extends JFrame
{
   private RoutineCheckBoxPanel routinePanel;
               // A panel to hold check boxes
   private GreetingPanel greet;
               //A panel to greet the user.
   private NonRoutinePanel extrasPanel;
               //Panel for parts and labor
   private Container contentPane;
               //Reference to  contentPane
   private JPanel buttonPanel;
               //A panel to hold buttons
   private JButton calcButton;//To calculate the cost
   private JButton exitButton;//To exit the application
   private final double TAX_RATE = 0.06;//Sales tax rate

   //****************************************************
   // Constructor creates a window
   //****************************************************
   public AutomotiveInvoiceWindow()
   {
      //Create a titled window
      super("Service Invoice Calculator");

      //Specify what happens when close button is clicked
      setDefaultCloseOperation(JFrame.EXIT_ON_CLOSE);

      //Get a reference to the content pane
      contentPane = getContentPane();

      //Create a BorderLayout manager
      contentPane.setLayout(new BorderLayout());
```

```
      //Create the custom panels
      routinePanel = new RoutineCheckBoxPanel();
      extrasPanel = new NonRoutinePanel();
      greet = new GreetingPanel();

      //Create a button panel
      buildButtonPanel();

      //Add components to content pane
      contentPane.add(routinePanel,BorderLayout.CENTER);
      contentPane.add(extrasPanel, BorderLayout.EAST);
      contentPane.add(greet, BorderLayout.NORTH);
      contentPane.add(buttonPanel, BorderLayout.SOUTH);

      //Pack contents of the window and display it.
      pack();
      setVisible(true);
   }

   //*****************************************************
   //The buildButtonPanel builds the button panel
   //*****************************************************
   public void buildButtonPanel()
   {
      //Create a panel
      buttonPanel = new JPanel();

      //Create buttons
      calcButton = new JButton("Calculate");
      exitButton = new JButton("Exit");

      //Connenct the buttons with the event listeners
      calcButton.addActionListener(
            new CalcButtonListener());
      exitButton.addActionListener(
            new ExitButtonListener());

      //Add buttons to panel
      buttonPanel.add(calcButton);
      buttonPanel.add(exitButton);
   }

   //*****************************************************
   // Private inner class that handles the event when the
   // user clicks on the calculate button
   //*****************************************************
   private class CalcButtonListener implements
                                ActionListener
   {
      public void actionPerformed (ActionEvent e)
      {
         double subtotal;
         double total;
         double tax;
         DecimalFormat money;

         money = new DecimalFormat("#,##0.00");
```

```
            //Calculate subtotal for all services
            subtotal = routinePanel.getRoutineCost() +
               extrasPanel.getNonRoutineCost();

            //Calculate sales tax
            tax = subtotal * TAX_RATE;

            //Calculate total
            total = subtotal + tax;

            //Display the charges
            JOptionPane.showMessageDialog(null,
               "Subtotal:  $" + money.format(subtotal)+
               "\nTax:  $" + money.format(tax) +
               "\nTotal:  $" + money.format(total));
         }
      }

      private class ExitButtonListener implements ActionListener
      {
         public void actionPerformed(ActionEvent e)
         {
            System.exit(0);
         }
      }

      public static void main(String [] args)
      {
         AutomotiveInvoiceWindow invoice;
         invoice = new AutomotiveInvoiceWindow();
      }
   }
```

Program Output

Original GUI

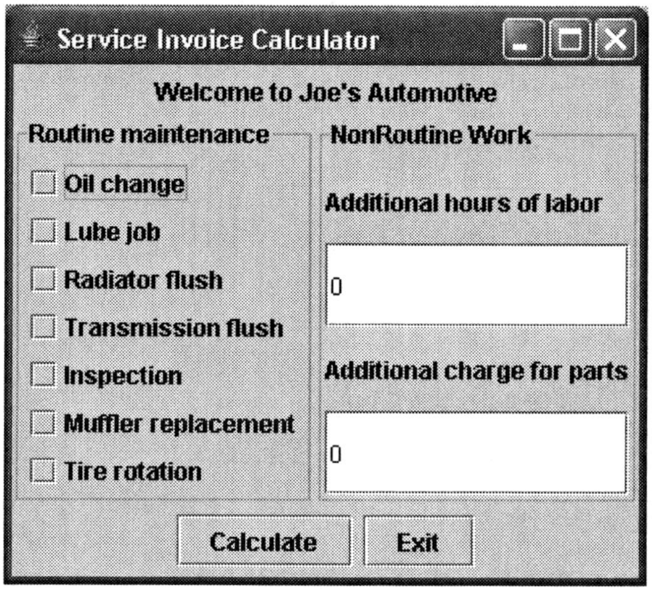

User enters choices for routine maintenance, hours of labor and parts for non-routine work.

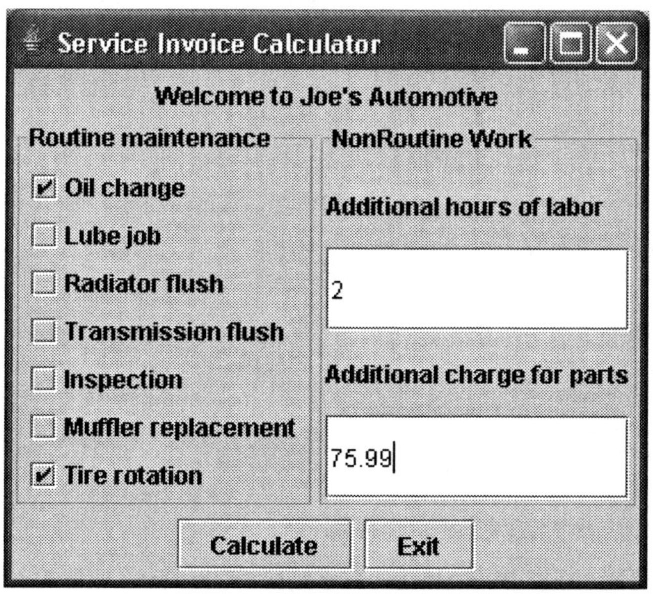

Window that appears when user clicks calculate button.

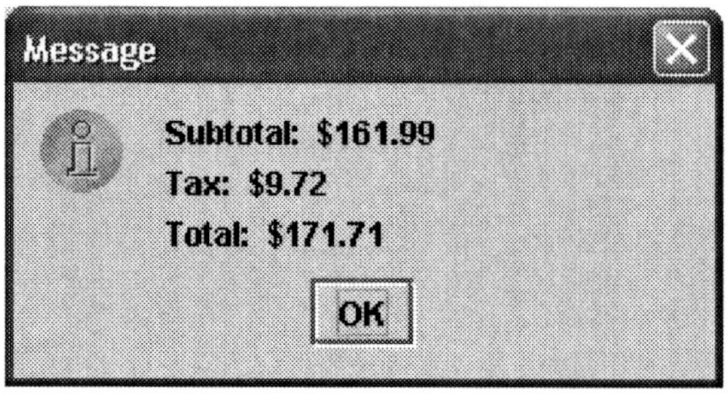
Message
Subtotal: $161.99
Tax: $9.72
Total: $171.71
OK

CHAPTER 12

GUI Applications—Part 2

Solutions

- ✦ Programming Challenge 2: Image Viewer
- ✦ Programming Challenge 4: Skateboard Designer
- ✦ Programming Challenge 6: Cell Phone Packages

Programming Challenge 2: Image Viewer

Problem Statement:

Write an application that allows the user to view image files. The application should use either a button or a menu item that displays a file chooser. When the user selects an image file, it should be loaded and displayed.

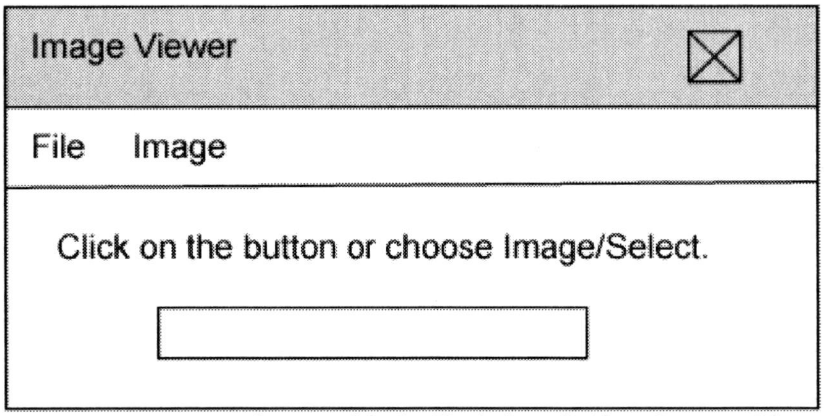

Figure 12-1 Sketch of the Image Viewer Window

Solution The ImageViewer Class:

Define What The Program Is To Do

Purpose	To create window allowing the user to view a selected image file.	
Fields	imagePanel	A panel to the image
	buttonPanel	A panel to hold the button
	imageLabel	Instructions for the user
	contentPane	A reference to the contentPane
	button	The button to click to select the image to view
	menuBar	The menu bar at the top of the window
	fileMenu	The file menu
	exitItem	An item to exit the application
	imageMenu	The image menu
	selectorItem	An item to select the image to view
Constructor	ImageViewer()	Creates an image viewer window.

Methods	buildMenuBar	Creates a menu bar
	buildImageMenu	Creates a drop down menu for image commands
	buildFileMenu	Creates a drop down menu for file commands
	buildImagePanel	Creates a panel with instructions that will be replaced by the image to view
	buildButtonPanel	Creates a panel with a button on it.
Private Inner Class	ExitListener	Handles the event when the user selects Exit from the File menu.
	method actionPerformed	Exits the program
Private Inner Class	ImageSelectorListener	Handles the event that is generated when the user selects Select from the Image menu or clicks on the button.
	method actionPerformed	Allows viewing of an image selected by the user.

Pseudocode for ImageViewer Class

1) This class will extend JFrame.

2) Declare fields for window objects.

3) Constructor.

   a) Create a window with a title by calling the super constructor and passing it the title.

   b) Build a menu bar and panels for the image and the button, then add them to the content pane.

   c) Pack and display the window.

4) The buildMenuBar method.

   a) Create the menu bar.

   b) Create menus and add them to the menu bar.

   c) Put the menu bar in the window.

5) The buildImageMenu

a) Create the menu item to select the image.

b) Connect it to the listener.

c) Create the menu and add the menu item to it.

6) The buildExitMenu

a) Create the menu item to exit the program.

b) Connect it to the listener.

c) Create the menu and add the menu item to it.

7) The buildImagePanel method.

a) Create a panel.

b) Create a label with instructions for the user.

c) Add the label to the panel.

8) The buildButtonPanel method.

a) Create a panel.

b) Create a button.

c) Connect the button to the listener.

d) Add the button to the panel.

9) The private inner class ImageSelectorListener.

a) This class will implement ActionListener.

b) The actionPerformed method.

i) Create a file chooser.

ii) Get the value which indicates the action taken by the user to close the dialog box.

iii) If the user clicked on the open or save button

(1) Get the file name.

iv) Create an image icon.

v) Put the icon on the label.

vi) Remove any text.

vii) Resize to accomodate the image.

10) The private inner class ImageSelectorListener.

a) This class will implement ActionListener.

b) The actionPerformed method.

i) Exit the program.

Code Listing 12-1 (ImageViewer.java)

```
//**********************************************************
// Written by Diane Christie
// Chapter 12
// Programming Challenge 2:  Image Viewer
//**********************************************************

//**********************************************************
// Write an application that allows the user to view image
// files.  The application should use either a button or a
// menu item that displays a file chooser.  When the user
// selects an image file, it should be loaded and displayed.
//**********************************************************

//**********************************************************
// The ImageViewer class allows the user to use either a
// button or a menu item to choose an image file to view.
//**********************************************************

import java.awt.*;
import java.awt.event.*;
import javax.swing.*;
import java.io.*;

public class ImageViewer extends JFrame
{
   private JPanel imagePanel;//A panel to the image
   private JPanel buttonPanel;//A panel to hold the button
   private JLabel imageLabel;//Instructions for the user
   private Container contentPane;//Reference to contentPane
   private JButton button;//The button to select the image
   private JMenuBar menuBar;//The menu bar
   private JMenu fileMenu;//The file menu
   private JMenuItem exitItem;//An item to exit application
   private JMenu imageMenu;//The image menu
   private JMenuItem selectorItem;//An item to select image

   //*****************************************************
   // Constructor
   //*****************************************************
   public ImageViewer()
   {
      //Creates a titled window
      super("Image Viewer");

      //Specify what happens when the close button is clicked
```

```
      setDefaultCloseOperation (JFrame.EXIT_ON_CLOSE);

      //Get the content pane and set the layout manager
      contentPane = getContentPane();
      contentPane.setLayout(new BorderLayout());

      //Build the menu bar
      buildMenuBar();

      //Build the image panel
      buildImagePanel();

      //Build the button panel
      buildButtonPanel();

      //Add the panels to the window
      contentPane.add(imagePanel, BorderLayout.CENTER);
      contentPane.add(buttonPanel, BorderLayout.SOUTH);

      //size the window to fit the contents and display it
      pack();
      setVisible(true);
   }

   //********************************************************
   // The buildMenuBar method creates a menu bar
   //********************************************************
   public void buildMenuBar()
   {
      // Create the menu bar
      menuBar = new JMenuBar();

      // Build menus
      buildImageMenu();
      buildFileMenu();

      // Add menus to menu bar
      menuBar.add(fileMenu);
      menuBar.add(imageMenu);

      //place menu bar in window
      setJMenuBar(menuBar);
   }

   //********************************************************
   // The buildImageMenu method creates a drop down menu
   // for image commands
   //********************************************************
   public void buildImageMenu()
   {
      //Create item
      selectorItem = new JMenuItem("Select");

      //Add short cut key for item
      selectorItem.setMnemonic(KeyEvent.VK_S);

      //Connect it with a listener
      selectorItem.addActionListener(
   new ImageSelectorListener());

      //Create the menu
```

```
      imageMenu = new JMenu("Image");

      //Add a short cut key for menu
      imageMenu.setMnemonic(KeyEvent.VK_I);

      //Add the item to the menu
      imageMenu.add(selectorItem);
   }

   //*****************************************************
   // The buildFileMenu method creates a drop down menu for
   // file commands
   //*****************************************************
   public void buildFileMenu()
   {
      //Create item
      exitItem = new JMenuItem("Exit");

      //Add a short cut key for item
      exitItem.setMnemonic (KeyEvent.VK_X);

      //Connect it with a listener
      exitItem.addActionListener(new ExitListener());

      //Create the menu
      fileMenu = new JMenu("File");

      //Add a short cut key for the menu
      fileMenu.setMnemonic (KeyEvent.VK_F);

      //Add the item to the menu
      fileMenu.add(exitItem);
   }

   //*****************************************************
   // The buildImagePanel method creates a panel with
   // instructions that will be replaced by the image
   // to view
   //*****************************************************
   public void buildImagePanel()
   {
      //Create the panel
      imagePanel = new JPanel();

      //Create a label with instructions for the user
      imageLabel = new JLabel("Click on the button or" +
         " choose Image/Select.");

      //Add the label to the panel
      imagePanel.add(imageLabel);
   }

   //*****************************************************
   // The buildButtonPanel method creates a panel with a
   // button on it.
   //*****************************************************
   public void buildButtonPanel()
   {
      //Create the panel
      buttonPanel = new JPanel();
```

```
      //Create the button
      button = new JButton("Select an image to view");

      //Connect the button to the listener
      button.addActionListener(new ImageSelectorListener());

      //Add the button to the panel
      buttonPanel.add(button);
   }

   //*****************************************************
   // Private inner class that handles the event that is
   // generated when the user selects Exit from the File
   // menu.
   //*****************************************************
   private class ExitListener implements ActionListener
   {
      public void actionPerformed(ActionEvent e)
      {
         System.exit(0);
      }
   }

   //*****************************************************
   // Private inner class that handles the event that is
   // generated when the user selects Select from the Image
   // menu or clicks on the button.
   //*****************************************************
   private class ImageSelectorListener implements ActionListener
   {
      public void actionPerformed(ActionEvent e)
      {
         File selectedFile;
         String fileName;

         //Create a file chooser
         JFileChooser fileChooser = new JFileChooser();

         //Get the value which indicates the action
         //taken by the user to close the dialog box
         int status = fileChooser.showOpenDialog(null);

         //if the user clicked on the open or save button
         if (status == JFileChooser.APPROVE_OPTION);
         {
            //get the file name
            selectedFile = fileChooser.getSelectedFile();
            fileName = selectedFile.getPath();
         }

         //Create an image icon
         ImageIcon fileImage = new ImageIcon(fileName);


         //put the icon on the label
         imageLabel.setIcon(fileImage);

         //remove any text
         imageLabel.setText(null);

         //resize to accomodate the image
```

```
            pack();
         }
      }

      public static void main(String [] args)
      {
         ImageViewer view = new ImageViewer ();
      }
   }
```

Program Output

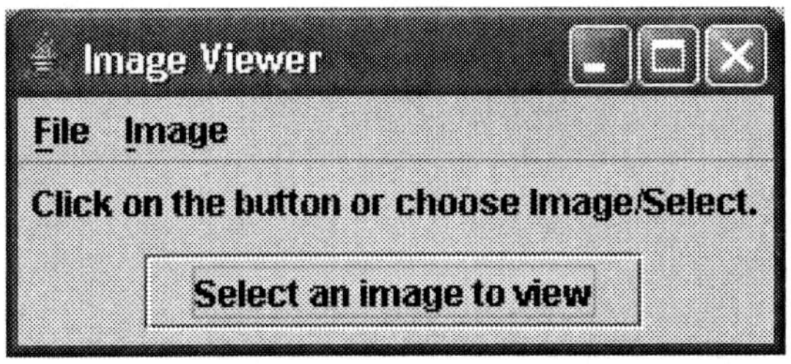

When the user clicks on the button or the Image/Select

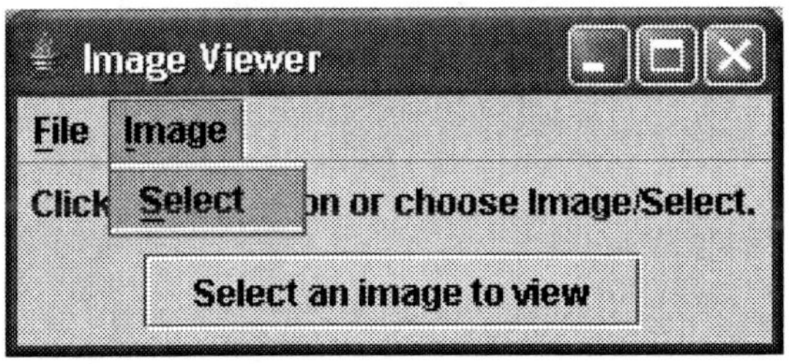

The following window appears

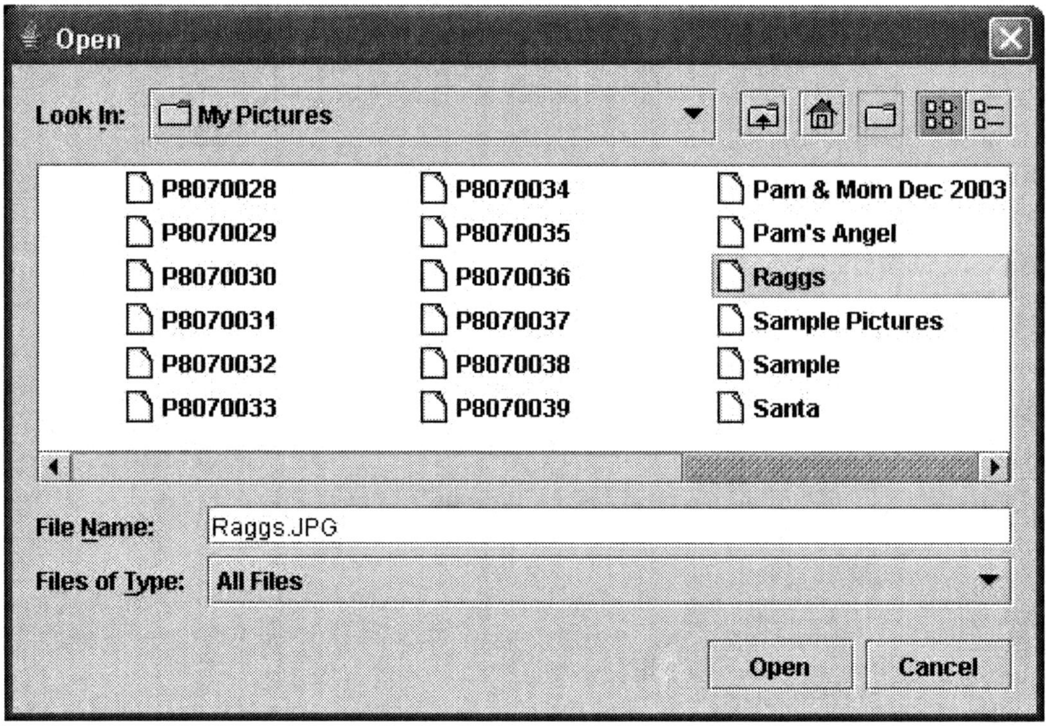

When the user chooses a file and clicks on the open button the following window appears

Image Viewer
File
Image
Select an image to view

Programming Challenge 4: Skateboard Designer

Problem Statement:

The Skate Shop sells the skateboard products listed below

Decks	Truck Assemblies	Wheels
The Master Thrasher $60	7.75 inch axle $35	51 mm $20
The Dictator $45	8 inch axle $40	55 mm $22
The Street King $50	8.5 inch axle $45	58 mm $24
		61 mm $28

In addition, the Skate Shop sells the following miscellaneous products and services:

Grip tape: $10

Bearings: $30

Riser pads: $2

Nut & Bolts kit: $3

Create an application that that allows the user to select one deck, one truck assembly, and one wheel set from either list components or combo boxes. The application should also have a list component that allows the user to select multiple miscellaneous products. The application should display the subtotal, the amount of sales tax (at 6%), and the total of the order.

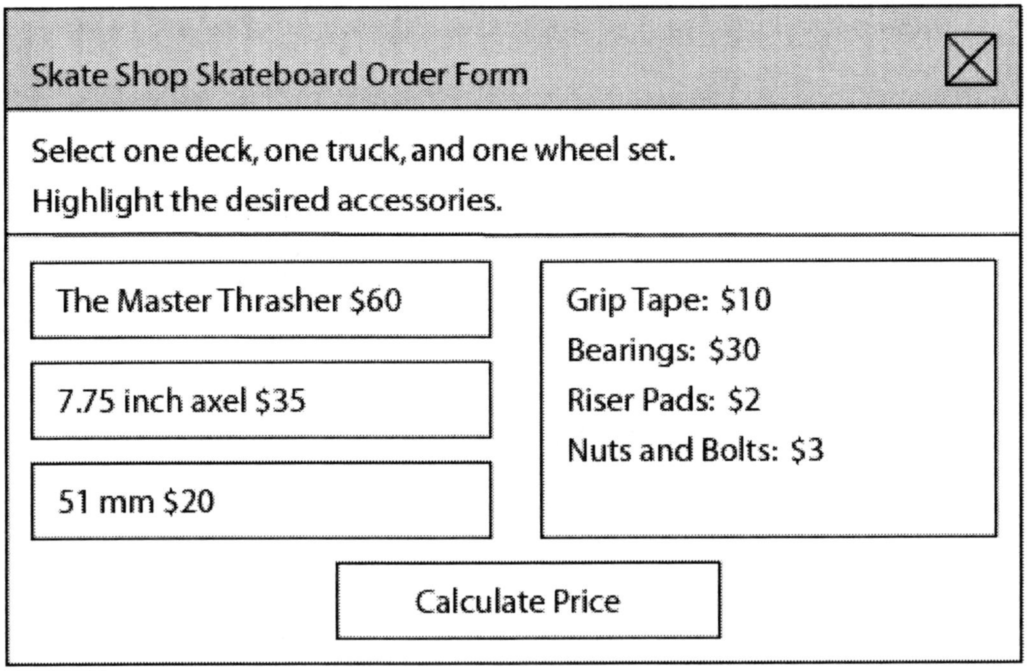

Figure 12-2 Sketch of Skate Shop Custom Skateboard Order Window

Solution:

The desired layout can be achieved by using a BorderLayout manager with the SkateboardDesigner's content pane. Each panel can be created separately and added to the content pane. We will need the following panels:

- InstructionPanel. This panel contains the labels that appears in the window's north region.
- ComboPanel. This panel contains the combo boxes for the decks, trucks, and wheels.
- ListPanel. This panel contains the list box listing available accessories.
- ButtonPanel. This panel contains the button to calculate the price of the skateboard.

The SkateboardDesigner Class

Define What the Class Is To Do

Purpose	To create a window allowing the user to design a skateboard.	
Fields	decks	An array of Strings containing a list of decks.
	trucks	An array of Strings containing a list of trucks.
	wheels	An array of Strings containing a list of wheels.
	miscellaneous	An array of Strings containing a list of accessories.
	deckBox	A combo box containing decks to choose from.
	truckBox	A combo box containing trucks to choose from.
	wheelBox	A combo box containing wheels to choose from.
	comboPanel	A panel containing all combo boxes
	listPanel	A panel containing a list box.
	buttonPanel	A panel containing a button.
	instPanel	A panel containing instructions for the user.
	button	The button to allow the user to calculate the price of the skateboard.
	miscList	A list of available accessories,
	instructions1	A label with instructions for the user to use the combo boxes.
	Instructions2	A label with instructions for the user to use the list box.
	contentPane	A reference to the contentPane.
Constructor	SkateboardDesigner()	Creates a SkateboardDesigner window.
Methods	buildInstructionPanel()	Creates a panel containing instructions for the user.
	buildComboPanel()	Creates a panel containing the combo boxes containing choices for decks, trucks, and wheels.
	buildListPanel()	Creates a panel containing a list of accessories.
	buildButtonPanel()	Creates a panel contining the

		button to calculate the price of the skateboard.	
Private Inner Class	ButtonListener	Handles the event that is generated when the user clicks on the button.	
	method	actionPerformed()	Calculates the price of the skateboard with the user's choice of deck, truck, and wheels, along with all chosen accessories.

Pseudocode for the SkateboardDesigner Class

1) This class will extend JFrame.

2) Declare fields for window objects.

3) Constructor.

   a) Create a window with a title by calling the super constructor and passing it the title.

   b) Build panels for the combo boxes, list boxes, button, and instructions, and then add them to the content pane.

   c) Pack and display the window.

4) The buildInstructionPanel method.

   a) Create a panel with a grid layout.

   b) Create labels with instructions for user.

   c) Add labels to panel.

5) The buildComboPanel method.

   a) Create a panel with a grid layout.

   b) Create the combo boxes.

   c) Add combo boxes to the panel.

6) The buildListPanel method.

   a) Create a panel.

   b) Create a list of accessories.

c) Add list to panel.

7) The buildButtonPanel method.

a) Create a panel containing the button.

b) Create the button and connect to the listener.

c) Add the button to the panel.

8) The private inner class ButtonListener.

a) This class will implement ActionListener.

b) The actionPerformed method.

i) Get the user's accessory choices.

ii) Add the price of each accessory chosen to total.

iii) Get the selection for the skateboard deck.

iv) Add the price of the deck to the total.

v) Get the selection for the skateboard truck.

vi) Add the price of the truck to the total.

vii) Get the selection for the skateboard wheels.

viii) Add the price of the wheels to the total.

ix) Calculate the tax and add to get a final price.

x) Display results in a dialog box.

Code Listing 12-2 (SkateboardDesigner.java)

```
//***********************************************************
// Written by Diane Christie
// Chapter 12
// Programming Challenge 4:  Skateboard Designer
//***********************************************************

//***********************************************************
// The Skate Shop sells the skateboard products listed below
// Decks            Truck Assemblies   Wheels
// Master Thrasher $60  7.75 inch axle $35    51 mm $20
// Dictator $45         8 inch axle $40       55 mm $22
// Street King $50      8.5 inch axle $45 58 mm $24
//                                  61 mm $28
// In addition, the Skate Shop sells the following
// miscellaneous products and services:
// Bearings:  $30
// Riser pads: $2
```

```
// Nut & Bolts kit: $3
// Create an application that that allows the user to
// select one deck, one truck assembly, and one wheel set
// from either list components or combo boxes.  The
// application should also have a list component that
// allows the user to select multiple miscellaneous
// products.  The application should display the subtotal,
// the amount of sales tax (at 6%), and the total of the
// order.
//*********************************************************

//*********************************************************
// The SkateboardDesigner class creates a window that
// allows the user to choose parts to design a skateboard.
//*********************************************************

import java.awt.*;
import java.awt.event.*;
import javax.swing.*;
import java.text.DecimalFormat;

public class SkateboardDesigner extends JFrame
{
   private String [] decks = {"The Master Thrasher $60",
      "The Dictator $45", "The Street King $50"};
   private String [] truckAssemblies = {"7.75 inch axle $35",
      "8 inch axle $40", "8.5 inch axle $45"};
   private String [] wheels = {"51 mm $20", "55 mm $22",
      "58 mm $24", "61 mm $28"};
   private String [] miscellaneous = {"Grip tape: $10",
      "Bearings:  $30", "Riser pads:  $2",
      "Nuts & bolts:  $3"};
   private JComboBox deckBox;//contains deck selections
   private JComboBox truckBox;//contains truck selections
   private JComboBox wheelBox;//contains wheel selections
   private JPanel comboPanel;//contains all combo boxes
   private JPanel listPanel;//contains list boxes
   private JPanel buttonPanel;//contains buttons
   private JPanel instPanel;//contains instructions for user
   private JButton button;//button to calculate price
   private JList miscList;//list of accessories
   private JLabel instructions1;//instructions for combo boxes
   private JLabel instructions2;//instructions for list
   private Container contentPane;//content pane of window

   //*******************************************************
   // Constructor
   //*******************************************************
   public SkateboardDesigner()
   {
      //Creates a titled window
      super("Skate Shop Skateboard Order Form");

      //Specify what happens when the close button is clicked
      setDefaultCloseOperation (JFrame.EXIT_ON_CLOSE);

      //Get the content pane and set the layout manager
      contentPane = getContentPane();
      contentPane.setLayout(new BorderLayout());

      //Build various panels
```

```
    buildInstructionPanel();
    buildComboPanel();
    buildListPanel();
    buildButtonPanel();

    //Add panels to content pane of window
    contentPane.add(instPanel, BorderLayout.NORTH);
    contentPane.add(comboPanel, BorderLayout.WEST);
    contentPane.add(listPanel, BorderLayout.EAST);
    contentPane.add(buttonPanel, BorderLayout.SOUTH);

    //size the window to fit the contents and display it
    pack();
    setVisible(true);
}

//*******************************************************
// The buildInstructionPanel method creates a panel
// containing instructions for the user.
//*******************************************************
public void buildInstructionPanel()
{
    //Create a panel with a grid layout
    instPanel = new JPanel();
    instPanel.setLayout(new GridLayout(2,0));

    //Create labels with instructions for user
    instructions1 = new JLabel("Select one deck, one "
        + "truck assembly, and one wheel set.");
    instructions2 = new JLabel("Highlight desired " +
        "accessories.");

    //Add labels to panel
    instPanel.add(instructions1);
    instPanel.add(instructions2);
}

//*******************************************************
// The buildComboPanel method creates a panel containing
// the combo boxes containing choices for decks, trucks,
// and wheels.
//*******************************************************
public void buildComboPanel()
{
    //Create a panel with a grid layout
    comboPanel = new JPanel();
    comboPanel.setLayout(new GridLayout(3,0));

    //Create the combo boxes
    deckBox = new JComboBox(decks);
    truckBox = new JComboBox(truckAssemblies);
    wheelBox = new JComboBox(wheels);

    //Add combo boxes to the panel
    comboPanel.add(deckBox);
    comboPanel.add(truckBox);
    comboPanel.add(wheelBox);
}

//*******************************************************
// The buildListPanel method creates a panel containing
```

```
// a list of accessories.
//*****************************************************
public void buildListPanel()
{
   //Create a panel
   listPanel = new JPanel();

   //Create a list of accessories
   miscList = new JList(miscellaneous);

   //Add list to panel
   listPanel.add(miscList);
}

//*****************************************************
// The buildButtonPanel methos creates a panel contining
// the button to calculate the price of the skateboard.
//*****************************************************
public void buildButtonPanel()
{
   //Create a panel containing the button
   buttonPanel = new JPanel();

   //Creaate the button and connect to the listener
   button = new JButton("Calculate Price");
   button.addActionListener(new ButtonListener());

   //Add the button to the panel
   buttonPanel.add(button);
}

//*****************************************************
// Private inner class that handles the event that is
// generated when the user clicks on the button.
//*****************************************************
private class ButtonListener implements ActionListener
{
   public void actionPerformed(ActionEvent e)
   {
      DecimalFormat money = new DecimalFormat("0.00");
      String selection;
      double total = 0;//Total price before tax
      double finalTotal;//Total price after tax
      double tax;//Sales tax
      final double TAX_RATE = 0.06;

      //get the user's accessory choices
      Object[] selections = miscList.getSelectedValues();

      //add the price of each accessory chosen to total
      for (int i = 0; i < selections.length; i++)
      {
         if(selections[i].equals("Grip tape: $10"))
            total += 10;
         if(selections[i].equals("Bearings:  $30"))
            total += 30;
         if(selections[i].equals("Riser pads:  $2"))
            total += 2;
         if(selections[i].equals("Nuts & bolts:  $3"))
            total += 3;
      }
```

```
            //get the selection for the skateboard deck
            selection = (String) deckBox.getSelectedItem();

            //add the price of the deck to the total
            if (selection.equals("The Master Thrasher $60"))
               total += 60;
            else if (selection.equals("The Dictator $45"))
               total += 45;
            else if (selection.equals("The Street King $50"))
               total += 50;

            //get the selection for the skateboard truck
            selection = (String) truckBox.getSelectedItem();

            //add the price of the truck to the total
            if (selection.equals("7.75 inch axle $35" ))
               total += 35;
            else if (selection.equals("8 inch axle $40"))
               total += 40;
            else if (selection.equals("8.5 inch axle $45"))
               total += 45;

            //get the selection for the skateboard wheels
            selection = (String) wheelBox.getSelectedItem();

            //add the price of the wheels to the total
            if (selection.equals("51 mm $20"))
               total += 20;
            else if (selection.equals("55 mm $22"))
               total += 22;
            else if (selection.equals("58 mm $24"))
               total +=24;
            else if (selection.equals("61 mm $28"))
               total += 28;

            //calculate the tax and add to get a final price
            tax = total * TAX_RATE;
            finalTotal = total + tax;

            //Display results
            JOptionPane.showMessageDialog(null,
               "Subtotal:  $" + money.format(total) +
               "\nTax:  $" + money.format(tax) +
               "\nTotal:  $" + money.format(finalTotal));
         }
      }

      public static void main(String [] args)
      {
         SkateboardDesigner skateboard =new SkateboardDesigner();
      }
   }
```

Program Output

Original GUI

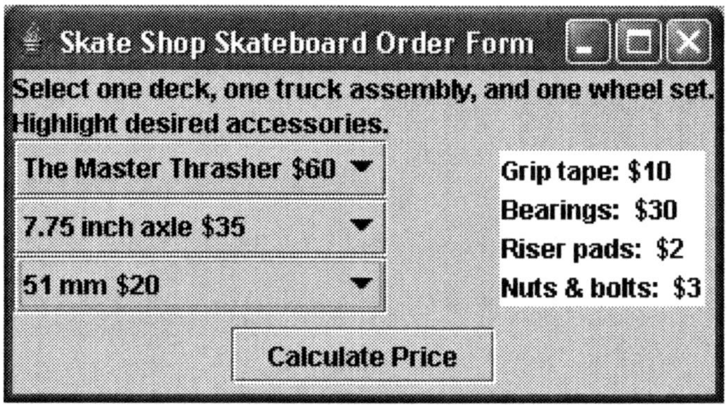

User enters choices for deck, truck, and wheel set. The user highlights the accessories required.

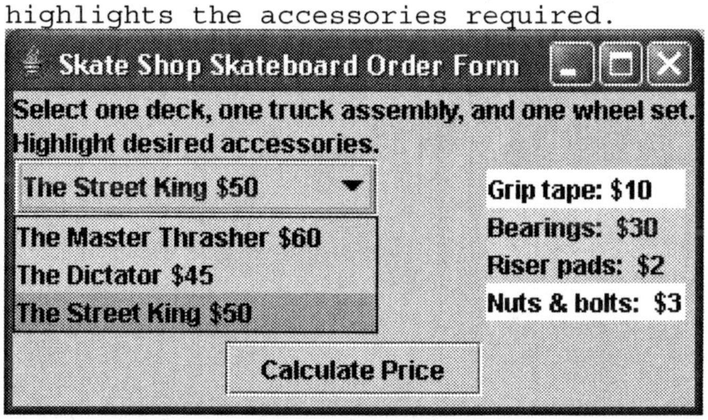

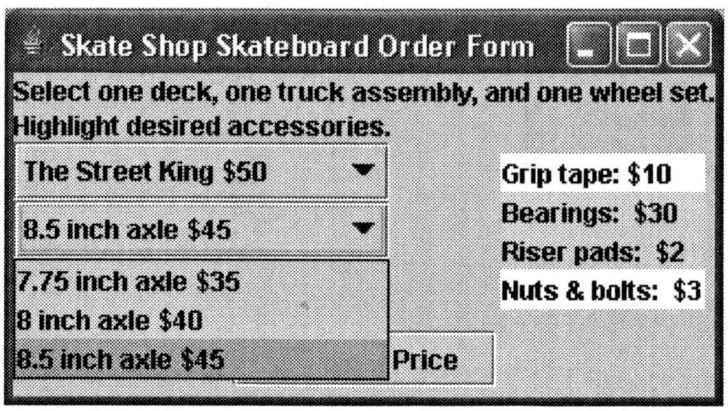

After the user makes his or her choices. This window appears when user clicks calculate button.

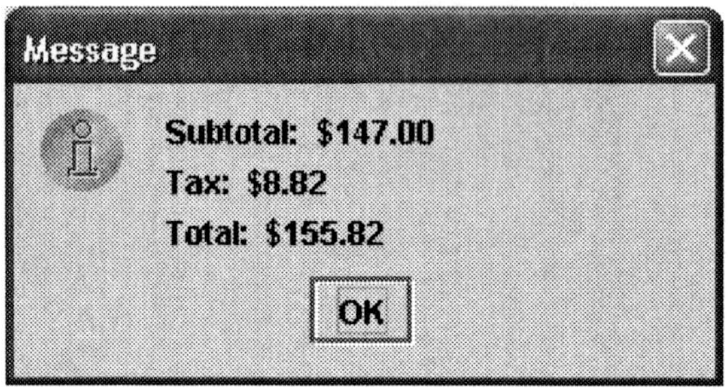
Message
Subtotal: $147.00
Tax: $8.82
Total: $155.82
OK

Programming Challenge 6: Cell Phone Packages

Problem Statement:

Cell Solutions, a cell phone provider, sells the following packages:

300 minutes per month: $45.00 per month

800 minutes per month: $65.00 per month

1500 minutes per month: $99.00 per month

The provider sells the following phones. (A 6% sales tax applies to the sale of a phone.)

Model 100: $29.95

Model 110: $49.95

Model 200: $99.95

Customers may also select the following options:

Voice mail: $5.00 per month

Text messaging: $10.00 per month

Write an application that displays a menu system. The menu system should allow the user to select one package, one phone, and any of the options desired. As the user selects items from the menu, the applications should show the prices of the items selected.

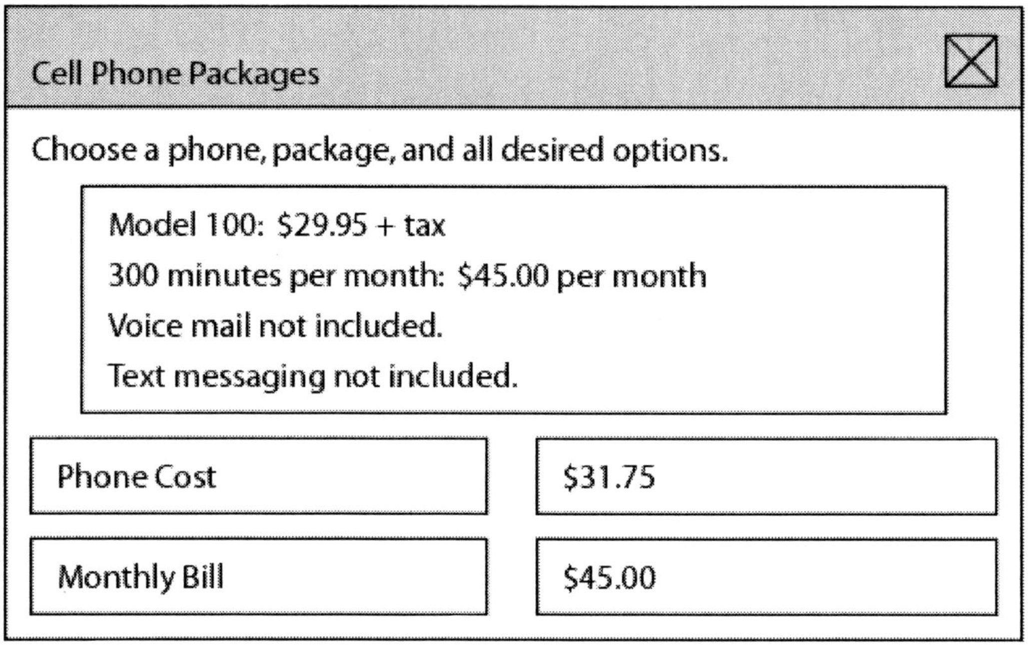

Figure 12-3 Sketch of the Cell Phone Window

Solution:

The desired layout can be achieved by using a BorderLayout manager with the CellPhone's content pane. Each panel can be created separately and added to the content pane. We will need the following panels:

- InstructionPanel. This panel contains the labels that appears in the window's north region.
- ListPanel. This panel contains the list box listing user choices and prices.
- PricePanel. This panel contains the labels and text boxes that contain total costs output to the user.

We also need a menu system.

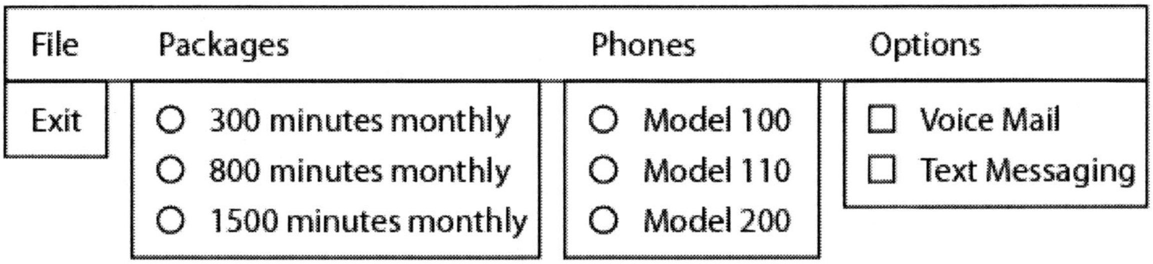

Figure 12-4 Sketch of CellPhone class's menu system

Solution:

Define What the Class Is To Do

Purpose	**To create a window allowing the user to select a cell phone, a package, and desired options.**	
Fields	**TAX_RATE**	**The sales tax rate of 6%.**
	listPanel	**A JPanel to hold the list of choices.**
	pricePanel	**A JPanel to hold the prices.**
	instructionsPanel	**A JPanel containing instructions to the user.**
	instructions	**A JLabel has instructions for the user.**
	phoneCostLabel	**A JLabel indicating which number is the price of the phone.**
	monthlyCostLabel	**A JLabel indicating which number is the monthly bill.**
	phoneCostOutput	**A JTextField holding the price of the phone.**
	monthlyCostOutput	**A JTextField holding the monthly cost of the cell phone plan.**
	list	**A Jlist holding the user's choices.**
	choices	**An array of strings which are the user's choices for cell phone, package, and options.**
	phoneCost	**The number representing the cost of the selected phone.**
	packageCost	**The number representing the cost of the selected package.**
	optionsCost	**The number representing the cost of the selected options.**

		cost of the selected options.
	contentPane	A reference to the content pane.
	menuBar	A JMenuBar which will go at the top of the window and contain other menus.
	fileMenu	A JMenu containing file commands.
	phoneMenu	A JMenu containing radio buttons to choose a phone model.
	packageMenu	A JMenu containing radio buttons to choose a cell phone package.
	optionsMenu	A JMenu containing check boxes to choose desired options.
	exitItem	A JMenuItem to allow the user to exit the program.
	voiceItem	A JMenuItem to allow the user to select voice mail as an option.
	textItem	A JMenuItem to allow the user to select text messaging as an option.
	minutes300	A JMenuItem to allow the user to select a package having 300 monthly minutes.
	minutes800	A JMenuItem to allow the user to select a package having 800 monthly minutes.
	minutes1500	A JMenuItem to allow the user to select a package having 1500 monthly minutes.
	model100	A JMenuItem to allow the user to select a model 100 cell phone.
	model10	A JMenuItem to allow the user to select a model 110 cell phone.
	model200	A JMenuItem to allow the user to select a model 200 cell phone.
Constructors	CellPhone()	Creates a CellPhone object.
Methods	buildMenuBar()	Creates a menu bar.

	buildInstructionsPanel ()	Creates a panel that contains instructions for the user.	
	buildPhoneMenu()	Creates a drop down menu with choices for a cell phone.	
	buildPackageMenu()	Creates a drop down menu with choices for a cell phone packages.	
	buildOptionsMenu()	Creates a drop down menu with choices for a cell phone options.	
	buildFileMenu()	Creates a drop down menu for file commands.	
	buildListPanel()	Creates a panel with a list of user choices.	
	buildPricePanel()	Creates a panel with the cost on it.	
Private Inner Class	PhoneListener	Handles the event that is generated when the user selects a phone model from the phone menu.	
	Method	actionPerfor med	Displays the model and cost of the selected phone.
Private Inner Class	PackageListener	Handles the event that is generated when the user selects a cell phone package from the package menu.	
	method	actionPerformed	Displays the number of minutes and cost of the selected package.
Private Inner Class	OptionsListener	Handles the event that is generated when the user selects the desired options from the options menu.	
	method	actionPerformed	Displays the status and cost of the selected options.
Private Inner Class	ExitListener	Handles the event that is generated when the user selects exit from the	

		file menu.	
	method	actionPerformed	Exits the program

Pseudocode for CellPhone class

1) This class will extend JFrame.

2) Declare fields for window objects.

3) Constructor.

   a) Create a window with a title by calling the super constructor and passing it the title.

   b) Build a menu bar and panels for the instructions, list of choices, and the price output, then add them to the content pane.

   c) Pack and display the window.

4) The buildMenuBar method.

   a) Create the menu bar.

   b) Create menus and add them to the menu bar.

   c) Put the menu bar in the window.

5) The buildInstructionsPanel method.

   a) Create a panel.

   b) Create a label with user instructions.

   c) Add the label to the panel.

6) The buildPhoneMenu method.

   a) Create radio button items, model 100 is default.

   b) Calculate price for default model.

   c) Connect each item with a listener.

   d) Group the radio buttons.

   e) Create the menu.

   f) Add the items to the menu.

7) The buildPackageMenu method.

a) Create radio button items, 300 minutes is default.

b) Calculate price for default package.

c) Connect each item with a listener.

d) Group the radio buttons.

e) Create the menu.

f) Add the items to the menu

8) The buildOptionsMenu method.

a) Create check box items.

b) Connect each item with a listener.

c) Create the menu.

d) Add the items to the menu.

9) The buildFileMenu method.

a) Create the exit item.

b) Add a short cut key for item.

c) Connect it with a listener.

d) Create the menu.

e) Add a short cut key for the menu.

f) Add the item to the menu.

10) The buildListPanel method.

a) Create the panel.

b) Create a label with instructions for the user.

c) Set the number of visible rows to 6.

d) Add the list to the panel.

11) The buildPricePanel method.

a) Create a panel with 2 rows and 2 columns.

b) Create a label and non-editable text field for the phone cost.

c) Output the default phone price.

d) Create a label and non-editable text field for the monthly bill.

e) Output the default monthly bill.

f) Add pieces to the panel.

12) The private inner class ExitListener.

a) This class will implement ActionListener.

b) The actionPerformed method.

i) Exit the program.

13) The private inner class PhoneListener.

a) This class will implement ActionListener.

b) The actionPerformed method.

i) Calculate price (with sales tax) and set output string depending on user choice.

ii) Redisplay list of choices and price of phone.

14) The private inner class PackageListener.

a) This class will implement ActionListener.

b) The actionPerformed method.

i) Set montly rate and output string depending on user choice.

ii) Redisplay list of choices and monthly bill.

15) The private inner class OptionsListener.

a) This class will implement ActionListener.

b) The actionPerformed method.

i) Calculate monthly cost of options and set output strings depending on user choice.

ii) Redisplay list of choices and monthly bill.

Code Listing 12-3 (CellPhone.java)

```
//***********************************************************
```

```
// Written by Diane Christie
// Chapter 12
// Programming Challenge 6:  Cell Phone Package
//*******************************************************

//*******************************************************
// Cell Solutions, a cell phone provider, sells the
// following packages:
//    300 minutes per month:  $45.00 per month
//    800 minutes per month:  $65.00 per month
//    1500 minutes per month:  $99.00 per month
// The provider sells the following phones. (A 6% sales
// tax applies to the sale of a phone.)
//       Model 100:  $29.95
//    Model 110:  $49.95
//    Model 200:  $99.95
// Customers may also select the following options:
//    Voice mail: $5.00 per month
//    Text messaging: $10.00 per month
// Write an application that displays a menu system.  The
// menu system should allow the user to select one package,
// one phone, and any of the options desired.  As the user
// selects items from the menu, the applications should
// show the prices of the items selected.
//*******************************************************

//*******************************************************
// The CellPhone class allows the user to select a cell
// phone package, a cell phone, and any options desired.
//*******************************************************

import java.awt.*;
import java.awt.event.*;
import javax.swing.*;
import java.io.*;
import java.text.DecimalFormat;

public class CellPhone extends JFrame
{
   private final double TAX_RATE = 0.06;//Sales tax rate

   // Array holding user choices
   private String [] choices = {"Model 100:  $29.95 + tax",
      "300 minutes per month:  $45.00 per month",
      "Voice mail not included",
      "Text messaging not included"};

   private JLabel phoneCostLabel;//phone price label
   private JLabel monthlyCostLabel;//monthly price label
   private JTextField phoneCostOutput;//price of phone
   private JTextField monthlyCostOutput;//price per month
   private JPanel listPanel;//A panel to hold selections
   private JPanel pricePanel;//A panel to hold prices
   private JPanel instructionsPanel;//Holds instructions
   private JLabel instructions; //User instructions
   private JList list;//List of choices
   private Container contentPane;//ContentPane reference
   private JMenuBar menuBar;//The menu bar
   private JMenu fileMenu;//The file menu
   private JMenuItem exitItem;//Item to exit application
   private JMenu packageMenu;//The package menu
```

```
private JMenuItem minutes300;//A package item
private JMenuItem minutes800;//A package item
private JMenuItem minutes1500;//A package item
private JMenu phoneMenu;//The phone menu
private JMenuItem model100;//The model 100 phone
private JMenuItem model110;//The model 110 phone
private JMenuItem model200;//The model 200 phone
private JMenu optionsMenu;//The options menu
private JMenuItem voiceItem; //voice mail
private JMenuItem textItem; //text messaging
private double phoneCost;//price for phone
private double packageCost;//monthly package bill
private double optionsCost;//monthly options bill

DecimalFormat money = new DecimalFormat("0.00");

//**************************************************
// Constructor
//**************************************************
public CellPhone()
{
   //Creates a titled window
   super("Cell Phone Packages");

   //Specify what happens when close button is clicked
   setDefaultCloseOperation (JFrame.EXIT_ON_CLOSE);

   //Get the content pane and set the layout manager
   contentPane = getContentPane();
   contentPane.setLayout(new BorderLayout());

   //Build the menu bar
   buildMenuBar();

   //Build instructions panel
   buildInstructionsPanel();

   //Build the image panel
   buildListPanel();

   //Build the output panel
   buildPricePanel();

   //Add the panels to the window
   contentPane.add(instructionsPanel, BorderLayout.NORTH);
   contentPane.add(listPanel, BorderLayout.CENTER);
   contentPane.add(pricePanel, BorderLayout.SOUTH);
   //contentPane.add(buttonPanel, BorderLayout.SOUTH);

   //create the array for the user's choices
   //size the window to fit the contents and display it
   pack();
   setVisible(true);

}

//**************************************************
// The buildMenuBar method creates a menu bar
//**************************************************
public void buildMenuBar()
{
```

```
   // Create the menu bar
   menuBar = new JMenuBar();

   // Build menus
   buildPhoneMenu();
   buildPackageMenu();
   buildOptionsMenu();
   buildFileMenu();

   // Add menus to menu bar
   menuBar.add(fileMenu);
   menuBar.add(packageMenu);
   menuBar.add(phoneMenu);
   menuBar.add(optionsMenu);

   //place menu bar in window
   setJMenuBar(menuBar);
}

//*****************************************************
// The buildInstructionsPanel method creates a panel
// that contains instructions for the user.
//*****************************************************
public void buildInstructionsPanel()
{
   //Create the panel
   instructionsPanel = new JPanel();

   //Create a label with instructions for the user
   instructions = new JLabel("Choose a phone, package,"
      + " and all desired options.");

   //Add the label to the panel
   instructionsPanel.add(instructions);
}

//*****************************************************
// The buildPhoneMenu method creates a drop down menu
// with choices for a cell phone.
//*****************************************************
public void buildPhoneMenu()
{
   //Create items, model 100 is default
   model100 = new JRadioButtonMenuItem("Model 100", true);
   //price for default model 100
   phoneCost = (1 + TAX_RATE) * 29.95;
   model110 = new JRadioButtonMenuItem("Model 110");
   model200 = new JRadioButtonMenuItem("Model 200");

   //Connect each with a listener
   model100.addActionListener(new PhoneListener());
   model110.addActionListener(new PhoneListener());
   model200.addActionListener(new PhoneListener());

   //Group the radio buttons
   ButtonGroup group = new ButtonGroup();
   group.add(model100);
   group.add(model110);
   group.add(model200);

   //Create the menu
```

```
      phoneMenu = new JMenu("Phones");

      //Add the items to the menu
      phoneMenu.add(model100);
      phoneMenu.add(model110);
      phoneMenu.add(model200);
   }

   //*****************************************************
   // The buildPackageMenu method creates a drop down menu
   // with choices for a cell phone packages.
   //*****************************************************
   public void buildPackageMenu()
   {
      //Create items, 300 minutes is default
      minutes300 = new JRadioButtonMenuItem(
         "300 minutes monthly", true);
      //price for default package of 300 minutes
      packageCost = 45.0;
      minutes800= new JRadioButtonMenuItem(
         "800 minutes monthly");
      minutes1500 = new JRadioButtonMenuItem(
         "1500 minutes monthly");

      //Connect each with a listener
      minutes300.addActionListener(new PackageListener());
      minutes800.addActionListener(new PackageListener());
      minutes1500.addActionListener(new PackageListener());

      //Group the radio buttons
      ButtonGroup group = new ButtonGroup();
      group.add(minutes300);
      group.add(minutes800);
      group.add(minutes1500);

      //Create the menu
      packageMenu = new JMenu("Packages");

      //Add the item to the menu
      packageMenu.add(minutes300);
      packageMenu.add(minutes800);
      packageMenu.add(minutes1500);
   }

   //*****************************************************
   // The buildOptionsMenu method creates a drop down menu
   // with choices for a cell phone options.
   //*****************************************************
   public void buildOptionsMenu()
   {
      //Create items
      voiceItem = new JCheckBoxMenuItem("Voice mail");
      textItem= new JCheckBoxMenuItem("Text messaging");
      optionsCost = 0;//no options in default

      //Connect each with a listener
      voiceItem.addActionListener(new OptionsListener());
      textItem.addActionListener(new OptionsListener());

      //Create the menu
      optionsMenu = new JMenu("Options");
```

```
      //Add the item to the menu
      optionsMenu.add(voiceItem);
      optionsMenu.add(textItem);
   }

   //*****************************************************
   // The buildFileMenu method creates a drop down menu
   // for file commands.
   //*****************************************************
   public void buildFileMenu()
   {
      //Create item
      exitItem = new JMenuItem("Exit");

      //Add a short cut key for item
      exitItem.setMnemonic (KeyEvent.VK_X);

      //Connect it with a listener
      exitItem.addActionListener(new ExitListener());

      //Create the menu
      fileMenu = new JMenu("File");

      //Add a short cut key for the menu
      fileMenu.setMnemonic (KeyEvent.VK_F);

      //Add the item to the menu
      fileMenu.add(exitItem);
   }

   //*****************************************************
   // The buildListPanel method creates a panel with
   // a list of user choices.
   //*****************************************************
   public void buildListPanel()
   {
      //Create the panel
      listPanel = new JPanel();

      //Create a label with instructions for the user
      list = new JList(choices);

      //Set the number of visible rows to 6
      list.setVisibleRowCount(6);

      //Add the list to the panel
      listPanel.add(list);
   }

   //*****************************************************
   // The buildPricePanel method creates a panel with the
   // cost on it.
   //*****************************************************
   public void buildPricePanel()
   {
      //Create a panel with 2 rows and 2 columns
      pricePanel = new JPanel();
      pricePanel.setLayout(new GridLayout(2,2));

      //Create a label and non-editable text field
```

```
        phoneCostLabel = new JLabel("Phone cost");
        phoneCostOutput = new JTextField(10);
        phoneCostOutput.setEditable(false);
        //Output the default phone price
        phoneCostOutput.setText("$" +
           money.format(phoneCost));

        //Create a label and non-editable text field
        monthlyCostLabel = new JLabel("Monthly bill");
        monthlyCostOutput = new JTextField(10);
        monthlyCostOutput.setEditable(false);
        //Output the default monthly bill
        monthlyCostOutput.setText("$" +
           money.format(packageCost + optionsCost));

        //Add pieces to the panel
        pricePanel.add(phoneCostLabel);
        pricePanel.add(phoneCostOutput);
        pricePanel.add(monthlyCostLabel);
        pricePanel.add(monthlyCostOutput);
     }

     //*****************************************************
     // Private inner class that handles the event that is
     // generated when the user selects Exit from the File
     // menu.
     //*****************************************************
     private class ExitListener implements ActionListener
     {
        public void actionPerformed(ActionEvent e)
        {
           System.exit(0);
        }
     }

     //******************************************************
     // Private inner class that handles the event that is
     // generated when the user chooses a cell phone.
     //*****************************************************
     private class PhoneListener implements ActionListener
     {
        public void actionPerformed(ActionEvent e)
        {
           //calculate price and set output string depending on
           //user choice
           if (model100.isSelected())
           {
              phoneCost = (1 + TAX_RATE) * 29.95;
              choices[0] = "Model 100: $29.95 + tax";
           }
           else if (model110.isSelected())
           {
              phoneCost = (1 + TAX_RATE) * 49.95;
              choices[0] = "Model 110: $49.95 + tax";
           }
           else if (model200.isSelected())
           {
              phoneCost = (1 + TAX_RATE) * 99.95;
              choices[0] = "Model 200: $99.95 + tax";
           }
```

```
         //redisplay
         list.setListData(choices);
         phoneCostOutput.setText("$" +
            money.format(phoneCost));

      }
   }

   //******************************************************
   // Private inner class that handles the event that is
   // generated when the user chooses a package.
   //******************************************************
   private class PackageListener implements ActionListener
   {
      public void actionPerformed(ActionEvent e)
      {
         //change price and output string depending on
         //user choice
         if (minutes300.isSelected())
         {
            choices[1] = "300 minutes per month: $45.00" +
               " per month";
            packageCost = 45.0;
         }
         else if (minutes800.isSelected())
         {
            choices[1] = "800 minutes per month: $65.00" +
               " per month";
            packageCost = 65.0;
         }
         else if (minutes1500.isSelected())
         {
            choices[1] = "1500 minutes per month: $99.00" +
               " per month";
            packageCost = 99.0;
         }

         //redisplay
         monthlyCostOutput.setText("$" +
            money.format(packageCost+optionsCost));
         list.setListData(choices);
      }
   }

   //******************************************************
   // Private inner class that handles the event that is
   // generated when the user chooses options.
   //******************************************************
   private class OptionsListener implements ActionListener
   {
      public void actionPerformed(ActionEvent e)
      {
         //reset options to none
         optionsCost = 0;

         //change price and output string depending on
         //user choice
         if (voiceItem.isSelected())
         {
            choices[2] = "Voice mail: $5.00 per month";
            optionsCost += 5.0;
```

```
            }
            else
            {
               choices[2] = "Voice mail not included";
            }
            if (textItem.isSelected())
            {
               choices[3] = "Text messaging: $10.00 per month";
               optionsCost += 10.0;
            }
            else
            {
               choices[3] = "Text messaging not included";
            }

            //redisplay
            monthlyCostOutput.setText("$" +
               money.format(packageCost+optionsCost));
            list.setListData(choices);

         }
      }

      public static void main(String [] args)
      {
         CellPhone phonePlan = new CellPhone();
      }
}
```

Program Output

The original window

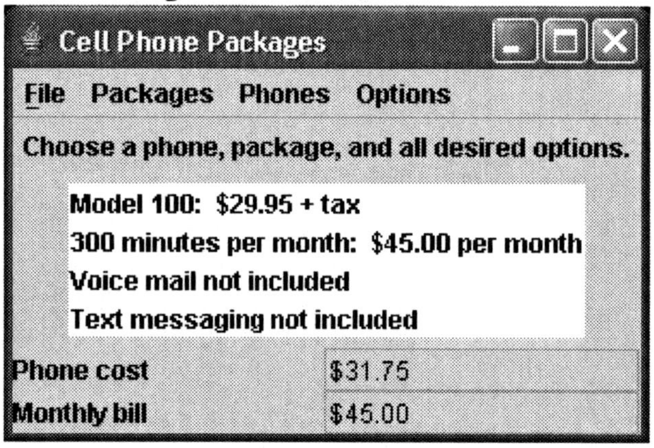

User can select a different model phone than the default model

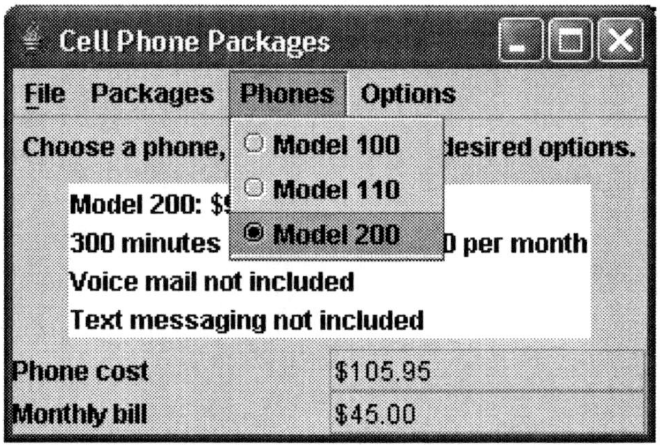

or a different package than the default

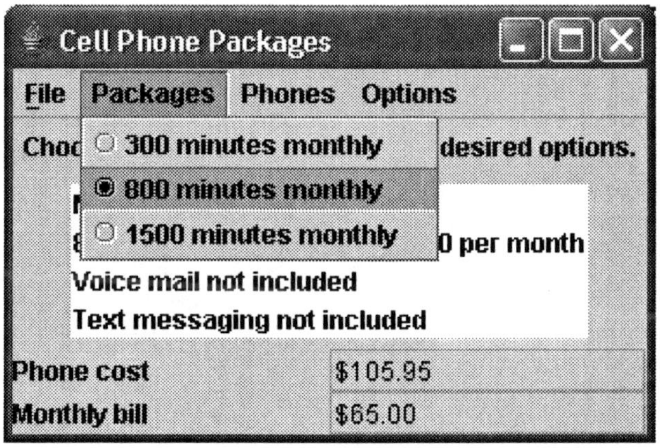

User may also select 0 (default), 1, or 2 options

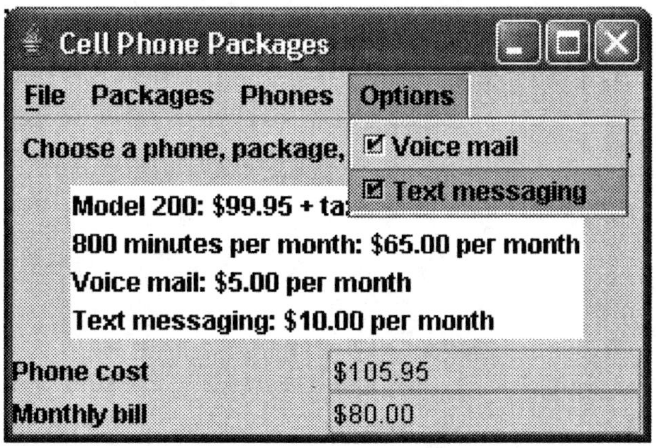

NOTES

CHAPTER 13

Applets and More

Solutions

- Programming Challenge 3: WatchMe Applet
- Programming Challenge 4: Thermometer Applet
- Programming Challenge 6: GridFiller Applet

Programming Challenge 3: WatchMe Applet

Problem Statement:

Write an applet that displays a drawing of two eyes in the center of its window. When the mouse cursor is not inside the window, the eyes should look ahead. When the mouse cursor is inside the window, the eyes should follow the cursor.

Figure 13-1 Sketch of the Applet Window

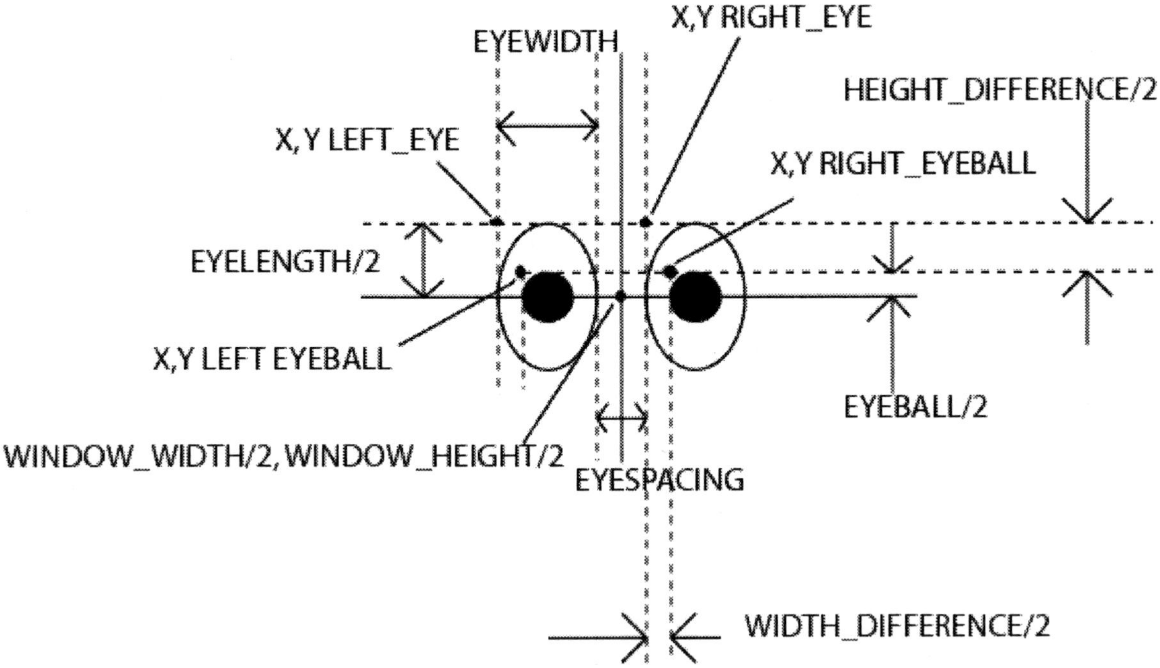

Figure 13-2 Sketch of eyes

Preliminary calculations:

We need to center the eyes in the window. The center of the window has

```
X = WINDOW_WIDTH/2
Y = WINDOW_HEIGHT/2
```

When drawing graphical shapes, the X and Y coordinates are in the upper left hand corner of the shape. The Y coordinate for each eye will be the same, but there will be a right eye X and a left eye X. So the top of the eye is at

```
EYE_Y = WINDOW_HEIGHT/2 - EYELENGTH/2
```

The left side of the right eye is located at

```
RIGHT_EYE_X = WINDOW_WIDTH/2 + EYESPACING/2
```

and the left side of the left eye is at

```
LEFT_EYE_X = WINDOW_WIDTH/2 - EYEWIDTH - EYESPACING/2
```

Similarly for the eyeballs, they need to be centered in the eyes. The spacing around the eyeball is the WIDTH_DIFFERENCE (in X direction) and LENGTH_DIFFERENCE (in Y direction).

INITIAL_EYEBALL_Y = WINDOW_HEIGHT/2 - EYEBALL/2

INITIAL_RIGHT_EYEBALL_X = WINDOW_WIDTH/2 + EYESPACING/2 + WIDTH_DIFFERENCE/2

INITIAL_LEFT_EYEBALL_X = WINDOW_WIDTH/2 - EYESPACING/2 - WIDTH_DIFFERENCE/2 - EYEBALL

All that leaves is to calculate how much to move the eyes and in what direction. Since we don't want to have the eyeballs past the eyes, we don't want to go the entire space between the eyeballs and the eyes. Pick something smaller than WIDTH_DIFFERENCE/2 and LENGTH_DIFFERENCE/2.

MOVE_LEFT_RIGHT = WIDTH_DIFFERENCE/3

MOVE_UP_DOWN = LENGTH_DIFFERENCE/3

We need to look left if the mouse is left of the eyes, right if the mouse is right of the eyes, up if the mouse is above the eyes, and down if the mouse is below the eyes. If the mouse leaves the window, or is in the eye area, the eyes will look ahead (initial position).

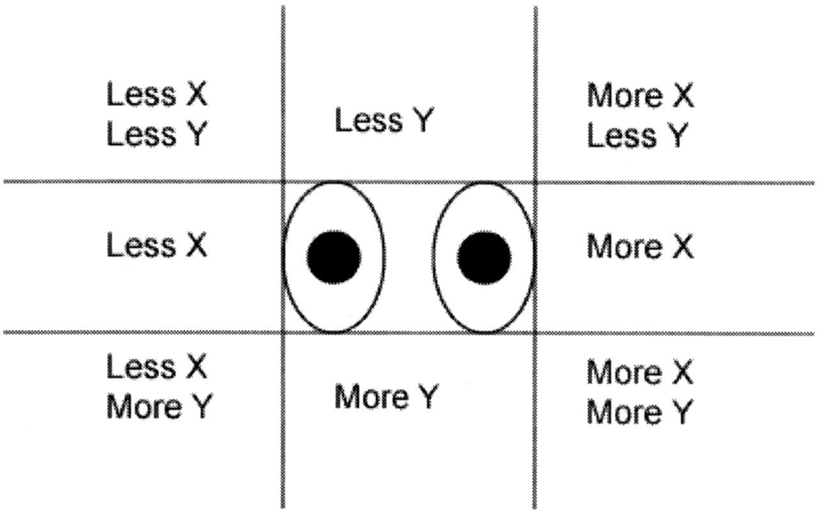

Figure 13-3 Position of mouse relative to eyes

Purpose	To display eyes that follow the movement of the mouse.	
Fields	EYELENGTH	The constant length of the outside of the eyes.
	EYEWIDTH	The constant width of the outside of the eyes.
	EYEBALL	The constant diameter of the eyeball.
	WINDOW_WIDTH	The constant width of the window.
	WINDOW_HEIGHT	The constant height of the window.
	EYESPACING	The constant space between outside of the eyes.
	WIDTH_DIFFERENCE	The constant difference in the width of the outside of the eye and the eyeball.
	LENGTH_DIFFERENCE	The constant difference in the height of the outside of the eye and the eyeball.
	RIGHT_EYE_X	The constant X value for the outside of the right eye.
	INITIAL_RIGHT_EYEBALL_X	The constant X value for the right eyeball when it is centered in the right eye.
	LEFT_EYE_X	The constant X value for the outside of the left eye.
	INITIAL_LEFT_EYEBALL_X	The constant X value for the left eyeball when it is centered in the left eye.
	EYE_Y	The constant Y value for the outside of the eyes.
	INITIAL_EYEBALL_Y	The constant Y value for the eyeballs when they are centered in the eyes.
	MOVE_LEFT_RIGHT	The constant amount to move the eyeballs right or left.
	MOVE_UP_DOWN	The constant amount to move the eyeballs up or down.
	rightEyeballX	The current X position for the right eyeball.
	leftEyeballX	The current X position for the left eyeball.
	eyeballY	The current Y position for both eyeballs.

Methods	init	Initializes variables, sets window size, and connects mouse listeners with applet window.
	paint	Draws the graphical shapes.
Private Inner Class	MyMouseListener	Extends the Mouse Adapter class and handles the event when the user moves the mouse out of the window.
	method mouseExited	Centers the eyeballs in the eyes.
Private Inner Class	MyMouseMotionListener	Extends the MouseMotion Adapter class and handles the event when the user moves the mouse.
	method mouseMoved	Moves the eyeballs to follow the mouse.

Pseudocode for WatchMe Class

1) This class will extend JApplet.

2) Declare constants and fields for X and Y values for eyeballs.

3) The init method.

   a) Get the content pane

   b) Set the background color to white

   c) Set the size of the applet window

   d) Connect the listeners to the applet window

   e) Intialize variables

4) The paint method.

   a) Call the base class paint method.

   b) Draw eyes and eyeballs.

5) The private inner class MyMouseListener.

   a) This class will extend MouseAdapter.

b) The mouseExited method.

i) Reinitialize variables to center the eyeballs

ii) force a call to the paint method.

6) The private inner class MyMouseMotionListener.

a) This class will extend MouseMotionAdapter.

b) The mouseMoved method.

i) If currentX < LEFT_EYE_X

(1) Move eyeballs left

(2) If currentY < EYE_Y

(a) Move eyeballs up

(3) Else if currentY > EYE_Y + EYELENGTH

(a) Move eyeballs down

(4) else

(a) Eyeballs not up or down

ii) Else if currentX > RIGHT_EYE_X + EYEWIDTH

(1) Move eyeballs right

(2) If currentY < EYE_Y

(a) move eyeballs up

(3) Else if currentY > EYE_Y + EYELENGTH

(a) Move eyeballs down

(4) Else

(a) Eyeballs not up or down

iii) Else

(1) Eyeballs not left or right

(2) If currentY < EYE_Y

(a) Move eyeballs up

(3) Else if currentY > EYE_Y + EYELENGTH

(a) Move eyeballs down

(4) Else

(a) Eyeballs not up or down

iv) Force a call to the paint method.

Code Listing 13-1 (WatchMe.java)

```
//*******************************************************************
// Written by Diane Christie
// Chapter 13
// Programming Challenge 3:  WatchMe Applet
//*******************************************************************

//*******************************************************************
// Write an applet that displays a drawing of two eyes in the center
// of its window.  When the mouse cursor is not inside the window,
// the eyes should look ahead.  When the mouse cursor is inside the
// window, the eyes should follow  the cursor.
//*******************************************************************

import java.awt.*;
import java.awt.event.*;
import javax.swing.*;

public class WatchMe extends JApplet
{
   //the length of the outer eye
   private final int EYELENGTH = 100;

   //the width of the outer eye
   private final int EYEWIDTH = 80;

   //the diameter of the eyeball
   private final int EYEBALL = 40;

   //the width of the applet window
   private final int WINDOW_WIDTH = 400;

   //the height of the applet window
   private final int WINDOW_HEIGHT = 300;

   //the space between the outer eyes
   private final int EYESPACING = 40;

   //the difference in the width of the outer eye and the
   //diameter of the eyeball
   private final int WIDTH_DIFFERENCE = EYEWIDTH-EYEBALL;
```

```
//the difference in the height of the outer eye and the
//diameter of the eyeball
private final int LENGTH_DIFFERENCE = EYELENGTH-EYEBALL;

//the X value for drawing the right outer eye
private final int RIGHT_EYE_X = WINDOW_WIDTH/2 + EYESPACING/2;

//the X value for drawing the right eyeball centered in the
//right outer eye
private final int INITIAL_RIGHT_EYEBALL_X = WINDOW_WIDTH/2 +
               EYESPACING/2 + WIDTH_DIFFERENCE/2;

//the X value for drawing the left outer eye
private final int LEFT_EYE_X = WINDOW_WIDTH/2 - EYEWIDTH -
               EYESPACING/2;

//the X value for drawing the left eyeball centered in the
//left outer eye
private final int INITIAL_LEFT_EYEBALL_X = WINDOW_WIDTH/2 -
               EYESPACING/2 - WIDTH_DIFFERENCE/2 - EYEBALL;

//the Y value for drawing the outer eyes
private final int EYE_Y = WINDOW_HEIGHT/2 - EYELENGTH/2;

//the Y value for drawing the eyeballs centered in the
//outer eyes
private final int INITIAL_EYEBALL_Y = WINDOW_HEIGHT/2 - EYEBALL/2;

//the amount to move the eyeballs right or left
private final int MOVE_LEFT_RIGHT = WIDTH_DIFFERENCE/3;

//the amount to move the eyeballs up or down
private final int MOVE_UP_DOWN = LENGTH_DIFFERENCE/3;

//the current X value for the right eyeball
private int rightEyeballX;

//the current X value for the left eyeball
private int leftEyeballX;

//the current Y value for the eyeballs
private int eyeballY;

//****************************************************************
// init method
//****************************************************************

public void init()
{
   //Get the content pane
   Container contentPane = getContentPane();

   //Set the background color to white
   contentPane.setBackground(Color.white);

   //Set the size of the applet window
   resize(WINDOW_WIDTH, WINDOW_HEIGHT);
```

```
      //Connect the listeners to the applet window
      addMouseListener(new MyMouseListener());
      addMouseMotionListener(new MyMouseMotionListener());

      //intialize variables
      rightEyeballX = INITIAL_RIGHT_EYEBALL_X;
      leftEyeballX = INITIAL_LEFT_EYEBALL_X;
      eyeballY = INITIAL_EYEBALL_Y;
   }

   //*****************************************************************
   // paint method
   //*****************************************************************
   public void paint(Graphics g)
   {
      // Call the base class paint method.
      super.paint(g);

      //Draw eyes
      g.setColor(Color.black);
      //right eye
      g.drawOval(RIGHT_EYE_X, EYE_Y, EYEWIDTH, EYELENGTH);
      //left eye
      g.drawOval(LEFT_EYE_X, EYE_Y, EYEWIDTH, EYELENGTH);
      //right eyeball
      g.fillOval(rightEyeballX, eyeballY, EYEBALL, EYEBALL);
      //left eyeball
      g.fillOval(leftEyeballX, eyeballY, EYEBALL, EYEBALL);
   }

   //*****************************************************************
   // Mouse listener class
   //*****************************************************************
   private class MyMouseListener extends MouseAdapter
   {
      public void mouseExited(MouseEvent e)
      {
         //center the eyeballs
         rightEyeballX = INITIAL_RIGHT_EYEBALL_X;
         leftEyeballX = INITIAL_LEFT_EYEBALL_X;
         eyeballY = INITIAL_EYEBALL_Y;

         //force a call to the paint method
         repaint();
      }
   }

   //*****************************************************************
   // Mouse Motion listener class
   //*****************************************************************
   private class MyMouseMotionListener extends MouseMotionAdapter
   {
      public void mouseMoved (MouseEvent e)
      {
         //Get the X and Y coordinates of the mouse cursor.
         int currentX = e.getX();
         int currentY = e.getY();

         if(currentX < LEFT_EYE_X)
```

```
{
   //move eyeballs left
   leftEyeballX = INITIAL_LEFT_EYEBALL_X - MOVE_LEFT_RIGHT;
   rightEyeballX = INITIAL_RIGHT_EYEBALL_X - MOVE_LEFT_RIGHT;

   if (currentY < EYE_Y)
   {
      //move eyeballs up
      eyeballY = INITIAL_EYEBALL_Y - MOVE_UP_DOWN;
   }
   else if (currentY > EYE_Y + EYELENGTH)
   {
      //move eyeballs down
      eyeballY = INITIAL_EYEBALL_Y + MOVE_UP_DOWN;
   }
   else
   {
      //eyeballs not up or down
      eyeballY = INITIAL_EYEBALL_Y;
   }
}
else if (currentX > RIGHT_EYE_X + EYEWIDTH)
{
   //move eyeballs right
   leftEyeballX = INITIAL_LEFT_EYEBALL_X + MOVE_LEFT_RIGHT;
   rightEyeballX = INITIAL_RIGHT_EYEBALL_X + MOVE_LEFT_RIGHT;
   if (currentY < EYE_Y)
   {
      //move eyeballs up
      eyeballY = INITIAL_EYEBALL_Y - MOVE_UP_DOWN;
   }
   else if (currentY > EYE_Y + EYELENGTH)
   {
      //move eyeballs down
      eyeballY = INITIAL_EYEBALL_Y + MOVE_UP_DOWN;
   }
   else
   {
      //eyeballs not up or down
      eyeballY = INITIAL_EYEBALL_Y;
   }
}
else
{
   //eyeballs not left or right
   leftEyeballX = INITIAL_LEFT_EYEBALL_X;
   rightEyeballX = INITIAL_RIGHT_EYEBALL_X;
   if (currentY < EYE_Y)
   {
      //move eyeballs up
      eyeballY = INITIAL_EYEBALL_Y - MOVE_UP_DOWN;
   }
   else if (currentY > EYE_Y + EYELENGTH)
   {
      //move eyeballs down
      eyeballY = INITIAL_EYEBALL_Y + MOVE_UP_DOWN;
   }
   else
   {
```

```
                //eyeballs not up or down
                eyeballY = INITIAL_EYEBALL_Y;
            }
        }

        //force a call to the paint method
        repaint();

    }
  }
}
```

Program Output

The initial applet window

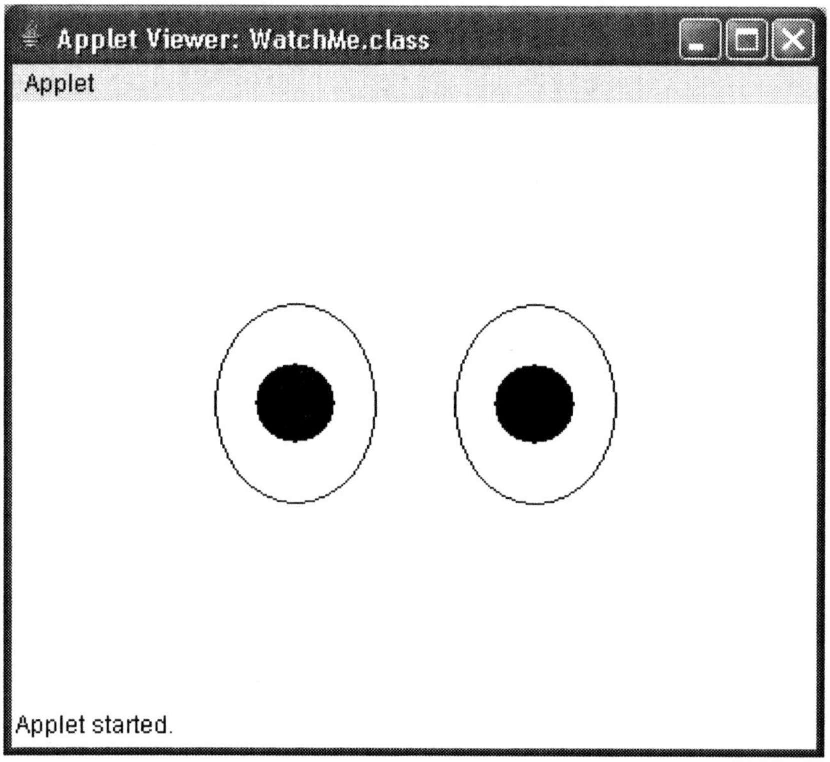

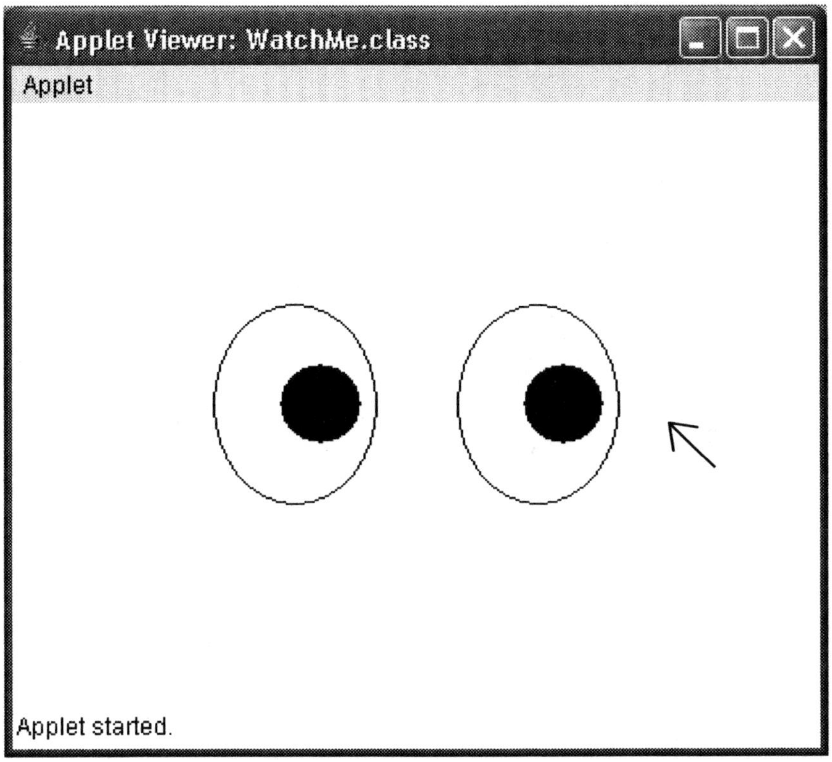

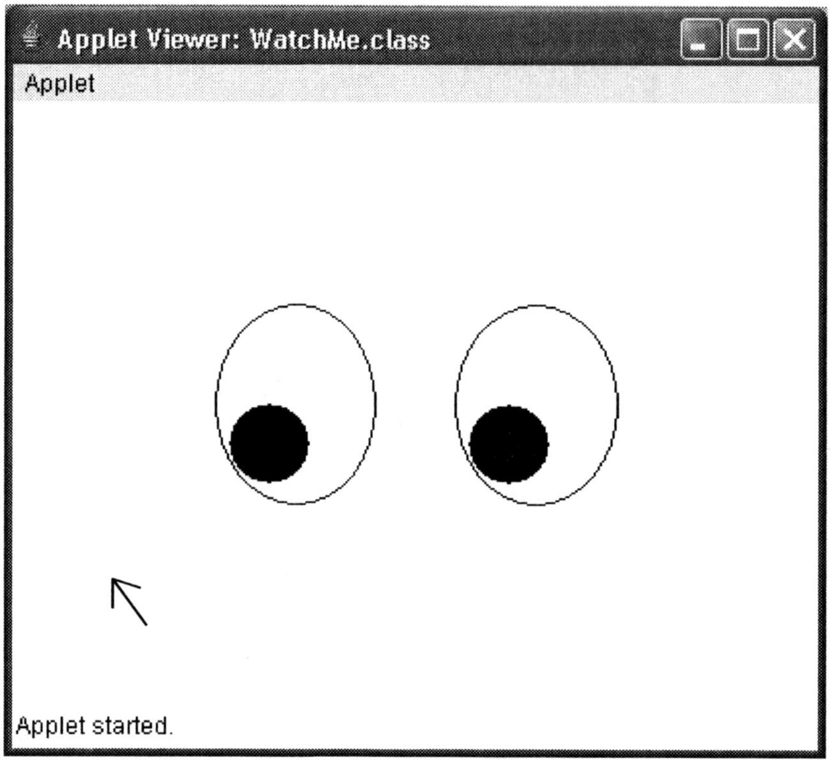
Applet Viewer: WatchMe.class
Applet
Applet started.

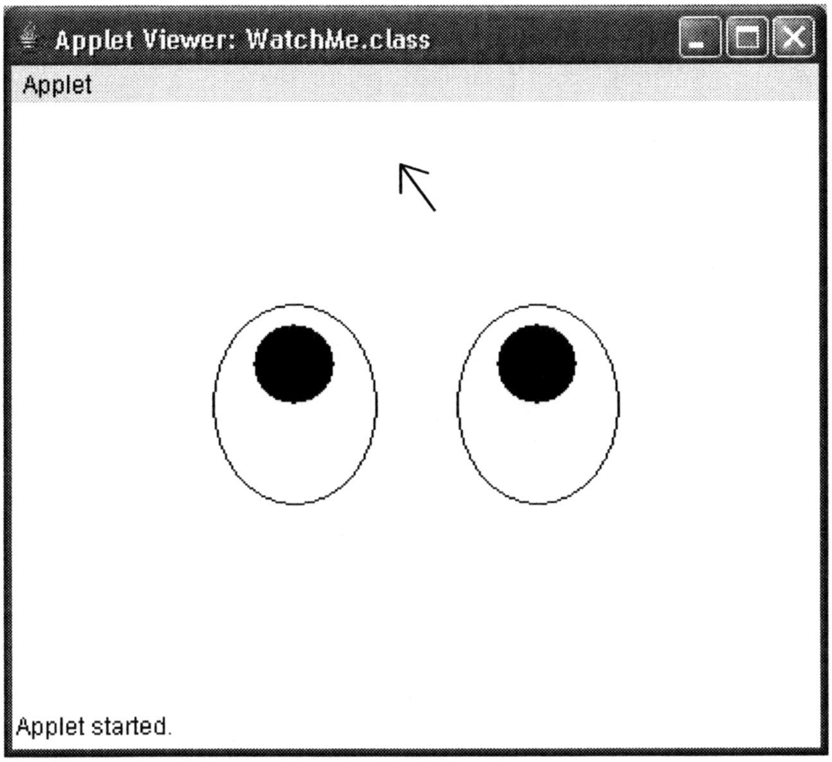
Applet Viewer: WatchMe.class
Applet
Applet started.

Programming Challenge 4: Thermometer Applet

Problem Statement:

Write an applet that displays a thermometer. The user should be able to control the temperature with a slider component. When the user moves the slider, the thermometer should show the corresponding temperature.

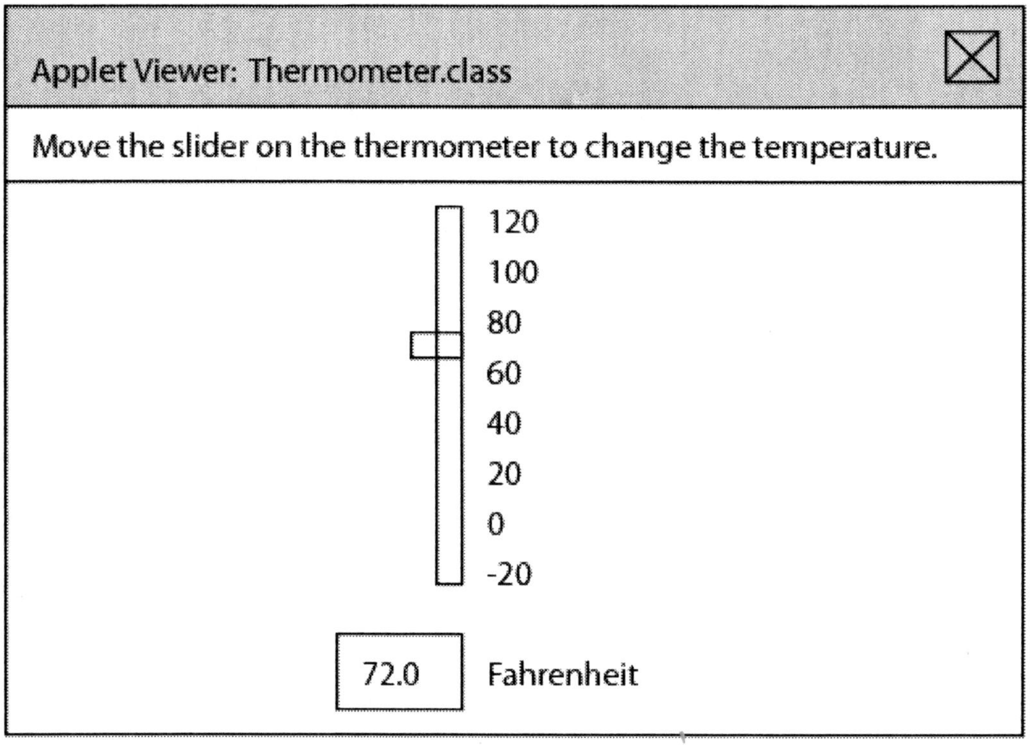

Figure 13-4 Sketch of Thermometer Applet Window

Solution:

The desired layout can be achieved by using a BorderLayout manager with the Thermometer's content pane. Each panel can be created separately and added to the content pane. We will need the following panels:

- InstructionPanel. This panel contains the labels that appears in the window's north region.
- SliderPanel. This panel contains the slider for the thermometer.

- ReadOutPanel. This panel contains the digital readout in a text box with the appropriate label.

The Thermometer Class

Define What the Class Is To Do

Purpose	**To allow the user to use a slider on a thermometer to change the temperature.**	
Fields	**contentPane**	**A reference to the contentPane.**
	sliderPanel	**A JPanel containing the thermometer slider.**
	readOutPanel	**A JPanel containing the digital readout of the temperature.**
	instructionsPanel	**A JPanel containing instructions for the user.**
	slider	**A JSlider that represents a thermometer.**
	instructions	**A JLabel that contains instructions for the user.**
	label	**A JLabel that indicates the temperature is in Fahrenheit.**
	temp	**A value representing the temperature.**
Methods	**init()**	**Sets the layouts, builds the panels, and adds the panels the content pane.**
	buildInstructionPanel()	**Creates a panel containing instructions for the user.**
	buildSliderPanel()	**Creates a panel containing the slider for the thermometer.**
	buildReadOutPanel()	**Creates a panel containing a the digital readout of the temperature.**
Private Inner Class	**SliderListener**	**Handles the event that is generated when the user moves the slider.**
	method	**stateChanged()** — **Sets the digital read out to the temperature on the thermometer.**

Pseudocode for the Thermometer Class

1) This class will extend JApplet.

2) Declare fields for applet objects.

3) The init method.

   a) Get a reference to the content pane.

   b) Set the layout to BorderLayout.

   c) Build the panels.

   d) Add panels to content pane.

4) The buildInstructionPanel method.

   a) Create a panel.

   b) Create labels with instructions for user.

   c) Add labels to panel.

5) The buildSliderPanel method.

   a) Create a panel.

   b) Create the slider.

   c) Connect the slider to the listener.

   d) Add slider to the panel.

6) The buildReadOutPanel method.

   a) Create a panel.

   b) Create an uneditable text field.

   c) Create a label.

   d) Add the components to the panel.

7) The private inner class SliderListener.

   a) This class will implement ChangeListener.

   b) The stateChanged method.

      i) Get the value of the slider.

ii) Set the text field to the value.

Code Listing 13-2 (Temperature.java)

```
//********************************************************************
// Written by Diane Christie
// Chapter 13
// Programming Challenge 4:  Thermometer Applet
//********************************************************************

//********************************************************************
// Write an applet that displays a thermometer.  The user should be
// able to control the temperature with a slider component.  When
// the user moves the slider, the thermometer should show the
// corresponding temperature.
//********************************************************************

import java.awt.*;
import java.awt.event.*;
import javax.swing.*;
import javax.swing.event.*;

public class Thermometer extends JApplet
{
   private Container contentPane;//A reference to the content pane
   private JPanel sliderPanel;//A panel containing the slider
   private JPanel readOutPanel;//A panel containing a digital temp
   private JPanel instructionPanel;//A panel with user instructions
   private JSlider slider;//A slider representing a thermometer
   private JLabel instructions;//A label with instructions
   private JLabel label;//Fahrenheit scale
   private JTextField temp;//The current temperature

   //*****************************************************************
   // init method
   //*****************************************************************

   public void init()
   {
      //Get the content pane
      contentPane = getContentPane();

      //Set the layout
      contentPane.setLayout(new BorderLayout());

      //build the panels
      buildInstructionPanel();
      buildSliderPanel();
      buildReadOutPanel();

      //add the panels
      contentPane.add(instructionPanel, BorderLayout.NORTH);
      contentPane.add(sliderPanel, BorderLayout.CENTER);
      contentPane.add(readOutPanel, BorderLayout.SOUTH);
   }

   //*****************************************************************
   // The buildInstructionPanel method creates a panel for user
```

```
// instructions.
//*****************************************************************
public void buildInstructionPanel()
{
   //Create a panel
   instructionPanel = new JPanel();

   //Create a label with instructions
   instructions = new JLabel("Move the slider on the thermometer "
      + "to change the temperature");

   //Add the label to the panel
   instructionPanel.add(instructions);
}

//*****************************************************************
// The buildSliderPanel method creates a panel that has a slider
// which resembles a thermometer.
//*****************************************************************
public void buildSliderPanel()
{
   //Create the panel
   sliderPanel = new JPanel();

   //Create a slider that resembles a thermometer
   slider = new JSlider(JSlider.VERTICAL, -40, 120, 72);
   slider.setMajorTickSpacing(20);
   slider.setMinorTickSpacing(5);
   slider.setPaintTicks(true);
   slider.setPaintLabels(true);

   //Connect the slider with a listener
   slider.addChangeListener(new SliderListener());

   //Add the slider to the panel
   sliderPanel.add(slider);
}

//*****************************************************************
// The buildReadOutPanel method creates a panel that has a digital
// temperature readout.
//*****************************************************************
public void buildReadOutPanel()
{
   //Create a panel
   readOutPanel = new JPanel();

   //Create an uneditable textbox
   temp = new JTextField("72", 5);
   temp.setEditable(false);

   //Create a label
   label = new JLabel ("Fahrenheit");

   //Add components to the panel
   readOutPanel.add(temp);
   readOutPanel.add(label);
}
```

```
   //*************************************************************
   // The private inner class SliderListener handles the change
   // in the slider (thermometer).
   //*************************************************************
   private class SliderListener implements ChangeListener
   {
      public void stateChanged(ChangeEvent e)
      {
         double temperature;  //represents the value on the slider

         //get the value set on the slider
         temperature = slider.getValue();

         //set the digital readout to that value
         temp.setText(Double.toString(temperature));
      }
   }
}
```

Program Output

Original GUI

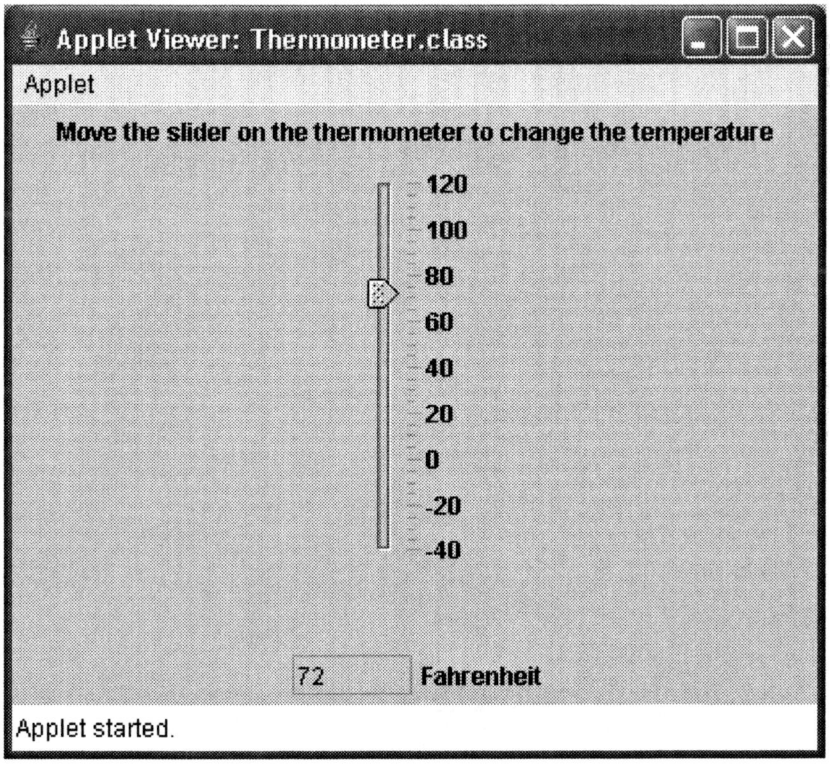

After the user makes changes the temperature on the slider, the digital read out reflects the change.

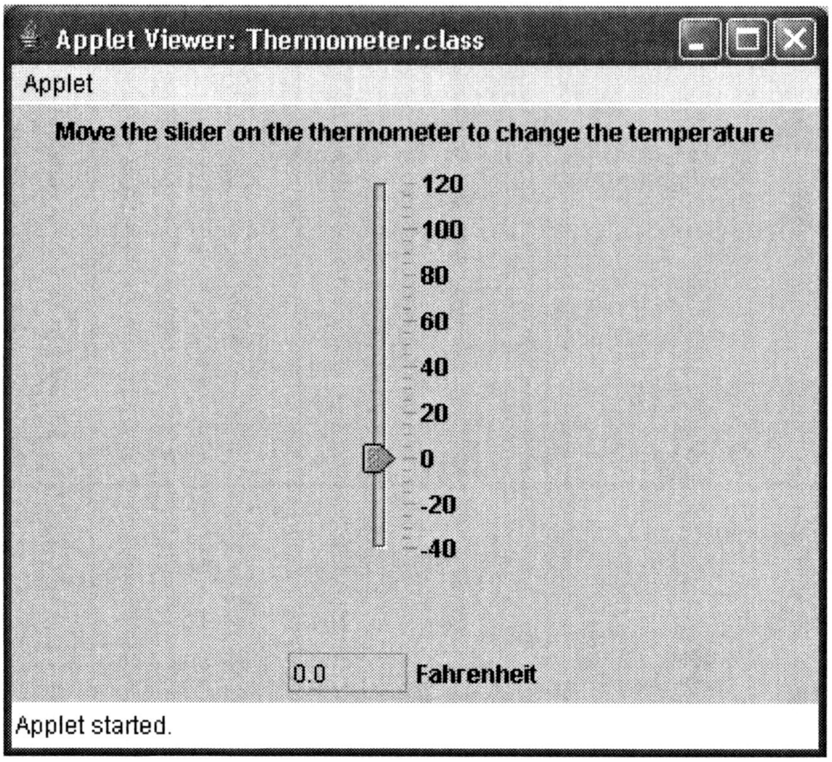
Applet Viewer: Thermometer.class
Applet
Move the slider on the thermometer to change the temperature
120
100
80
60
40
20
0
-20
-40
0.0
Fahrenheit
Applet started.

Programming Challenge 6: GridFiller Applet

Problem Statement:

Write an applet that displays a four by four grid. When the user clicks on a square in the grid, the applet should draw a filled circle in it. If the square already has a circle, clicking on it should cause the circle to disappear.

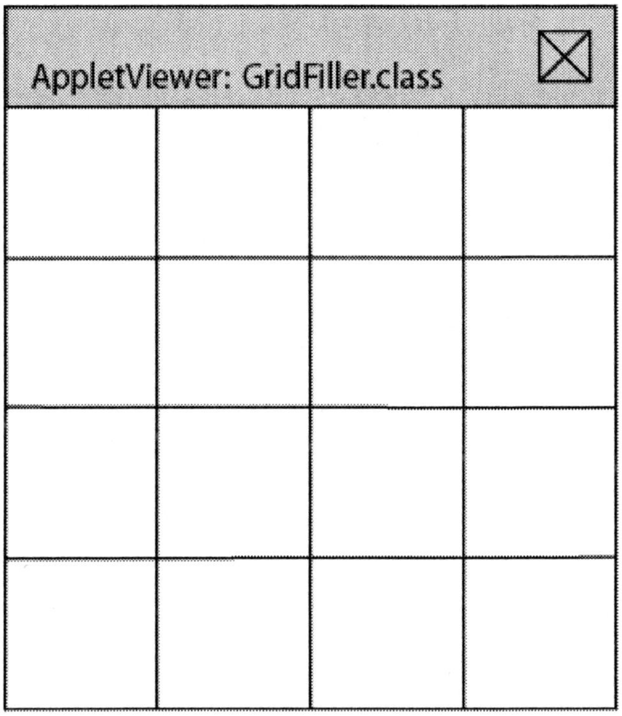

Figure 13-5 Sketch of the GridFiller Applet

Solution:

We need to have an array that holds information of which squares should have a filled circle. Use an array of boolean values to determine this, since making them disappear will simply mean changing the state. Determining where to draw the circles can be handled by using integer division. We want the X,Y coordinate of the filled circle to be at the upper left corner of the square no matter where you click on that square. We can accomplish this by dividing the coordinates X and Y by the width of one square. This will give a 0 quotient for anything that is less than one square width. This corresponds to the 0 index of the array. This idea will work for both X and Y.

Define What the Class Is To Do

Purpose	To allow the user to add or remove filled circles in grid squares by clicking on the squares.		
Fields	holding	A two dimensional array that holds a grid of Boolean values. The value true indicates that a filled circle is present in the corresponding grid on the applet window.	
Methods	init()	Initializes the applet window.	
	initializeArray()	Initializes all values in the two dimensional array to false.	
	paint()	Draws the grid and filled circles in the squares that correspond to true values in the two dimensional array.	
Private Inner Class	MyMouseListener	Handles the event that is generated when the user clicks in the grid on the applet window.	
	method	MouseClicked	Gets the X,Y coordinate of the mouse click, changes the state of the Boolean in the corresponding grid and redraws the applet window.

Pseudocode for GridFiller class

1) This class will extend JApplet.

2) Declare fields for the two dimensional array.

3) The init method.

   a) Resize the applet window to 400 x 400.

   b) Initialize the two-dimensional array.

   c) Connect the applet window with a mouse listener.

4) The initializeArray method.

   a) Set each element in the array to false.

5) The paint method.

a) Call the super constructor.

b) Draw the grid lines.

c) Draw a filled circle in the grid if the array contains a true value in the corresponding location.

6) The private inner class MyMouseListener.

a) This class will extends MouseAdapter.

b) The mouseClicked method.

i) Get the X,Y coordinate of the mouse click.

ii) Convert the X,Y coordinate to a location on the grid.

iii) Change the state of the corresponding value in the two dimensional array.

iv) Force a call to the paint method.

Code Listing 13-3 (GridFiller.java)

```
//********************************************************************
// Written by Diane Christie
// Chapter 13
// Programming Challenge 6:  GridFiller Applet
//********************************************************************

//********************************************************************
// Write an applet that displays a four by four grid.  When the user
// clicks on a square in the grid, the applet should draw a filled
// circle in it.  If the square already has a circle, clicking on it
// should cause the circle to disappear.
//********************************************************************

import java.awt.*;
import java.awt.event.*;
import javax.swing.*;

public class GridFiller extends JApplet
{
   //A 4 by 4 array that represents the grid squares.  If the square
   //contains a filled circle, the element is true.  If the square
   //is empty, the element is false.
   private boolean [][] holding = new boolean [4][4];

   //*****************************************************************
   // init method
   //*****************************************************************
   public void init()
   {
      //Get the content pane
      Container contentPane = getContentPane();
```

```
      //Set the background color to white
      contentPane.setBackground(Color.white);

      //set the size of the applet window
      resize (400, 400);

      //initialize holding array
      initializeArray();

      //Connect to listener
      addMouseListener(new MyMouseListener());
   }

   //****************************************************************
   // The initializeArray method sets all elements to false.  The
   // array is 4 by 4 to correspond to the grid squares.
   //****************************************************************
   public void initializeArray()
   {
      //set all elements in array to false (no filled circle)
      for (int i = 0; i < 4; i++)
         for (int j = 0; j < 4; j++)
            holding[i][j] = false;
   }

   //****************************************************************
   // paint method
   //****************************************************************
   public void paint(Graphics g)
   {
      // Call the base class paint method.
      super.paint(g);

      //draw grid lines
      g.drawLine(100, 0, 100, 400);
      g.drawLine(200, 0, 200, 400);
      g.drawLine(300, 0, 300, 400);
      g.drawLine(0, 100, 400, 100);
      g.drawLine(0, 200, 400, 200);
      g.drawLine(0, 300, 400, 300);

      //draw filled circle in each square that corresponds to a
      //true element from the array
      for (int i = 0; i < 4; i++)
         for (int j = 0; j < 4; j++)
            if (holding[i][j])
               g.fillOval(i*100, j*100, 100, 100);
               //this converts the array index back to a coordinate
               //which corresponds with the upper left corner of the
               //square.
   }

   //****************************************************************
   // Mouse listener class
   //****************************************************************
   private class MyMouseListener extends MouseAdapter
   {
      public void mouseClicked(MouseEvent e)
```

```
        {
           //get coordinates of mouse click
           int newX = e.getX();
           int newY = e.getY();

           //change the X,Y coordinates into row and column in grid
           int newRow = newX/100;
           int newCol = newY/100;

           //change state of the element that corresponds to
           //the square that was clicked
           holding[newRow][newCol] = !holding[newRow][newCol];

           //force a call to the paint method
           repaint();
        }
    }
}
```

Program Output

The original window

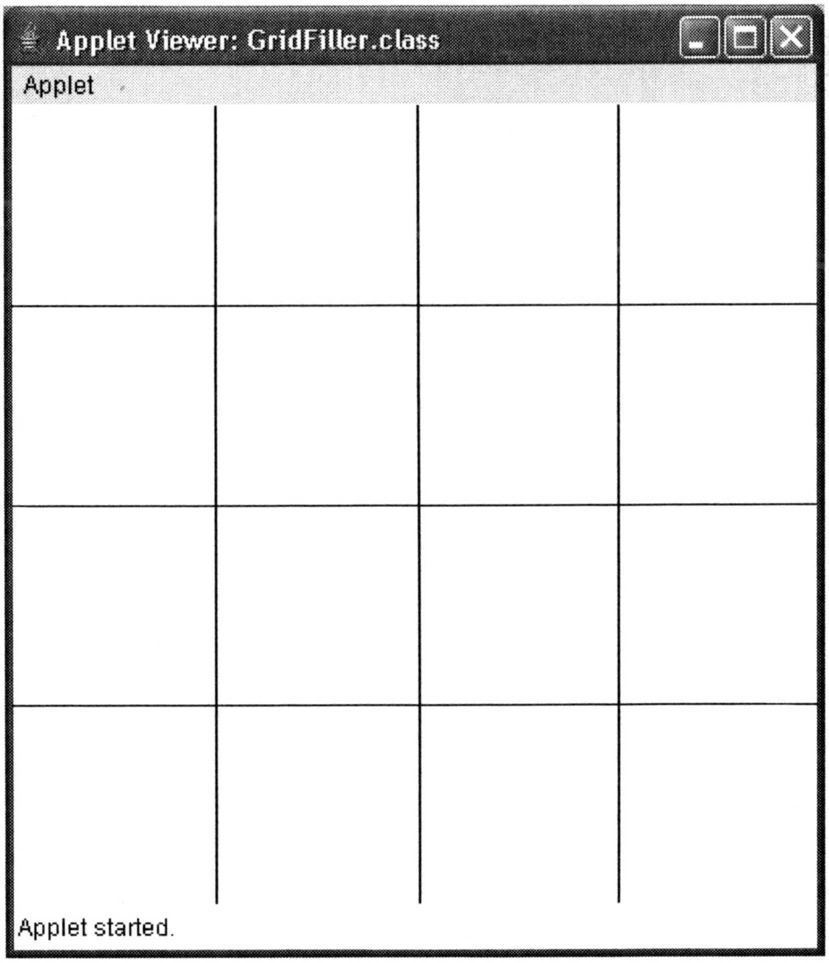

User can click on squares to add a filled-circles in those squares:

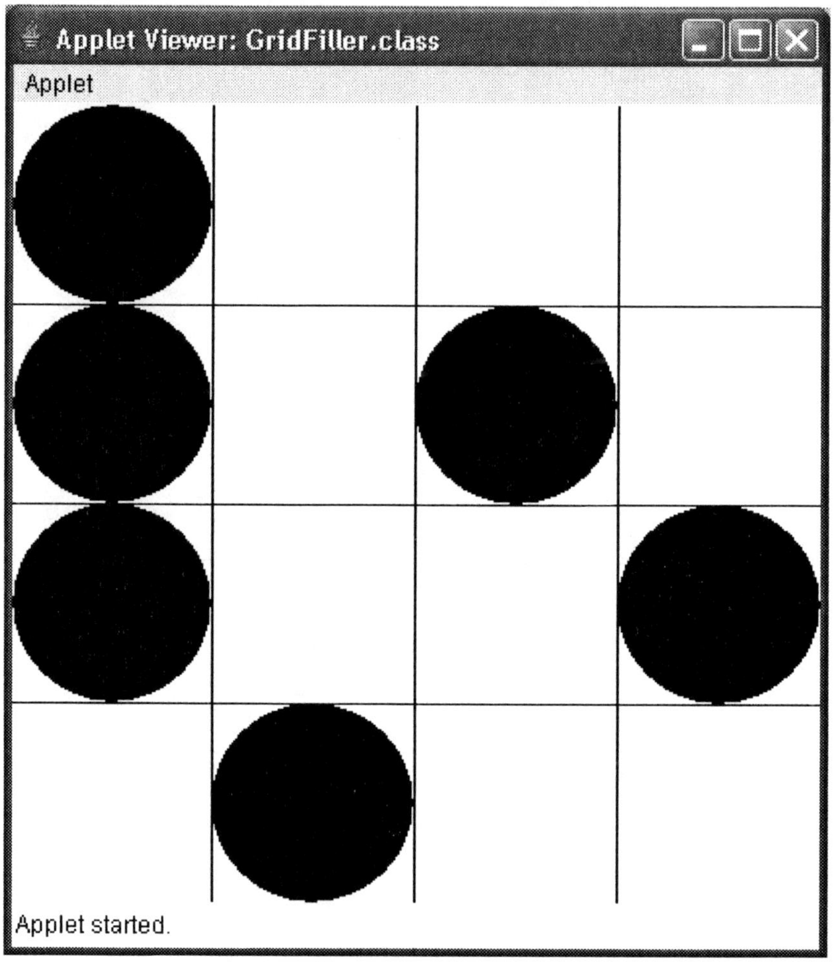

If the user clicks on a filled circle, it disappears.

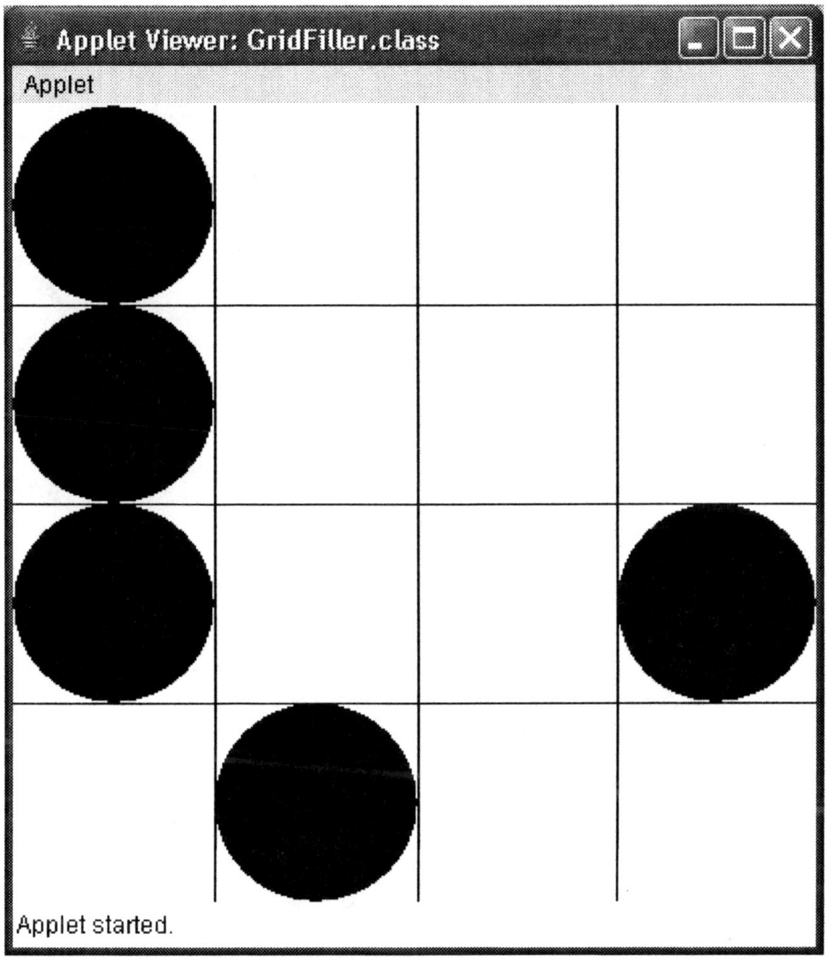

NOTES

CHAPTER 14

Recursion

Solutions

- Programming Challenge 1: Recursive Multiplication
- Programming Challenge 7: Recursive Power Method
- Programming Challenge 8: Sum of Numbers

Programming Challenge 1: Recursive Multiplication

Problem Statement:

Write a recursive function that accepts two arguments into the parameters x and y. The function should return the value of x times y. Remember, multiplication can be performed as repeated addition.

Solution:

Define What The Program Is To Do

Purpose	**To perform multiplication by repeated addition.**	
Input	**The two numbers to be multiplied.**	
Process	**Get the numbers to multiply from the user, then call the recursive method multiply.**	
Methods	**multiply**	**If the first argument is 0, return 0, else return the second argument plus a call to the multiply method.**
Output	**The product of the two numbers.**	

Pseudocode for MultiplicationDemo Class

1) Read in two numbers to be multiplied.

2) Call the recursive method multiply and print the result.

3) The multiply method.

   a. The base case, repeated add a number 0 times.

   b. The recursive case, add the number to a recursive call to multiply the number by one less.

Code Listing 14-1 (MultiplicationDemo.java)

```
//*******************************************************************
// Written by Diane Christie
// Chapter 14
// Programming Challenge 1:  Recursive Multiplication
//*******************************************************************
```

```
//***************************************************************
// Write a recursive function that accepts two arguments into the
// parameters x and y.  The function should return the value of x
// times y.  Remember, multiplication can be performed as repeated
// addition.
//***************************************************************

import java.util.Scanner;

public class MultiplicationDemo
{
   public static void main(String [] args)
   {
      int x, y;

      //Create a Scanner object to read from the keyboard
      Scanner keyboard = new Scanner(System.in);

      //Get two numbers from the user
      System.out.print("Enter the first number to multiply:  ");
      x = keyboard.nextInt();
      System.out.print("Enter the second number to multiply:  ");
      y = keyboard.nextInt();

      //Print out the results
      System.out.println("The product is " + multiply(x,y));
   }

   //***********************************************************
   // The multiply method uses recursion to multiply numbers using
   // repeated addition.
   //***********************************************************
   public static int multiply(int x, int y)
   {
      //base case
      if (x == 0)
         return 0;
      //recursive case
      else
         return (y + multiply(x-1, y));
   }

}
```

Program Output

```
Enter the first number to multiply:  7
Enter the second number to multiply:  4
The product is 28
```

Programming Challenge 7: Recursive Power Method

Problem Statement:

Write a method that uses recursion to raise a number to a power. The method should accept two arguments: the number to be raised and the exponent. Assume that the exponent is a nonnegative integer. Demonstrate the method in a program.

Solution:

Define what the program is to do

Purpose	**To calculate the result of a number raised to a power.**	
Input	**The number to be raised and the exponent.**	
Process	**Get the number and the power and call the recursive method power.**	
Method	**power**	**If the second argument is 0, return 1, else return the first argument times a call to the power method.**
Output	**The result of the first number raised to the power of the second number.**	

Pseudocode for the PowerDemo Class

1) Read in the number to be raised and the power to which to raise it.

2) Call the recursive method power and print the result.

3) The power method.

   a. The base case, any number raised to the 0th power is 1.

   b. The recursive case, multiply the number to be raised by a recursive call to power using one less for the exponent.

Code Listing 14-2(PowerDemo.java)

```
//*****************************************************************
// Written by Diane Christie
// Chapter 14
// Programming Challenge 7:  Recursive Power Method
//*****************************************************************

//*****************************************************************
// Write method that uses recursion to raise a number to a power.
// The method should accept two arguments:  the number to be raised
```

```
// and the exponent.  Assume that the exponent is a nonnegative
// integer.  Demonstrate the method in a program.
//*******************************************************************

import java.util.Scanner;

public class PowerDemo
{
   public static void main(String [] args)
   {
      int x, y;

      //Create a Scanner object to read from the keyboard
      Scanner keyboard = new Scanner(System.in);

      //Get two numbers from the user
      System.out.print("Enter the number to be raised:  ");
      x = keyboard.nextInt();
      System.out.print("Enter the exponent:  ");
      y = keyboard.nextInt();

      //Print out the results
      System.out.println("The result is " + power(x,y));
   }

   //**************************************************************
   // The power method uses recursion to calculate the result
   // of raising a number to a power.  The power (the second
   // argument) must be a nonnegative integer).
   //**************************************************************
   public static double power(double base, int pow)
   {
      //base case
      if (pow ==0)
         return 1;
      //recursive case
      else
         return (base * power(base, pow-1));

   }
}
```

Program Output

```
Enter the number to be raised:  2
Enter the exponent:  5
The result is 32.0
```

Programming Challenge 8: Sum of Numbers

Problem Statement:

Write a method that accepts an integer argument and returns the sum of all the integers from 1 up to the number passes as an argument. For example, if 50 is passed as an argument, the method will return the sum of 1, 2, 3, 4, …, 50. Use recursion to calculate the sum. Demonstrate the method in a program.

Solution:

Define what the program is to do:

Purpose	To calculate the sum of the numbers from 1 to the argument.	
Input	The number at which to stop summing.	
Process	Get the number and call the recursive method sum.	
Method	sum	If the argument is 1, return 1, else return the argument plus a call to the sum method.
Output	The result of the numbers from 1 to the argument.	

Pseudocode for the SumDemo Class

1) Read in the number at which to stop summing.

2) Call the recursive method sum and print the result.

3) The sum method.

   a. The base case, summing up to 1.

   b. The recursive case, sum the number at which to stop to a call to sum using an argument which is one less.

Code Listing 14-3(SumDemo.java)

```
//*******************************************************************
// Written by Diane Christie
// Chapter 14
// Programming Challenge 8:  Sum of Numbers
//*******************************************************************

//*******************************************************************
// Write a method that accepts an integer argument and returns the
```